The Sociology of Gender

The Sociology of Gender

An Introduction to Theory and Research

Second Edition

Amy S. Wharton

WILEY-BLACKWELL

A John Wiley & Sons, Ltd., Publication

This second edition first published 2012
© 2012 John Wiley & Sons Ltd

Edition History: Blackwell Publishing Ltd (1e, 2005)

Wiley-Blackwell is an imprint of John Wiley & Sons, formed by the merger of Wiley's global Scientific, Technical and Medical business with Blackwell Publishing.

Registered Office
John Wiley & Sons Ltd, The Atrium, Southern Gate, Chichester, West Sussex, PO19 8SQ, UK

Editorial Offices
350 Main Street, Malden, MA 02148-5020, USA
9600 Garsington Road, Oxford, OX4 2DQ, UK
The Atrium, Southern Gate, Chichester, West Sussex, PO19 8SQ, UK

For details of our global editorial offices, for customer services, and for information about how to apply for permission to reuse the copyright material in this book please see our website at www.wiley.com/wiley-blackwell.

The right of Amy S. Wharton to be identified as the author of this work has been asserted in accordance with the UK Copyright, Designs and Patents Act 1988.

Library of Congress Cataloging-in-Publication Data
Wharton, Amy S.
  The sociology of gender : an introduction to theory and research / Amy S. Wharton.
–2nd ed.
     p. cm.
  Includes bibliographical references and index.
  ISBN 978-0-470-65568-9 (pbk.)
  1. Gender identity.   2. Sex differences.   3. Sex role.   4. Equality.   I. Title.
  HQ1075.W48 2011
  305.3–dc22

                              2010049295

A catalogue record for this book is available from the British Library.

This book is published in the following electronic formats: ePDF 9781444397239; ePub 9781444397246

Set in 10.5 on 13.5 pt Palatino by Toppan Best-set Premedia Limited
Printed and bound in Singapore by C.O.S. Printers Pte Ltd

5   2015

Contents

Contents

Contents

Chapter 1

Introduction to the Sociology of Gender

Chapter Objectives

- Provide an overview of the book's general aims.
- Explain how sociologists approach the study of social life and gender, in particular.
- Define gender and other key terms, and understand the debates over their use.
- Identify the three frameworks sociologists use to examine this concept.
- Provide examples of the ways that gender shapes individuals, social interaction, and institutions.
- Explain the importance of considering gender from a cross-national and comparative perspective.

The Sociology of Gender: An Introduction to Theory and Research, Second Edition. Amy S. Wharton.
© 2012 John Wiley & Sons Ltd. Published 2012 by John Wiley & Sons Ltd.

Introduction

> Last summer at a family gathering, my mother asked what I would be
> working on during my sabbatical. "Gender," I responded. "You mean gender
> bias?" she asked helpfully. "No, gender," I said. There ensued an awkward
> silence, then my sixteen-year-old nephew quipped, "There are men and there
> are women. What more is there to say? Short book."

From "Confounding Gender" by Mary Hawkesworth

Introduction

I identify with the narrator in this story. Like her, I have often found
myself having to explain my interest in the topic of gender. Many
people share – at least implicitly, anyway – the teenage nephew's
belief that gender is something unproblematic, self-evident, and
uncontested. Is there anything more to say?

My belief that there is, indeed, more to say on the topic of gender
is the motivation for this book. In it, I hope to achieve two goals:
First, I aim to convince readers that understanding gender requires
us to go beyond the obvious and to reconsider issues we may think
are self-evident and already well understood. Challenging the
taken-for-granted is one essential component of the sociological
perspective. In fact, sociologists argue that what people view as
unproblematic and accept as "the way things are" may be most in
need of close, systematic scrutiny. A second goal of the book is to
demonstrate the ways that gender matters in social life. Though
complex and ever-changing, the social world is ordered and, at some
level, knowable. As a principle of social relations and organization,
gender is one of the forces that contribute to this patterning of social
life. By understanding gender, we understand more about the
social world.

Meeting these goals is more challenging than ever before.
Virtually all of the social sciences have produced a staggering
amount of empirical research on gender. Further, gender research
has proliferated across the globe, and the ability of scholars to communicate with and learn from one another across geographical and
disciplinary boundaries has expanded exponentially. This multi-

2

plicity of views and perspectives does not have to result in chaos and confusion, however. The field's conceptual and theoretical diversity can be a source of enrichment rather than fragmentation. In order to receive the benefits of this diversity, however, students of gender must be skilled at communicating across perspectives, identifying points of overlap, convergence, and opposition. Demonstrating how this can be accomplished while, at the same time, doing justice to the range and variety of the ever-expanding theory and research on gender presents challenges I hope to meet in the following pages.

Sociological Vantage Points

There are many ways to gather information and produce knowledge, including knowledge about gender. This book, however, is premised on my belief that sociology (and the social sciences) offers the most useful vantage points from which this topic can be understood. Sociology does not provide the *only* access to the social world, of course. Fiction, music, and art, for example, all may provide people with meaningful insights about their lives. As a scientific discipline, sociology values systematic, theoretically informed analyses of the empirical world. While personal narratives and experiences are undeniably important, relying exclusively on these sources of information may lead to the "fundamental attribution error" – the tendency to explain behavior by invoking personal dispositions while ignoring the roles of social structure and context (Aries 1996; Ross 1977). Only by moving away from the purely subjective can we understand the broader social forces that shape our lives. Sociologists employ a wide variety of quantitative and qualitative methods to gather the information that informs their empirical claims. They use these methods as means to insure that data are gathered and analyzed systematically, with the aim of explaining and extending knowledge.

Though embracing the assumptions and methods of science as it has traditionally been conceived, sociologists have – out of necessity

– also broadened these traditions. We recognize that the social world we study is complex and that this demands multiple forms of knowledge-gathering, some of which may be unique to the social (as opposed to the other) sciences. Models of science that work well for those studying the natural or physical world are not always applicable or desirable for studying the social world. As numerous social scientists have pointed out, humans – unlike other species – have tremendous capacities for reflection, creativity, and agency. People are neither programmable machines nor are they prisoners of their instincts. As a result, sociologists must contend with the fact that all people know something of the circumstances in which they act and thereby possess a degree of "sociological competence" (Lemert 1997, p. x). As sociologists, we are at our best when we can communicate with and learn from those we study. The sociological enterprise is further strengthened by its practitioners' capacities to critically reflect on the circumstances through which their knowledge is produced. The ability to engage in self-reflection and critique one's assumptions, methods, and conceptual orientations contributes vitally to the growth of sociological knowledge.

There are several, more specific characteristics of sociological knowledge –including knowledge about gender. Most important, this knowledge emanates from diverse theoretical perspectives and methodologies. Because they focus attention on different aspects of the social world and ask different kinds of questions, the interplay of diverse perspectives and methods helps facilitate the production of knowledge. I believe that the most useful sociological knowledge is produced collectively, through dialogue and debate, rather than in self-contained isolation. Sociological knowledge is not complete, seamless, or monolithic, however. Rather, like all knowledge grounded in the practices of science, this knowledge is incomplete, contingent, and often inconsistent.

These disciplinary characteristics have shaped what we know about gender and how we have come to know it. What follows thus draws on these characteristics. In my view, the tools of social science and sociology, in particular – while not flawless or complete – have been and continue to be the most useful in providing people with the means to challenge the taken-for-granted, understand their own lives and the world around them, and create possibilities for change.

A Brief History of the Sociological Study of Gender

Beginnings

I took my first course on gender as an undergraduate at the University of Oregon in 1975. As I recall, the course had only been in existence for a few years prior. "Gender" appeared nowhere in the course title: It was called "the sociology of women." My experience of being introduced to the study of *gender* through the sociology of *women* was fairly typical for sociology students of my generation. The study of gender in sociology grew out of the second wave of the women's movement. One expression of this movement in colleges and universities was its critique of academic disciplines, like sociology, for ignoring women. Women were rarely the subjects of research and activities heavily dominated by women (e.g., housework) received little attention. Critics thus claimed that sociology reflected a "male bias," generating knowledge most applicable to men's lives rather than to the lives of women and to society defined more broadly. The challenge for sociology at that time was best captured in the question posed by the late sociologist, Jessie Bernard (1973a, p. 781): "Can [sociology] become a science of society rather than a science of male society?"

While the term "gender" gradually began to enter the sociological literature, gender scholars for many years devoted considerably more attention to women – and topics related to femininity – than to men and topics related to masculinity. In addition, much more was written about differences between women and men than was written about *variations among women* and *among men*. Perhaps more fundamental was the persistent, often implicit, assumption that sociology as a discipline could accommodate new knowledge about gender without having to rethink some of its own key assumptions

5

about the social world. Each of these tendencies has been challenged in recent years.

Recent conceptual developments

The sociology of women has given way to a sociology of gender. On one level, this change is reflected in a growing literature on men and masculinity (Connell 1995; Schrock and Schwalbe 2009). Although men have long been of interest to sociologists, this recent literature focuses on men as gendered rather than generic beings. This development, in turn, has been accompanied by the recognition that gender itself is *relational*: Understanding what women are or can be thus requires attention to what men are or can be.

Another important development involves the growing recognition of variations among men and among women, resulting in increased attention to masculini*ties* and femininit*ies*. The acknowledgment of multiple rather than singular expressions of gender has been accompanied by a recognition that some forms of masculinity or femininity are more socially valued than others. In this view, relations between particular kinds of masculinity (or particular kinds of femininity) are understood as relations of domination and subordination. In addition, this formulation recognizes that "masculinities [and femininities] come into existence at particular times and places and are always subject to change" (Connell 1995, p. 185).

A related development in the sociology of gender is the field's increased concern with the relations between gender and other bases of distinction and stratification, such as age, race or ethnicity, sexual orientation, social class, or nation. This literature challenges the notion that women (or men) represent a homogeneous category, whose members can be automatically assumed to share common interests and experiences. For example, as studies of care work have shown, a global division of women's labor underlies this industry: Poor women from less affluent countries migrate to the richer West to care for the children and clean the houses of women who are more well-to-do (Ehrenreich and Hochschild 2002). Contained within the global gap between rich and poor is a gap among women and women's work activities. Though gender, race and ethnicity, and social class are analytically separate, as aspects of lived experience, they are highly intertwined.

Another aspect of gender scholarship is its attempt to transform sociological knowledge. It is insufficient to simply add knowledge about gender to existing sociological literatures. Instead, we should rethink taken-for-granted sociological concepts and ideas, with the aim of refashioning these literatures. Purportedly gender-neutral practices and institutions, such as law, work, and formal organization, have received new scrutiny from scholars interested in gender. These scholars' efforts have helped move the sociology of gender from the margins to the center of sociological thought. In turn, they have contributed to the growing recognition that gender scholarship has something to offer the sociological mainstream.

A related theme in gender scholarship is the belief that cross-national, comparative research is essential. Gender has long been of interest to researchers around the world, but the vast majority of studies focus on a single society. There are some good reasons for this. Comparative data are not always easy to come by, and cross-national research can be time-consuming and expensive. However, some of these logistical barriers to cross-national research have been overcome. New technologies have vastly expanded access to information and increased the possibilities for scholarly communication among those in different places on the globe.

This has enabled researchers to learn more about the role of societal-level influences on gender and how aspects of gender uncovered in one societal context may or may not be generalizable to other settings. For example, while studies conducted in Western societies show that acts of physical aggression towards a partner are committed by both men and women, this pattern is not found in all nations (Archer 2006). Cross-national research thus is important in helping us avoid the dangers of over-generalization, which occurs when one assumes that conclusions based on one group of women or men can be automatically extended to all women or all men. As we saw earlier, a similar kind of critique was what led sociologists to examine women in their own right in the first place.

7

The internationalization of gender scholarship has also helped facilitate new research agendas. A particular focus has been the ways that gender shapes and is shaped by macro-societal trends, processes, and institutions, such as globalization, migration, and state policies (O'Connor, Orloff, and Shaver 1999).

Nevertheless, it is important not to throw the baby out with the bathwater. Cross-national research on gender has taught us much about the ways that gender operates differently across societies and revealed the implications of those differences for women's and men's lives. Ironically, however, looking across boundaries in this way has also reinforced scholars' view that gender's role in social organization is fundamental: "In virtually every culture, gender difference is a pivotal way in which humans identify themselves as persons, organize social relations, and symbolize meaningful natural and social events and processes" (Harding 1986, p. 18).

In considering the history of gender scholarship, one final point to keep in mind is the relationship between how social scientists think about gender and events in the larger society. Gender scholarship emerged during the women's movement, a time when middle-class women in the West were responding to growing educational and economic opportunities. Trends in gender scholarship in the current era are similarly linked to the social forces that are shaping the twenty-first century, such as globalization, neoliberalism, and the explosive growth of new modes and technologies of communication.

Defining Gender

Following Ridgeway and Smith-Lovin (1999, p. 192), I view **gender** as a "system of social practices"; this system creates and maintains gender distinctions and it "organizes relations of inequality on the basis of [these distinctions]." In this view, gender involves the creation of both differences *and* inequalities. But which social practices are most important in creating gender distinctions and inequalities, and how do these practices operate? The book's primary aim is to examine alternative answers to these questions. In the process, students will be introduced to the range and diversity of sociological understandings of gender.

Three features of this definition are important to keep in mind. First, gender is as much a process as a fixed state. This implies that gender is being continually produced and reproduced. Stated differently, we could say that gender is enacted or "done," not merely expressed. Understanding the mechanisms through which this occurs thus is an important objective. Second, gender is not simply a characteristic of individuals but occurs at all levels of the social structure. This is contained in the idea of gender as a "system" of practices that are far-reaching, interlocked, and exist independently of individuals. Gender is a multilevel phenomenon (Risman 1998). This insight enables us to explore how social processes, such as interaction, and social institutions, such as work, embody and reproduce gender. Third, this definition of gender refers to its importance in organizing relations of inequality. Whether gender differentiation must necessarily lead to gender inequality is a subject of debate that we will take up in the next chapter. For now, however, the important point is that, as a principle of social organization, gender is one critical dimension upon which social resources are distributed.

Gender is sometimes used interchangeably with the term "sex." In fact, there is no firm consensus on the appropriate use of these two terms among gender scholars. Some reject the term "sex" altogether and refer only to "gender." Others use them synonymously, while still others employ both concepts and recognize a clear distinction between them. These differences in usage are not merely semantic, but reflect more fundamental differences in perspective and theoretical orientation. Understanding the sociological meaning of sex and its relationship to gender thus is our next order of business in this chapter.

Sex and sex category

In conversation people often refer to men or women as the "opposite sex." The term "opposite sex" implies that men and women belong to completely separate categories. Are women and men truly opposites? In fact, human males and females share many character-istics, especially biological characteristics. For example, both nor-mally have 23 pairs of chromosomes and they are warm-blooded: In other respects, however, male and female bodies differ. These distinguishing characteristics, which include chromosomal differ-ences, external and internal sexual structures, hormonal produc-tion, and other physiological differences, and secondary sex characteristics, signify **sex**.

The claim that sex marks a distinction between two physically and genetically discrete categories of people is called **sexual dimor-phism**. Many view sexual dimorphism in humans as a biological fact; they believe that sexual differentiation creates two "structur-ally distinguishable" categories of humans (Breedlove 1994, p. 390). Others are more skeptical, arguing that social rather than biological forces produce two sexes in humans. This disagreement, which I will return to below, is an important area of debate among gender scholars.

In addition to the concept of sex, sociologists also use terms such as **sex assignment** or **sex category**. These concepts describe the processes through which social meanings are attached to biological sex. Sex assignment refers to the process – occurring at birth or even prenatally – by which people are identified as male or female (their sex category). Sex assignment is guided, at least in part, by socially agreed upon criteria for identifying sex, such as external genitalia. In most cases, sex assignment is a straightforward matter. Yet, this is not always the case. Researchers estimate that in as many as 2 percent of all live births, infants cannot be easily categorized as male and female (Blackless et al. 2000). In these cases, the sex chromo-somes, external genitalia, and/or the internal reproductive system do not fit the standard for males or females. These individuals are called **intersexuals**.

Lessons from the intersexed

Intersexuals have been a subject of fascination and debate through-out recorded history (Kessler 1998). More than any other group, however, the medical profession has defined the issue of intersexuality and societal responses to it. Not surprisingly, as medical technology has become more sophisticated, intersexuality has come to be defined as a condition requiring medical intervention – as a "correctable birth defect" (Kessler 1998, p. 5). In these cases, doctors perform complicated surgery designed to provide an infant with "normal" genitals – that is, with genitals that match a particular sex category.

In recent years, some intersexuals have begun to speak out against this practice of surgically altering children born with ambiguous genitalia. In 1992, Cheryl Chase, an intersex woman, founded an organization called the Intersex Society of North America (ISNA). This group's primary goal is to reduce, if not eliminate, genital surgery on intersex infants. Instead, members of INSA believe that surgery should be a choice made when the intersexed person is old enough to give informed consent. In 1996, members of INSA demonstrated at the American Academy of Pediatrics annual meeting in Boston, advocating "an avoidance of unnecessary genital surgery, family counseling with regard to the child's future medical needs and options, complete disclosure of medical files, referral of the adolescent to peer support, and the fully informed consent of the intersexual youth to any or all medical procedures" (Turner 1999, p. 457). INSA also advocates for people's right to remain intersexed and to gain social acceptance for this status. Members of the ISNA thus reject the belief that everyone must fall into one of two sex categories, and they envision a society where genital variation is accepted.

INSA's goals may sound unrealistic. The fact that it is difficult to imagine a world where genitals no longer anchor people's understanding of male and female underscores the close ties between genitals and gender in people's taken-for-granted reality. This taken-for-granted reality represents the "natural attitude" toward gender; it comprises a set of beliefs that on the surface appear "obvious" and thus not open to examination or questioning. Among these "unquestionable axioms" are: "the beliefs that there are two and only two genders; gender is invariant; genitals are the essential

signs of gender; the male/female dichotomy is natural; being masculine or feminine is not a matter of choice; all individuals can (and
must) be classified as masculine or feminine" (Hawkesworth 1997,
p. 649; see also Garfinkel 1967; Kessler and McKenna 2000). By
raising the possibility that genitals are not definitive evidence of
one's maleness or femaleness, intersexuals are challenging "the
natural attitude."

Sex or gender?

INSA and research on intersexuals have helped reveal the social
processes that shape assignment to (and, in the case of many intersexuals) construction of a sex category. These efforts can be seen as
part of a broader attempt to understand the links between sex and
gender. Most now agree that the biological or genetic aspects of
maleness and femaleness cannot be understood as fully separate
and distinct from the social processes and practices that give
meaning to these characteristics. As Hoyenga and Hoyenga (1993,
p. 6) explain, "We are the products of both our biologies and our
past and present environments, simultaneously and inseparably;
we are bodies as well as minds at one and the same time."

This view – that biology and society interact to shape human
behavior – may not seem controversial, but researchers disagree
over exactly how this interaction should be understood. Is sex
the biological and genetic substrate from which gender distinctions emerge, or do gender distinctions lead us to perceive two,
easily distinguishable sexes? Is sexual dimorphism itself a social
construction?

The two positions in this discussion represent fairly distinct conceptions of the body (Connell 1995) and hence a disagreement over
the *degree to which they see sex as socially constructed*. At one end of
the spectrum are those who believe that gender is not grounded in
any biological or genetic reality (Lorber 1994). In this view, the body
"is a more or less neutral surface or landscape on which a social
symbolism is imprinted" (Connell 1995, p. 46). Accordingly, sexual
dimorphism, from this perspective, is less an objective reality than

a socially constructed distinction. In Kessler and McKenna's (1978, p. 163) words, "Scientists construct dimorphism where there is continuity. … Biological, psychological, and social differences do not lead to our seeing two genders. Our seeing of two genders leads to the 'discovery' of biological, psychological, and social differences." In other words, first we have social understandings of what men and women are, or should be, and then we perceive sex differences.

Kessler and McKenna (1978) suggest that, while assignment to a sex category occurs first at birth (or perhaps even prenatally), people continue to categorize one another as males or females throughout life. This continual process of categorization (or, in their words, "attribution") is the means through which gender distinctions emerge and are reproduced. As these authors explain, however, adults typically lack the kind of information about others' bodies that is used to assign sex category at birth. In particular, since clothing usually hides people's genitals from the views of others, people rely on other "markers" to assign a sex category. These markers may include physical characteristics, such as hair, body type, or voice, or they may include aspects of dress, mannerisms or behavior. What count as markers of sex category depend heavily on cultural circumstances and thus vary widely across time, place, and social group. Assignment to sex categories thus relies heavily on social criteria. As views on what are acceptable ways to express oneself as a male or female change, so too do markers of sex category.

These processes are further complicated by Kessler and McKenna's observation that, regardless of what criteria are invoked to assign sex category, there is none that works in every circumstance to distinguish males from females:

If we ask by what criteria a person might classify someone as being either male or female, the answers appear so self-evident as to make the question trivial. But consider a list of items that differentiate males from females. There are none that always and without exception are true of only one gender. No behavioral characteristic (e.g.,

> crying or physical aggression) is always present or never present for one gender. Neither can physical characteristics –either visible (e.g., beards), unexposed (e.g., genitals), or normally unexamined (e.g., gonads) – always differentiate the genders. (Kessler and McKenna 1978, pp. 1–2)

What are the implications of these claims? Most important is the view that sex distinctions are not based on any fully "objective" characteristics of human beings; rather, they are themselves social constructions. Further, this implies that it is impossible to conceive of sex apart from gender. Rather than sex being the basis for gender distinctions, as some claim, this view argues that gender is the basis for distinctions based on sex.

From this perspective, the fact that most people *believe* in the existence of two, objectively identifiable and, hence, "real" sex categories is what requires explanation. Researchers like Kessler and McKenna want to explain how sex distinctions take on their self-evident quality and why belief in these distinctions is so "incorrigible," as they put it, and thus resistant to change (Garfinkel 1967, pp. 122–8).

Kessler and McKenna's perspective may be difficult to grasp, since a belief in objectively real sex categories is a widely shared view in Western thought. Ironically, however, the very taken-for-grantedness of this belief fuels Kessler and McKenna's interest in understanding how such a widely shared view emerges in daily life. If gender meanings have their roots in the social world, as this position implies, then social, rather than biological or genetic, processes are the key to understanding gender. These social processes might include individually focused practices, such as socialization (discussed in the next chapter) or they could include social practices operating at other levels of analysis, such as those occurring within groups or organizations. These latter sources of gender will be discussed in Parts II and III.

On the other side of this debate are sociologists who emphasize the ways in which biology sets limits on what societal influences can achieve (Rossi 1977; Udry 2000). Sometimes referred to as **bio-**

social perspectives, these views treat sex as objectively, identifiable "real" distinctions between males and females that are rooted in human physiology, anatomy, and genetics. These distinctions become the raw material from which gender is constructed. Sociologists who embrace this view would not necessarily deny that assignment to sex categories reflects socially agreed-upon rules, nor would they deny that gender shapes what counts as a marker of sex category. However, these sociologists draw a clear distinction between sex and gender, arguing that sex limits the construction of gender.

I present these views to show that differences in how sociologists define sex and gender reflect more than debates over terminology. Underlying these disagreements are fundamental differences in the kinds of questions researchers ask and the kinds of knowledge they hope to gain. For example, the biosocial perspective is most strongly identified with research seeking to identify biological, genetic, or evolutionary contributions to male and female behaviors and characteristics. We will discuss this research later in this chapter. Those agreeing with Kessler and McKenna, on the other hand, take a different view. While recognizing biological influences on the physical body, Kessler and McKenna object to the notion that biology is the "bedrock" of gender (Kessler and McKenna 2000, p. 69). From their view, adherents to a biosocial perspective take for granted precisely what is most in need of explanation: people's belief in the existence of two, discrete sex categories.

Like most sociologists, I believe that the biological and the social worlds are interdependent and mutually influential. The biological or genetic aspects of maleness and femaleness cannot be understood as fully separate and distinct from the social processes and practices that give meaning to these characteristics. It is thus impossible to neatly separate the realm of sex from that of gender when we are trying to explain any aspect of social life. This view thus is somewhere between Kessler and McKenna's and the biosocial account. Accordingly, I will use the term "gender," rather than "sex" or "sex category," most often throughout the book. When discussing a particular theory or body of work that uses sex instead of gender, however, I will adopt the terminology used by the proponents of that perspective.

Three Frameworks for Understanding Gender

Three broad frameworks will be used to organize the material presented in this book. These frameworks correspond generally to where the "sociological action" is with respect to the social practices that produce gender: For some, this action resides in individuals – their personalities, traits, emotions, etc. This "individualist" approach will be highlighted in Part I, but will appear in other chapters as well. The social practice most closely associated with this framework is socialization, the subject of Chapters 2 and 3. For others, gender is created through social interaction and is inherently contextual in its impact. This implies that gender cannot be reduced to an identity or set of personality traits. Still others argue that gender is embedded in the structures and practices of organizations and social institutions, which appear on the surface to be gender-neutral. I refer to these latter two approaches as "contextual," as they locate the forces producing gender outside the person. These approaches will be highlighted in Chapter 4 and discussed throughout Parts II and III.

Each framework focuses attention on different aspects of the social world. As a result, each asks different kinds of questions and draws different kinds of conclusions. I envision these frameworks as being somewhat like lenses in that each brings certain issues into sharp focus, while others remain outside the field of vision and are ignored or overlooked. A particular framework thus may enable its users to perceive something they may not have noticed using another framework. At the same time as frameworks enable perception, however, they also limit what is seen by excluding other issues from view.

The fact that all frameworks are necessarily partial and selective is the basis for gender scholars' growing awareness that one alone is insufficient for understanding a topic as complex as gender. Fundamentally, gender is a multilevel system whose effects can be seen at all levels of social life. This does not mean that the frameworks we will be using fit together like pieces of a single puzzle, with the truth revealed in the whole. As we will see, pieces of one framework may be compatible with pieces of another, though this is not necessarily the case. Moving between frameworks or combining them in creative ways requires intellectual effort. What we can do here is examine the different angles of vision sociologists have used to address gender, explore the knowledge each has produced and the questions each leaves unanswered, and develop ways to navigate between perspectives.

The three frameworks for understanding gender to be used in this book include: individualist, interactional, and institutional approaches. While each framework contains within it a range of viewpoints, I believe that the differences between frameworks are more salient than differences among perspectives within each framework. For example, although each framework contains some more recent and some more classic perspectives on gender, the frameworks generally tended to emerge at different historical moments. As such, some have been used more extensively than others. Individualist approaches to gender have been used extensively by gender scholars throughout the social sciences and have most in common with lay understandings of gender. Included among individualist perspectives are theories drawn from psychology as well as from sociology. More recently, many theorists and researchers have moved toward a more relational understanding of gender, turning their attention to social interaction and social relations. Interactionists tend to draw on perspectives like ethnomethodology that focus on social situations. Gendered institutions is the most recent framework to emerge and thus is somewhat less theoretically developed than the others. Those with an institutional orientation often draw from more "macro-structural" sociological traditions and have been increasingly interested in relating gender to large-scale patterns, such as welfare states.

Is one perspective more "true" than another? While specific claims made by proponents of each perspective may be empirically tested and more (or less) supported by the evidence, the perspectives themselves cannot be judged as "true" or "false." Rather, as perspectives on a multilevel phenomenon, they should be viewed as providing guidelines for analysis and investigation. Perspectives tell us what we should most carefully attend to and what we can downplay or ignore. The perspectives covered in this chapter emphasize different domains of social life and each alerts students of gender to the ways that gender operates in that domain. Throughout the book I will refer to these perspectives as they become relevant when we discuss particular aspects of gender. Some perspectives will be more relevant for some issues than others. Sometimes more than one perspective will be relevant. I believe that one perspective alone is insufficient to cover contemporary gender scholarship.

Gender Matters

Why study gender? One of this book's major premises is that gender matters in social life – it is one of the organizing principles of the social world: it organizes our identities and self-concepts, structures our interactions, and is one basis upon which power and resources are allocated. Moreover, gender is a tenacious and pervasive force, its existence extending across space and time. Understanding how and, to some extent, why gender matters are issues to be taken up in the following chapters. To preview this discussion, however, we can draw on the three gender frameworks described above. First, gender matters because it shapes the identities and behavioral dispositions of individuals. Researchers disagree over the means through which these gendered characteristics are acquired and precisely how they become a part of the person, but they agree that gender enters into how people see themselves, the ways they behave, and how they view others. While modern life enables people to have many identities, gender identity may be among the most influential in shaping the standards people hold for themselves.

Second, gender matters in the ways that it shapes social interaction. Identities, of course, are products of and sustained through interactions with others. Social interaction thus is an important setting in which gender emerges and is enacted. Social interaction also seems to require sex categorization (Ridgeway 1997). That the identification of someone as female or male facilitates social interaction testifies to this category's power in social life.

Finally, gender also organizes social institutions. By "**social institution**," I mean the "rules" that constitute some area of social life (Jepperson 1991). Social institutions include large, formally organized, public sectors of society, such as education, religion, sports, the legal system, and work, and they include the more personal, less formally organized areas of life, such as marriage, parenthood, and family. One trend in recent gender scholarship is attention to large-scale institutional trends and policies, such as globalization, migration, and neoliberalism (e.g., Calás, Smircich, Tienari, and Ellehave 2010; Davids and van Driel 2005). While social institutions may vary in the degree to which they are "gendered," many institutions cannot be understood without attention to the ways they embody and hence reinforce gender meanings.

As this discussion implies, gender gives shape and meaning to individuals, social relations, and institutions. We cannot fully understand the social world without attending to gender. But the flip side is equally true: We cannot understand gender without understanding the social world. As social life unfolds, gender is produced. As gender is produced, social life unfolds.

Who is to Blame?
Understanding Gender Inequality

One inadvertent consequence of an individualist view of gender is that women and men are often portrayed as either villains or victims – oppressing, exploiting, or defending against each other. While inequality does not just happen, how it happens is more complex than this. Just as gender must be viewed as not solely a property of individuals, so, too, gender inequality must be understood as the product of a more complex set of social forces. These may include the actions of individuals, but they are also to be found in the expectations that guide our interactions, the composition of our social groups, and the structures and practices of the institutions that surround us in daily life. These forces are subject to human intervention and change but are not always visible, known, or understood. They are subtle, may be unconscious, and are reproduced often without conscious intent or design. As we learn how gender operates, however, we will be better equipped to challenge it and remake it in ways we desire.

Chapter Summary

This chapter introduced some of the guiding themes of this book. They include my belief that gender is an important principle of social life and relations, and my contention that sociological vantage points represent the most useful way to understand these issues. Recent developments in this field include greater attention to men and masculinity, attention to variations within and between gender categories, a desire to rethink important sociological concepts and ideas from a gender perspective, and recognition of the value of a cross-national, comparative approach.

In addition, the chapter defined key terms, including gender. I discussed the distinction between sex and gender and introduced several other related concepts, including sexual dimorphism, sex assignment, and sex category. Sociologists disagree over how best to understand the relations between sex and gender, and these disagreements reflect more fundamental differences about the relations between the biological and the social. Finally, I provided an overview of the three frameworks that will be used to organize material in later chapters and discussed why and how gender matters in social life.

Further Reading

Bernard, Jessie. 1973a. "My four revolutions: An autobiographical history of the ASA." *American Journal of Society* 78: 773–791.

Kessler, Suzanne J. 1998. *Lessons from the Intersexed*. New Brunswick, NJ: Rutgers University Press.

Schrock, Douglas and Schwalbe, Michael. 2009. "Men, masculinity, and manhood acts." *Annual Review of Sociology* 35: 277–295.

Key Terms

Gender
Sex/sex category/sex assignment
Sexual dimorphism
Intersexual
Biosocial
Social institution

Critical Thinking Questions

1 Apply the three perspectives on gender to your daily life. Give examples of how gender operates at the individual, interactional, and institutional levels of analysis.

2 Instead of referring to women or men as the "opposite sex," try referring to them as the "other gender." Does this change your assumptions about the relationship between these two categories?

3 Do you agree with the claim that "sex is socially constructed"? What kinds of evidence can you find that supports your position?

Part I
Conceptual Approaches

Chapter 2

The Gendered Person

Chapter Objectives

- Critically evaluate psychological research on sex differences, including cross-national and comparative research.
- Critically evaluate research on the biological and genetic contributions to the study of sex differences.
- Critically evaluate sociological views of gender as an individual attribute.

For many sociologists and psychologists, personalities, minds, bodies, and all the other characteristics that comprise individuals are "where the action is" with respect to understanding gender. In this view, gender is reflected in who people are or how they behave; it is something that individuals possess as a part of themselves and that accompanies them as they move through life. This "something" may be understood in terms of masculinity or femininity, or it may be defined more specifically in terms of particular qualities or

The Sociology of Gender: An Introduction to Theory and Research, Second Edition. Amy S. Wharton.
© 2012 John Wiley & Sons Ltd. Published 2012 by John Wiley & Sons Ltd.

characteristics, such as an aptitude for math (Hyde and Mertz 2009; Penner 2008) or one's interest in politics (Mayer and Schmidt 2004). In all instances, however, gender is understood as something that resides in the individual. This way of thinking about gender – what I call the individualist perspective – is probably the most widely shared of the three frameworks we will be discussing in this book. In this chapter, we will critically examine this approach, looking at some of the many ways that sociologists and psychologists have applied this framework.

In addition to its focus on individuals, one further assumption of this framework is the implicit belief that average differences *between* women and men as groups are greater than the differences *within* each sex category. This is not a claim that all women are alike or all men are alike. Instead, the argument is that sex imposes limits or constraints on gender. The constraints imposed by sex come primarily from the different reproductive roles of women and men. Hence, those who view gender as an attribute of individuals tend to believe that there are some differences between the sexes that are relatively stable across situations.

Because an individualist approach sees differences between women as a group and men as a group as greater than differences within each category, researchers working within this framework generally pay less attention to differences *among* women (or men) with respect to race, ethnicity, sexual orientation, social class, and so on than do researchers adopting other frameworks (although this tendency has changed substantially in recent years). These researchers believe that sex distinctions are powerful organizers of human capabilities and behavior.

Much of this literature is comparative in that emphasis is placed on identifying differences between women and men. Psychologists and sociologists who embrace this perspective thus use sex rather than gender to describe the nature of the traits and dispositions they describe. Hence, the focus of this research tradition can be broadly described as "sex differences." Two topics have drawn most attention from these researchers: The first is an interest in the description and measurement of sex differences; the second involves an understanding of the origins of these differences, including their biological or genetic contributions.

Sex Differences in Traits, Abilities, or Behavioral Dispositions

Given its focus on individual characteristics, it is not surprising that sex difference research has been especially popular among psychologists, who are generally more interested in individual attributes than sociologists. Maccoby and Jacklin's (1974) treatise, *The Psychology of Sex Differences*, is widely regarded as the classic work in this area. In encyclopedic fashion, these authors reviewed and synthesized the existing literature on sex differences in temperament, cognition, and social behavior – no small feat, even in 1974. Examples of sex differences discussed by Maccoby and Jacklin include various intellectual capabilities, such as verbal and math skills and social behaviors, such as aggressiveness. Ironically, however, one of this book's most important conclusions was that differences between women and men were fewer and of less magnitude than many had assumed.

The women's movement was the impetus for many of these initial studies (Eagly 1995). Researchers were especially interested in challenging negative cultural stereotypes about women, and they believed that their empirical research would help serve this goal by demonstrating the essential similarities between men's and women's personalities and behavioral dispositions. In this respect, sex difference researchers were putting into practice Bernard's (1973) belief that scientific research on women and sex differences would help eliminate damaging stereotypes and cultural views that assumed women were inferior to men. Maccoby and Jacklin's (1974) work set into motion a tradition of sex difference research that continues today.

Literally hundreds of personality characteristics, capabilities, and behavioral orientations have been examined as researchers seek to identify differences (and, to a lesser extent, similarities) between women and men. For example, as mentioned above, researchers often study cultural stereotypes, such as nurturing interest and ability among women, or aggression among men (Eagly and Crowley 1986; Eagly and Steffen 1986). Studies have also explored sex differences in personality traits, such as assertiveness and self-esteem; in cognitive abilities, such as language use or mathematical aptitude; in attitudes, such as those related to sexuality; and in many other areas (Cohn 1991; Feingold 1993, 1994; Hyde 2005; Hyde and Linn 2006; Jones, Braithwaite, and Healy 2003; Moore and Johnson 2008; Oliver and Hyde 1993; Voyer, Voyer, and Bryden 1995).

Size and consistency of sex differences

What is the significance of these sex differences? To answer this question, we have to examine two related issues: (a) the magnitude or size of sex differences; and (b) the consistency of these differences across samples, time periods, and situations. These are important issues because there are virtually no traits or behaviors that reliably distinguish all men from all women. Hence, whenever sex differences are found, they represent *average* differences between the sexes, not categorical distinctions. That men and women differ, on average, implies that their responses are, to some degree, overlapping. Understanding the degree of overlap allows researchers to determine whether a particular sex difference is large or small, relative to other kinds of differences between individuals.

In considering the size of a sex difference, researchers begin by collecting all the relevant research findings related to the difference being considered. In their research on sex differences in classroom cheating behavior, for example, Whitley, Nelson, and Jones (1999) gathered thirty-six studies that addressed this issue. These studies were analyzed using a statistical technique called meta-analysis. This technique allows researchers to estimate the magnitude of a sex difference by taking into account the results of multiple studies and samples. Meta-analysis is a rigorous way to synthesize findings from many studies and draw conclusions about the average size of any particular sex difference.

This approach views the size of a sex difference in terms of the degree of overlap in women's and men's scores (Hyde 2005). When 85 percent or more of the scores of women and men overlap, it is typically considered a small average difference. When 65 percent of the scores overlap, it is considered a medium, average difference. When half of the scores overlap, it is considered a large average difference. This means that even when large differences between the sexes are found, there is still considerable overlap in women's and men's scores. In fact, for many of the characteristics examined by sex difference researchers, women and men are much more similar than different (Hyde 2005). In their meta-analysis of sex differences in cheating behavior, Whitley et al. (1999) found a very small, average difference between the sexes, with men more likely to engage in cheating than women.

Understanding the magnitude of any particular sex difference is extremely important. Failure to address this issue helps perpetuate one of two kinds of bias (Hare-Mustin and Marecek 1988). The "alpha bias" is the tendency to exaggerate sex differences, thus creating the impression that women and men are, as the saying goes, "opposites," when in fact, even the most robust sex differences are still average differences, not categorical ones. On the other hand, when relatively large sex differences are minimized or dismissed, researchers display the "beta bias." In this instance, researchers treat all sex differences as if they are trivial. Both kinds of bias can be avoided by careful attention to issues of magnitude.

The *consistency* of sex differences refers to their relative stability across different samples (such as samples differing by age, race or ethnicity, or social class), time periods, or social contexts. Meta-analysis can also be used to examine these issues, as researchers can compare the relative sizes of sex differences across age groups, time periods, countries, or other factors.

Like magnitude, consistency is, to some extent, a relative matter. Studies of a particular sex difference are rarely perfectly consistent; the same magnitude and even the direction (e.g., favoring females, favoring males, or no difference) of effect may vary from study to study. Given this, researchers sometimes assess whether a particular sex difference is more or less consistent across samples than are other kinds of personality or behavioral differences. Because there are many factors that make perfectly consistent results unattainable in the social sciences, researchers must be able to identify the reasons results vary, disentangling those having to do with sex difference from those having to do with other factors. Determining the degree of consistency is important because researchers can then link a particular trait or behavioral disposition with a particular sex, rather than with another social category, setting, or time period. If sex explains some aspect of human personality or behavior, then we would expect this association to persist across studies.

The magnitude and consistency of sex differences: An illustration from cross-national research

That women report more health complaints than men is a well-established research finding (Torsheim, Ravens-Sieberer, Hetland, Välimaa, Danielson, and Overpeck 2006; Van de Velde, Bracke, Levecque, and Meuleman 2010). But, like other sex differences, the magnitude and consistency of these differences varies across studies, even those focused on a single society. Torsheim et al.'s (2006) study of adolescent subjective health provides an example of sex difference research that illustrates these issues in a cross-national context.

These authors analyzed surveys of adolescents in 29 countries and regions. The survey measured the frequency with which respondents experienced a range of health issues, such as headaches, irritability, sleeping difficulties, nervousness, etc. Respondents were also asked questions about their alcohol use, living conditions, and level of social support from teachers and classmates. This individual-level information was combined with information on the respondents' countries, especially regarding the relative status of women and the country's gross domestic product (GDP), a measure of economic position.

For each health complaint and for all age groups in the study (ages 11, 13, and 15), girls reported more health complaints than boys. Sex differences were generally smaller at younger ages than among older adolescents. Figure 2.1 shows the results by country, focusing on sex differences in recurrent health complaints. The results are reported in odds ratios, which are a way of reporting the size of an effect. An odds ratio is a comparison of whether the probability of an event (in this case, any recurrent health complaints) is the same for two groups (in this case, girls and boys). Odds ratios greater than 1 indicate that the probability of reporting a recurrent health complaint is greater for girls than boys. Figure 2.1 shows that girls in all countries reported more recurrent health complaints than boys; this difference was smaller for the youngest age group; and the magnitude of sex differences varied by country. The researchers found that, generally speaking, countries in which women and men showed greater parity in areas such as education, income, and politics had smaller sex differences in adolescent health.

In sum, this study finds pervasive sex differences in adolescent subjective health across nations, coupled with cross-national variability in the magnitude of these differences. These findings underscore our preceding discussion of the complexities and contributions of sex difference research. Though sex differences in subjective health are well established and not unique to one particular culture, political system, or geographic location, these differences are not the same everywhere. The challenge for researchers is to understand the factors that both make gender a consistent force in shaping the lives of individuals *and* the factors that contribute to variability in its effects. Improvements in data quality and access have increased the amount and quality of cross-national research on sex differences and this has given researchers more tools with which to address these issues.

The Origins of Sex Differences

As the above example shows, identifying a sex difference inevitably prompts questions about its origins: *Why* are young women more

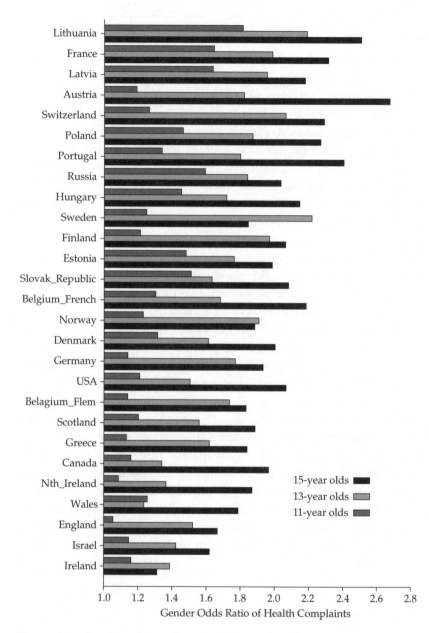

Figure 2.1 Gender odds ratios of adolescent health complaints.
Source: Torsheim et al. 2006. "Cross-national variation of gender differences in adolescent subjective health in Europe and North America." *Social Science and Medicine* 62(4): 815–827.

likely to report recurrent health complaints than their male peers? To explain their findings, most sex difference researchers consider a range of possible factors and recognize that even small differences may have multiple causes. In general, however, explanations can be divided into those that emphasize the primacy of biological or genetic factors and those emphasizing "environmental" causes. Note that even those emphasizing the primacy of biology acknowledge that environmental factors may also contribute, just as those emphasizing environmental factors may acknowledge biological contributions.

Biological or genetic explanations of sex differences

Whether there are biological or genetic contributions to sex differences is a subject of heated debate. Although researchers disagree on some points, many acknowledge that some sex differences may have biological or genetic contributions. At the same time, however, most sociologists (and many other scientists who study sex differences) insist that the impact of these biological or genetic contributions depends upon the environment or culture in which they emerge. In other words, accepting the possibility that biological or genetic factors may influence human personality and behavior does not imply that personality and behavior can be reduced to these factors (Freese 2008). Understanding how biology, genetics, and culture interact to shape personality and behavior, rather than examining each factor separately, is perhaps the best way to proceed as we explore these issues.

Research seeking to identify possible biological or genetic contributions to sex differences is certain to continue; we learn more and more about human biology, genetics, and evolution every day. Regarding genetics, in particular, sociologists Freese and Shostak (2009, p. 108) observe that: "The rapid maturation of this science and its human consequences seem likely to stand as one of the most important developments of our age." This makes it all the more important to understand how these factors may contribute to sex differences.

Epigenetic contributions to sex differences　From a biological or genetics perspective, interest in precisely how sex differences develop focuses on two general areas: epigenetic and evolutionary. **Epigenetic** research on sex differences is based on the notion that "both genes and environment, acting together at all times, determine the structure and function of brain cells and thus the behavior of the organism" (Hoyenga and Hoyenga 1993, p. 20). Studies from this perspective have examined prenatal sex hormones and their role in "priming" (i.e., predisposing) females and males to respond differently outside the womb (Hoyenga and Hoyenga 1993; Maccoby 1998). An epigenetic perspective also guides research on sex differences in perinatal (i.e., postnatal) hormones and brain organization.

Udry's (2000) research on the relationship between girls' exposure to prenatal androgens (i.e., male sex hormones) and their receptiveness to being socialized in a traditionally feminine way is a good example of an epigenetic approach. Udry's sample consisted of 163 white women ranging in age from 27 to 30. Because the women's mothers had supplied prenatal blood samples, Udry had a measure of the women's exposure to prenatal androgens. He also collected data on the women's gender socialization as children and their gendered adult behaviors, which he defined as having "feminine interests" (e.g., a concern with their physical appearance), characteristics of their job and home lives (e.g., marriage, children, and division of household labor), and their scores on personality measures of masculinity and femininity.

Udry found that women's level of exposure to prenatal androgens conditioned the relationship between their gender socialization as children and their gendered adult behaviors. For instance, women exposed to high doses of prenatal androgens were less receptive to traditional female socialization than girls who did not have high prenatal androgen exposure. In contrast, among women exposed to low doses of prenatal androgens, traditional female socialization had a strong effect on women's adult gendered behaviors. These findings imply that gender socialization may be, to some extent, conditioned by sex hormones.

Udry's (2000) research has been strongly criticized. Critics argue that his research is insufficiently attentive to the role of social forces in shaping behavior (Kennelly, Merz, and Lorber 2001; Miller and Costello 2001) and that he reduces gender to sex differences "or sex-dimorphism itself" (Risman 2001, p. 607). In short, they suggest that his biosocial model of gender places too much emphasis on the biological component of behavior.

Sex differences from an evolutionary psychology perspective   Evolutionary psychology, a field that explores links between psychology and genetic inheritance, has also attempted to explain sex differences. In fact, sex differences have received more attention from these researchers than almost any other topic (Freese, Li, and Wade 2003). Evolutionary psychologists believe that "males and females will be the same or similar in all those domains in which the sexes have faced the same or similar adaptive problems" (Buss 1995, p. 164). From this perspective, sex differences stem from differences in the adaptive problems each sex confronts during evolution. Evolutionary psychologists reject what they see as a "false dichotomy between biology and environment," arguing instead that humans develop through their attempts to effectively respond to their surroundings.

In which domains do women and men face different adaptive problems? Evolutionary psychologists argue that sexual selection is the key domain in which women and men confront different kinds of challenges. Sexual selection refers to "the causal process of the evolution of characteristics on the basis of reproductive advantage, as opposed to survival advantage" (Buss 1995, p. 165). Sexual selection occurs primarily through inter- and intrasex competition by both sexes. However, because of women's reproductive role, as well as other biological and physiological sex differences, evolutionary psychologists suggest that each sex faces unique sexual selection challenges. How each sex confronts these sex-specific challenges leads to sex differences in sexuality and mating.

Evolutionary psychologists have received their share of criticism. Many evolutionary biologists, as well as others in the natural sciences, have criticized evolutionary psychologists for ignoring the tremendous variability and flexibility in human and animal societies (Angier 1999) and for exaggerating the degree of difference between women and men. Learning and experience are also important factors in human and animal behavior, and these, too, have been downplayed by evolutionary psychologists. Anthropologists and sociologists suggest that the sex differences evolutionary psychologists attempt to explain could just as easily be explained by social processes. These debates are likely to continue, underscoring the difficulty of disentangling genetic effects from the many other forces shaping human social life.

Environmental Explanations of Sex Differences: Becoming Gendered

Of all sex difference researchers, those with an epigenetic or evolutionary perspective make the most direct connections between biological sex, personality, and behavior. Women and men are viewed as "hard-wired" for certain characteristics during their prenatal and perhaps even postnatal development. As a result, this research has been criticized for ignoring the role of social influences – or what are sometimes called "environmental" factors.

In discussing these factors, we will shift our attention from sex category to gender. This change in focus signals an emphasis on social, rather than biological, forces as the primary sources of differences between women and men. We will be looking at various kinds of social explanations for gender throughout the book. Here, we focus on those social influences that are believed to be relatively permanent and directly shape people early in life. Because our focus in this chapter is the individual, we will consider how people come to understand themselves as male or female and the consequences of those understandings.

To better grasp this idea, think back for a minute about your childhood and try to remember becoming aware of your gender for the first time. Do you recall your first memories of perceiving yourself or others around you as female or male? If these memories are too distant, have a conversation with a preschool age children about gender. See if you can learn how this child views the differences between girls and boys, and try to identify some of the meanings she or he associates with her or his own gender. If you take these suggestions, you will undoubtedly discover that gender – their own as well as others' – is a meaningful concept to children. By age three or so, most can identify themselves as female or male and associate particular qualities or characteristics with each gender.

Gender socialization

Socialization refers to the processes through which individuals take on gendered qualities and characteristics and acquire a sense of self. The socialization process transforms the "raw material" of biological sex into gender-differentiated personalities and behaviors. In other words, one's sex category sets into motion sex-specific processes of socialization. Socialization thus explains sex differences not by invoking biological or genetic factors, but rather by emphasizing how people's traits, aptitudes, and dispositions are shaped by their encounters with society. Sex differences (and similarities) are learned through specific processes that begin even before birth.

Through socialization, people learn what is expected of them as males or females. Even if these expectations are not realized fully, people learn that they will at some level be held accountable to them; that is, they will be assessed in part on the basis of whether they are "appropriately" masculine or feminine. These societal expectations are both powerful and subtle, as Cahill (1986) observed during his 18 months doing fieldwork at a preschool. Cahill reported that both adults and children pejoratively referred to a child behaving in a socially immature way as a "baby." When children behaved in more mature ways, however, they were labeled as "boy" or "girl." As Schrock and Schwalbe (2009) note, this does not merely signal to children that males are boys and females are girls. It also creates an association between being "grown up" and gaining others approval, and behaving as a "boy" or a "girl."

Gender socialization is a two-sided process. On one side is the *target* of socialization, such as a newborn, who encounters the social world through interactions with parents and caretakers. Through these encounters, children not only experience other people and the outside world, these interactions also help children become aware of themselves. The fact that information about gender is so essential to understanding and interacting with a newborn reveals just how deeply implicated gender is in the process of becoming human and developing a self. On the other side of the socialization process are the *agents* of socialization, the individuals, groups, and organizations who pass on cultural information. As we will see in Chapter 5, parents are the most important agent of socialization.

Learning gender: Theories of socialization

There are three major theories of socialization, each of which attempts to identify precisely how socialization occurs. These theories offer somewhat different explanations for how children come to understand themselves as female or male, take on characteristics seen as socially appropriate for their gender; and learn to use gender as a basis for organizing and assimilating information about themselves and others (Bem 1983). Two theories, **social learning** and **cognitive development**, are general learning theories that are also applicable to learning about gender, while the third perspective – **identification theory** – was developed specifically to explain gender socialization and, in particular, the acquisition of gender identity (Bem 1983; Stockard and Johnson 1992).

Social learning theory asserts that gender roles are learned through the reinforcements – positive and negative – children receive for engaging in gender-appropriate and gender-inappropriate behavior (Mischel 1970). This perspective also acknowledges that learning takes place through observation and modeling (Bandura and Walters 1963). According to social learning theorists, reinforcements, whether experienced directly in the form of rewards and punishments or vicariously experienced through observation, are the primary means through which children take on gender-appropriate behaviors. Differential treatment of female and male children by parents and other socializing agents creates gender differences in behavior. It is important to note that parents' responses to their children do not have to be conscious or intentional to have consequences. Indeed, parents' actions can be reinforcing regardless of intent or awareness.

The mechanisms of social learning can be easily illustrated. Imagine the responses of a parent to a three-year-old boy who falls down and begins to cry. The boy may be immediately picked up and comforted, he may simply be told to "be a big boy and stop crying," or perhaps he is simply ignored. Social learning theorists would argue that the child's future reactions to similar situations will be influenced by which of the above responses he receives. The child who is picked up and consoled may continue to display his feelings of pain and displeasure through tears, while boys who are scolded or ignored will gradually learn that crying or similar emotional expressions should not be expressed in these situations.

If parents of boys tend to respond one way and parents of girls tend to respond in another, social learning theorists would say that a gender-typed behavior has been created. A **gender-typed behavior**, then, is one that elicits different responses depending upon whether the person engaging in the behavior is female or male. Social learning theorists would argue that many sex differences are the result of gender-typing. That is, they are learned behaviors created by the mechanisms of reinforcement. Can you identify any other gender-typed behaviors?

Although reinforcement may be one mechanism through which gender roles are acquired, this theory does not fully explain this process (Bem 1983; Stockard and Johnson 1992). For example, evidence suggests that children, especially boys, may persist in gender-appropriate behaviors even when they are not reinforced for these activities, or even when they are negatively reinforced (Maccoby

1992; Stockard and Johnson 1992). More generally, research suggests that children are more actively involved in their own socialization than social learning theorists acknowledge Maccoby 1992). Regarding social learning theory, Bem (1983, p. 600) notes: "This view of the passive child is inconsistent with the common observation that children themselves frequently construct and enforce their own version of society's gender rules." To simplify somewhat, we can say that social learning theory tends to view children (and other targets of socialization) as lumps of clay that are molded by their environments. This approach reflects a view of the socialization process "from the outside." A cognitive perspective on gender socialization offers a different view.

Cognitive approaches How is *being* male or female expressed in people's *understandings* of themselves as masculine or feminine? Cognitive psychological approaches answer this question by examining how people internalize gender meanings from the outside world and then use those meanings to construct an identity consistent with them. This approach thus examines the connections between sex category membership and the meanings people attach to that membership (Bem 1993; Howard 2000). These meanings, in turn, are assumed to guide and help explain individual behavior.

Most closely associated with psychologists Lawrence Kohlberg (1966) and Sandra Bem (1983, 1993), cognitive theorists embrace a much more active view of children than proponents of social learning. Rather than focusing on the environment's role in molding children's behavior, cognitive theorists focus on the ways that children actively seek to understand themselves and their worlds. Part of this understanding involves recognizing different expectations for males and females. Once recognized, children are motivated to comply with these expectations. This approach thus provides a look at socialization from the "inside out," or from the perspective of the child and his or her thought processes.

Kohlberg's (1966) cognitive theory is based on the claim that gender learning can be explained using the principles of cognitive development (see also Piaget 1932). In this view, learning about gender occurs as part of a more general psychological process of cognitive maturation. Once children have labeled themselves as female or male, and recognize this as stable over time and situations, they are motivated to seek out gender-appropriate behaviors. In addition, children attach greater value to these behaviors and experience them as more positively reinforcing than gender-inappropriate behaviors. With age, children's abilities to interpret gender cues become more sophisticated and flexible, a pattern cognitive development theorists argue parallels intellectual development more generally.

While sympathetic to elements of this approach, some are skeptical of its claim that gender learning takes place only after children have labeled themselves as female or male. In addition, Bem (1983, 1993) argues that Kohlberg fails to sufficiently explain why and how children come to employ gender, rather than some other characteristic, as a cognitive organizing principle. These concerns have led to another kind of cognitive perspective, Bem's (1983, 1993) **gender schema theory**.

Bem (1983, 1993) argues that in cultures like American society, where gender distinctions are strongly reinforced, children learn to use gender to make sense of their experience and process new information. Through this process people acquire traits and personalities that are consistent with their understandings of themselves as male or female. They develop gender schemas, cognitive structures (or lenses) that help people assimilate and organize perception. As Bem (1993, p. 154) observes, "The gendered personality is more than a particular collection of masculine or feminine traits; it is also a way of looking at reality that produces and reproduces those traits during a lifetime of self-construction." In this view, the larger social world provides the "raw material" from which gender identities are constructed and these identities, in turn, guide perception and action.

Two other aspects of Bem's gender schema perspective are worth noting. The first is her contention that gender schemas in late twentieth-century American society emphasize **gender**

polarization – the belief that what is acceptable or appropriate for females is not acceptable or appropriate for males (and vice versa) and that anyone who deviates from these standards of appropriate femaleness and maleness is unnatural or immoral. Bem argues that these notions become part of children's internalized gender schemas, thus leading them to think of the other gender as the "opposite sex."

Another feature of gender schemas in American society, according to Bem (1993), is that they are **androcentric**. Androcentrism refers to a belief that males and masculinity are superior to females and femininity, and that males and masculinity are the standard or the norm. Not only do children internalize gender schemas that define males and females as inherently different, but they also internalize a sense that maleness and masculinity are more desirable and highly valued. For example, children may learn to associate dolls with girls and trucks with boys, but they will also learn that boys who play with dolls should be ridiculed while girls who play with trucks should be admired. In Bem's view, androcentrism damages both females *and* males. Regarding its effects on men, Bem says that androcentrism

> so thoroughly devalues whatever thoughts, feelings, and behaviors are culturally defined as feminine that crossing the gender boundary has a more negative cultural meaning for men than it has for women – which means, in turn, that male gender-boundary crossers are much more culturally stigmatized than female gender-boundary crossers. At the same time, androcentrism provides such an unreachable definition of what a real man is supposed to be that only a few men can even begin to meet it. (Bem 1993, pp. 149–50)

Bem's research suggests children use gender schemas because these categories are helpful in making sense of the social world. Extending this logic would lead us to predict that children would be more likely to attend to some social categories than others, and that these differences would be related to the category's usefulness in distinguishing between different kinds of people. Hirschfeld's (1996) research on preschoolers' awareness of social categories is consistent with this argument. He found that gender was salient in children's understanding and recall of visual and verbal narratives, but its relevance relative to other social categories, such as occupation and race, varied. Children use social categories like gender not simply because they are easily observed, but rather because they are curious about the social world and the kinds of people within it.

In sum, cognitive perspectives, such as those associated with Kohlberg and Bem, view children as, in important respects, socializing themselves. They imply that gender distinctions become very significant to children – as they are to adults – and that gender is therefore used to organize and process information from the environment. It is this process that creates sex differences. Moreover, for Bem, gender socialization not only involves learning about what is expected of one as male or female, but also the process of becoming gender schematic (i.e., of using gender schemas to process, organize, and interpret information). As she notes, "a gendered personality is both a product and a process. It is both a particular collection of masculine or feminine traits and a way of constructing reality that itself constructs those traits" (Bem 1993, p. 152). Because children are motivated to become "competent" members of their culture, they will learn to use the tools their culture provides (and values) to regulate their own behavior and interpret the world around them.

Social learning and cognitive approaches are not mutually exclusive. Rather, as I have stressed, social learning theory attends more to the ways that parents and others respond to children, while cognitive theories focus on children's efforts to make sense of the world around them. Both are important; we can only understand socialization if we examine the parent–child relationship itself, rather than focusing only on the parents' behavior or the child's (Maccoby 1992).

Identification theory: the psychoanalytic perspective Identification theory, the third major theory of socialization, differs from the previous two perspectives in significant ways. First, unlike social learning and cognitive development approaches, identification theory is explicitly concerned with gender, gender identity, and sexuality (Stockard and Johnson 1992). More important, however, this perspective disagrees that gender-appropriate behavior is learned through reinforcement, imitation, or reflects an intent to behave a particular way. Instead, drawing from the ideas of Freud and his followers, identification theorists assert that, at least some aspects of gender result from unconscious psychological processes (Chodorow 1978; Johnson 1988; Williams 1989).

The most influential version of psychoanalytic theory among sociologists of gender is the perspective developed by Nancy Chodorow in her 1978 classic, *The Reproduction of Mothering* and refined in her later writings. Chodorow's perspective focuses on how women and men develop a personal sense of what it means to be female or male. According to Chodorow, gender identity is formed during early childhood as children develop emotional attachments to a same-sex parent or adult. In cultures like the U.S. where women have primary responsibility for infant care, children of both sexes typically form their earliest emotional attachments to their mother – a woman. This attachment is important, given infants' extreme dependence on their mothers for the satisfaction of all their needs. For psychoanalytic theorists, infants' relations with mothers are emotionally significant and deeply meaningful, feelings that may be incorporated into the child's unconscious.

Despite these bonds, separation from the mother must eventually occur and this separation is a crucial step in child development. With the formation of **ego boundaries** – the sense of separation between "me" and "not me" – infants become aware of themselves and others as separate beings with an ability to influence their surroundings. Along with the formation of ego boundaries is a second developmental task: the formation of gender identity. **Gender identity** refers to people's own sense of themselves as males or females. In psychological terms, it is a "fundamental, existential sense of one's maleness or femaleness, an acceptance of one's gender as a social-psychological construction that parallels one's acceptance of one's biological sex" (Spence 1984, p. 84).

Not only must infants gain a sense of themselves as a separate entity in the world, they must also develop an awareness of themselves as male or female. For Chodorow and other psychoanalytic theorists, this awareness is helped by – perhaps even dependent upon – another kind of attachment: identification with a same-sex parent or adult. Through this bond children have an opportunity to learn what it means to be male or female. Identification is more than simply modeling an adult, however, but also has emotional significance for the child. Hence, gender identification gives children information about what it means to be male or female, and it motivates and sustains their interest in this aspect of themselves. Psychoanalytic theorists believe that gender identity remains significant to people and is a powerful force in their adult lives.

These processes operate somewhat differently for males and females, however. Because children of both sexes form a primary attachment first to their mother, male and female children face different challenges during early stages of development. The formation of males' ego boundaries is helped along by mothers' differences from their sons. Acquiring gender identity, by contrast, is potentially more problematic. Sons are forced to "switch" their identification from their mothers to their fathers, which is emotionally painful and difficult. This is made even harder when – as is typical even in two-parent households – fathers are less involved in caring for their children than mothers.

Girls' development unfolds somewhat differently. Because they are of the same sex as their mother, girls never have to give up their primary identification. Mothers' presence in girls' lives also gives girls a more concrete sense of what it means to be female than boys are likely to receive of what it means to be male from their fathers. What may become problematic for girls, however, is the formation of their ego boundaries – their sense of themselves as separate and independent from others.

These different paths to gender identification are responsible for gender-differentiated female and male personalities and form the backdrop against which males' and females' later development take place. The net result of these differences, according to psychoanalytic theorists, is that males and females acquire distinctly different gender identities, with different forms of "relational potential" (Chodorow 1978, p. 166). Male gender identity is, what Messner refers to as, "positional," meaning that the self "is solidified through separation from others" (1992, p. 32; see also Gilligan 1982). This implies that boys and men, more so than girls and women, will be more comfortable with separation and distance than with connection. In contrast, girls have "a basis for 'empathy' built into their primary definition of self in way that boys do not. Girls emerge with a stronger basis for experiencing another's needs or feelings as one's own (or of thinking that one is so experiencing another's needs and feelings)" (Chodorow 1978, p. 167). Women, more so than men, will feel more comfortable when connected to others and prefer relationship to separation. From a psychoanalytic perspective, then, the connection vs. separateness dimension is the basis from which other differences between the genders develop.

In addition, psychoanalytic theorists argue that gender identity will have a different significance for women and men. Because women's gender identity develops through their ongoing relations with their mothers, women are likely to acquire a relatively secure sense of themselves as women. Gender identity may be somewhat more amorphous and tenuous for men, who not only are forced to give up their primary attachment to their mother, but also must identify with a more distant father. As a result, while men may feel compelled to "prove" their masculinity to themselves and others, women believe that they are feminine as a result of being female. This difference helps to explain why men seem to have a greater psychic stake in gender than do women.

While this perspective has been embraced by some gender scholars, it has also been criticized on several counts. Some object to the perspective's Freudian roots, particularly its emphasis on unconscious processes. Critics claim that psychoanalytic arguments like Chodorow's are virtually impossible to systematically test or verify empirically. Another criticism is that this approach falsely universalizes a particular kind of mothering and family organization, thus ignoring how mothering and the creation of gender identity may differ in other social groups and contexts. In particular, some question Chodorow's implicit assumption that gender identity is separate from and develops independently of other identities, such as those involving race, ethnicity, or social class (Spelman 1988). Finally, some suggest that Chodorow's perspective reinforces exaggerated stereotypes about women and men. Her claim that women seek connection and men prefer separation strikes many as oversimplified and contributing to an unrealistic view of differences between women and men.

Although Chodorow acknowledges the limitations of her early viewpoint, she believes that gender has an important psychological component that must be taken into account. This component is primarily expressed through people's gender identities. While the specifics of gender identity are unique for each person, the contents of male and female gender identities are not random or arbitrary. As long as women continue to be primary caretakers of infants, and men have limited involvement in the early caretaking of children, women's and men's gender identities will evolve somewhat differently. For Chodorow (1995, p. 517): "each person's sense of gender – her gender identity or gendered subjectivity – is an inextricable fusion or melding of personally created (emotionally and through unconscious fantasy) and cultural meaning."

Gender theorists like Bem believe that people are capable of reflecting upon their own maleness or femaleness, and assigning meaning to their sex category membership. This perspective has a cognitive emphasis because it regards people's capacities to organize, select, and interpret information as important. Although psychoanalytic views of gender identity also recognize people's abilities to make sense of the world around them, psychoanalytic theorists emphasize unconscious and unreflective processes to a greater degree. Both views, however, share the belief that the meanings people assign to themselves as males or females play important roles in the production and reproduction of gender.

Summing up: Social explanations of gender differences

Theories of socialization address how people become gendered, or how they take on gender-appropriate traits or characteristics. Though each views the process somewhat differently, these perspectives all highlight the contribution of social factors in the creation of gender differences. They emphasize the power of societal expectations and show how children who are born into a world differentiated by gender come to embody those differences in their own personalities, preferences, and behaviors.

These theories focus on the acquisition of gender-appropriate characteristics, but they do not specify precisely what those characteristics are. What is considered appropriate for each gender varies according to societal and cultural context, time, and place, among other variables. Studies focused on the U.S. have become increasingly attentive to the ways that parental socialization varies by race and ethnicity (McLoyd, Cauce, Takeuchi, and Wilson 2000; Raffaelli and Ontai 2004). Cross-national research reveals how differences in gender expectations for children are linked to societal differences in culture, politics, and social structure (Sayer, Gauthier, and Furstenberg 2004).

Box 2.1   A university education is more important for a boy than a girl.

This table shows how people in 22 countries responded when asked their level of agreement with the statement that a university education is more important for a boy than a girl. How do you think these differences might be reflected in parental socialization practices?

Box 2.1 (*Continued*)

	Agree	Disagree	DK
	%	%	%
U.S.	15	83	2
Britain	9	87	3
France	14	87	0
Germany	16	83	1
Spain	7	93	0
Poland	34	58	8
Russia	22	73	5
Turkey	25	69	6
Egypt	50	47	3
Jordan	44	54	2
Lebanon	4	97	0
China	48	50	2
India	63	32	5
Indonesia	28	71	1
Japan	35	64	3
Pakistan	51	39	10
S. Korea	27	69	3
Argentina	10	88	2
Brazil	11	87	1
Mexico	14	84	3
Kenya	22	77	0
Nigeria	34	66	1

Pew Research Center Q33.

Source: "Gender Equality Universally Embraced, but Inequalities Acknowledged," July 1, 2010, the Pew Global Attitudes Project, a project of the Pew Research Center.

Sex Differences and Social Policy:
The Case of Mathematics Aptitude

Gender scholarship contributes to social policy debates at many levels. We focus here on the contributions of the individualist approach to gender – especially research on the magnitude, consistency, and causes of sex differences – to debates surrounding the underrepresentation of women in STEM (science, technology, engineering, and mathematics) fields. Women's underrepresentation in STEM disciplines has become an important public policy issue in the U.S.: in 2010, the U.S. House of Representatives passed legislation officially titled "Fulfilling the Potential of Women in Academic Science and Engineering," which promotes attempts to close the gender gap in this area. Closing this gap and encouraging all those interested in mathematics-intensive fields to pursue these areas are viewed as important for the U.S. (and world) economy.

As we consider how sex difference research contributes to knowledge about the causes of this gap, we will reprise several earlier points, including issues surrounding the size and consistency of sex differences; the relative importance of biological and social contributions to sex differences and the challenges of disentangling their effects; and the value of cross-national studies. Most important perhaps is the recognition that research can be a messy business, yielding incomplete answers and raising more questions than are answered. But empirical evidence is also a powerful tool for making sense of a complex world.

Biological contributions and their limits   Because women's representation in STEM fields has not increased as quickly as in some other academic areas, some argue that biological differences in women's and men's mathematical aptitudes or abilities may be partly to blame. Brain organization, hormones, and evolutionary factors have all been linked to sex differences in mathematical aptitude and put forward to explain women's underrepresentation in STEM fields (Ceci and Williams 2010; Hyde and Linn 2006; Penner 2008).

However, what Ceci and Williams (2010, p. 182) call "the strong biological position" regarding women's underrepresentation in STEM fields "is riddled with conflicting findings and claims."

For example, while neuroscientists are discovering some differences between male and female brains, they have not been able to link these differences to sex differences in intelligence or aptitude for high-level scientific or mathematical achievement. Some argue that in order to understand the underrepresentation of women in STEM fields we should not focus on mathematical ability per se, but rather the relative representation of women and men at the high end of the distribution (Hyde and Mertz 2009; Penner 2008). While studies have found variability in math aptitude, with males more likely to be represented at the high and low ends of the distribution, this variability cannot explain the low percentages of women in STEM.

Mathematical aptitude has been linked to spatial ability, and many who study the biological bases of women's underrepresentation in STEM fields focus on this set of skills. Researchers have found sex differences in certain types of spatial abilities. Voyer, Voyer, and Bryden (1995) analyzed 286 published studies of sex differences in spatial abilities conducted between 1970 and 1990, finding large sex differences favoring males for two of the three types of spatial skills measured. But studies of the relations between pre- or postnatal hormones on spatial abilities have failed to show a causal connection. While biological influences on women's underrepresentation in STEM fields are possible, they are likely to play only a secondary role.

Cross-national research on sex differences in math aptitude provides additional evidence for the insufficiency of biological explanations. Though sex differences in math aptitude are found in many countries, the magnitude and direction of these differences varies. Guiso, Monte, Sapienza, and Zingales (2008) examined the results of math and reading tests taken by almost 300,000 15 year-olds in 40 countries. They found that girls' math scores averaged 10.5 points lower than boys, while their reading scores averaged 32.7 points higher. As Figure 2.2 shows, this gap varies by country. Penner (2008, p. 163) reports similar findings, arguing that differences in

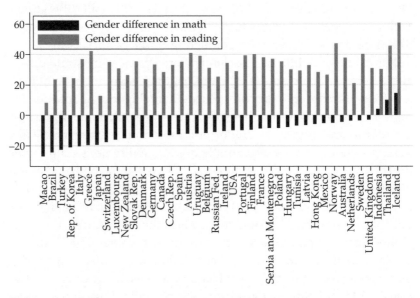

Figure 2.2 Difference between average girls' scores and average boys' scores in math and reading tests by country.

Source: Luigi Guiso, Ferdinando Monte, Paola Sapienza, and Luigi Zingales. 2008. "Gender, Science, and Math."*Science* 320: 1164–1332. Supporting Online Material for "Culture, Gender, and Math" (figure S1A, www.sciencemag.org/cgi/content/full/320/58801164/DC1

"country-specific socialization processes" might account for this variation. Penner also raises the possibility that the contribution of biological factors to sex differences in mathematics achievement may itself vary across societal contexts.

The role (and limits) of socialization Social factors may also help explain sex differences in mathematics aptitude. For example, Guiso et al. (2008) found that country-level variations in sex differences in mathematics performance (shown in Figure 2.2) were correlated with a country's level of gender equality. The more gender-equal a country, the smaller the gap in mathematics performance. Within the U.S., girls' performance on standardized mathematics tests has increased significantly over time, a finding attributed to girls taking more high school math and science courses (Hyde and Mertz 2009). Together, these findings suggest that sex differences in mathematics aptitude result in part from more traditional gender attitudes, especially those related to girls' pursuit of education and enrollment in math and science.

Despite this evidence, Ceci and Williams suggest that women's underrepresentation in STEM disciplines is due to more than socialization practices that discourage girls' pursuit of math:

> It asks too much of readers to accept that pervasive gender stereotypes, lack of parental encouragements, early toy use, and discriminatory teacher behaviors are a major cause of the lack of women in math-intensive STEM careers. How could such stereotypes be influential, given that girls elect to take as many advanced math courses as boys – and get better grades in them? (Ceci and Williams 2010, p. 183)

These authors do not dismiss the role of social factors altogether. Rather, they suggest that we look at women's and men's vocational interests and preferences as sources of influence on their career choices.

Consider the results of Su, Rounds, and Armstrong's (2009) meta-analysis of sex differences in vocational interests. These authors examined results from career interest inventories in use between 1964 and 2007. They found small to moderate sex differences in some areas and large differences in others. For example, women's and men's interest in careers that were data-oriented vs. idea-oriented differed barely at all, with over 90 percent overlap in their scores. Sex differences in other interest areas were much more pronounced. With respect to interest in "things" vs. "people," Su et al. (2009) found less than a 50 percent (46.9) overlap in women's and men's scores: Men reported stronger interest in "thing-oriented" careers than women, while women were more likely than me to be interested in careers that were people-oriented. Regarding an interest in engineering as a future vocation, the degree of overlap between women's and men's scores was even lower – just over 40 percent of scores overlapped. As we know from our earlier discussion of the size of sex differences, researchers consider these to be large sex differences.

How can this research contribute to an understanding of women's underrepresentation in STEM disciplines? Su et al. (2009) suggest that, because people's vocational interests seem to be established relatively early in life, those interested in increasing the percentage of women in STEM fields should focus more attention on these early years. In addition, Su et al. (2009, p. 879) propose that researchers learn more about the factors that shape women's and men's vocational interests by addressing such questions such as: "Why do some women become more interested in STEM fields than others? Which stage in the developmental process is critical for the development of science and engineering interests? What factors may thwart or promote the development of science and engineering interests?" Understanding these issues, they believe, will help educators and policy-makers create effective strategies for closing the STEM gender gap.

There is no easy answer to the question of why women are underrepresented in STEM fields, and there is no consensus about if or how this issue should be addressed through legislation or other social policies. I have discussed it here as a way to illustrate how the individualist approach to gender – and sex difference research in particular – can and has been used to address issues of social relevance. We conclude this chapter with a final look at the significance of sex differences.

Sex Differences and Gender Inequality

You may be wondering what is at stake in these debates about sex differences. As discussed earlier, a great deal of sex difference research has been motivated by the hope that findings would dispel cultural stereotypes about women, and in some cases, men. If research showed that the two groups were not really very different, according to this logic, it would be more difficult for societies to defend gender inequality. History provides some support for this argument. Unequal treatment has often been justified by supposed biological or genetic differences between women and men. Women in particular have been excluded from such domains as politics and employment on the basis of their differences from men. Hyde (2005, p. 589) suggests that these problems have not disappeared and she points out the continuing dangers of what she sees as "overinflated claims of gender differences." Racial and ethnic inequalities have also been justified on the basis of supposed biological or genetic differences between groups. It is always a good idea to be wary when social arrangements are justified by arguments about inherent differences between groups.

A focus on sex differences may be problematic for other reasons as well. Hollander and Howard (2000, p. 340) argue that a focus on group differences "may act as self-fulfilling prophecies, predisposing researchers to overlook group similarities and to exaggerate or even elicit information that confirms their preconceptions." This makes it all too easy for researchers to confirm gender stereotypes. According to these authors, a sex difference research is also problematic because it "often obscures the fact that different almost always means unequal" (Hollander and Howard 2000, p. 340). Differences, they argue, are almost never just differences, but instead reflect imbalances of power.

In response, others argue that denying differences is no more compatible with equality than acknowledging them, and they dispute the claim that differences must necessarily be seen as deficiencies on the part of one group. As Eagly (1995, p. 155) observes, "the sex differences that scientists have documented do not tell a simple tale of female inferiority." Eagly and others argue that equality is best served by having empirically supported knowledge about women and men. Differences do not imply inequality any more than similarity guarantees equal treatment. This view has received increasing support in recent years as researchers have developed more complex ways to understand the relations between gender difference and gender inequality.

Chapter Summary

The chapter reviewed several types of "individualist" approaches to gender. Used extensively by gender scholars, these perspectives have a long history of research and development. Individualist approaches treat gender as a characteristic of people. Proponents of these views focus their attention on women and men – their traits, characteristics, and identities – and suggest that gender operates primarily through these aspects of individuals.

The chapter examined sex difference research, including issues surrounding the measurement of these differences. We also considered the two primary explanations for sex differences. One set of explanations focuses on biological factors, while the second emphasizes social factors. For gender scholars with an individualist lens, the key social process that produces sex differences is socialization.

Socialization is the process through which people become gendered. They learn what is expected of them because they are female or male and how to display these characteristics. Because most sociologists consider gender distinctions as primarily social in origin, rather than biological, socialization is important to understand. Gender socialization has an especially central role to play in individualist understandings of gender, as these approaches emphasize the ways that gender is embodied in people. The three major theories of socialization – social learning, cognitive, and identification theories – each attempt to explain how people take on characteristics their society sees as appropriate for males and females.

The example of women's underrepresentation in STEM disciplines was used to illustrate how sex difference research can inform social policy debates. Researchers have studied both the biological and the social factors contributing to sex differences in mathematics aptitude. Though much is known about both sets of influences, our discussion also revealed the limits of our knowledge of sex differences.

Ultimately, all of the perspectives discussed in this chapter explore how much people's personal characteristics – traits, behaviors, and identities – are shaped by our sex category. They share a belief that people are gendered – that is, that the distinction between masculine and feminine is one that is expressed in individuals. In addition, most agree that sex distinctions are a primary reason for this. Sex, then, is a source of gender and sets limits on the traits, behaviors, and identities of people. Further, because gender is part of the person, it is assumed to be relatively stable. People do not put on and take off gender as they move from place to place, situation to situation, group to group.

In the following chapter, we will see how sociologists who adopt an interactionist or gendered institutions perspective account for gender's impact on everyday life. Interactionists believe that situational characteristics interact with, and sometimes offset, internalized personality attributes and behavioral dispositions to create gender distinctions. From a gendered institutions perspective, gender socialization is a less important source of gender distinctions than are features of social structure and social organization.

Further Reading

Ceci, Stephen J. and Williams, Wendy M. 2010. *The Mathematics of Sex: How Biology and Society Conspire to Limit Talented Women and Girls*. New York: Oxford University Press.

Chodorow, Nancy. 1978. *The Reproduction of Mothering*. Berkeley: University of California Press.

Hyde, Janet Shibley. 2005. "The Gender Similarities Hypothesis." *American Psychologist* 60: 581–592.

Key Terms

Epigenetic
Socialization

Conceptual Approaches

Social learning theory
Cognitive development theory
Identification theory
Gender-typed behavior
Gender schema theory
Gender polarization
Androcentric
Ego boundaries
Gender identity

Critical Thinking Questions

1 What are some commonly held beliefs about differences between women and men? How does the research discussed in this chapter challenge or support these beliefs?
2 Why might gender differences receive more attention from researchers than gender similarities?
3 What factors might explain why sex differences in gender and math aptitudes vary across societies?

Chapter 3

Gender in Interaction and Institutions

Chapter Objectives

- Critically evaluate the main elements of interactionist approaches to gender, including ethnomethodology, status characteristics theory, and homophily research.
- Critically evaluate the main elements of institutional approaches to gender.
- Discuss the major differences between individual, interactionist and institutional approaches to gender.

Have you ever found yourself the only woman (or man) in a group of people, such as a discussion group for a course or perhaps as a member of a work team? Now, think about situations where you were surrounded by others just like you – all women or all men. Did you feel differently in each situation? How did being a member

The Sociology of Gender: An Introduction to Theory and Research, Second Edition. Amy S. Wharton.
© 2012 John Wiley & Sons Ltd. Published 2012 by John Wiley & Sons Ltd.

of the majority or the minority (with respect to sex category) affect how you behaved and how others behaved toward you? These are among the issues explored by proponents of the frameworks presented in this chapter.

Recall that gender is a system of social practices that constitute people as different and that organizes relations of inequality. Thus far, we have looked at gender from the point of view of individuals and have focused on the social practices that produce the gendered person. But the social practices that constitute gender do not operate strictly at the individual level. These social practices also shape social relations and interaction patterns, and they operate as part of larger entities, such as organizations and institutions. In this chapter, we will explore these alternative frameworks. They include interactional approaches, which attend to social relations; and institutional perspectives, which highlight the structure and practices of organizations and social institutions. In contrast to individualist approaches, which focus on internalized and relatively stable characteristics of individuals, the two frameworks examined here emphasize social forces operating external to the person.

The perspectives examined in Chapter 2 share a belief that people are gendered – that is, that the distinction between masculine and feminine is one that is primarily expressed in individuals. In addition, most agree that sex distinctions are a primary reason for this. Sex, then, is a source of gender and sets limits on the traits, behaviors, and identities of people. Further, because gender is part of the person, it is assumed to be relatively stable – internal and unchangeable. People do not put on and take off gender as they move from place to place, situation to situation, group to group. This claim is disputed by the next set of perspectives we will examine.

Interactionist Views of Gender

Interactionist approaches to gender focus less on individuals and more on the social context within which individuals interact. Although these perspectives acknowledge that women and men may differ in some of the ways noted by individualists, interaction-ist approaches place greater attention on forces operating outside the individual. In contrast to individualists, who assume people's traits and abilities are relatively stable, interactionists argue that people's reactions and behaviors vary in response to the social context. The social context includes the other participants in a setting and features of the environment where the interaction takes place. These approaches, as Deaux and Major (1990, p. 91) explain, "presume[s] a repertoire of possibilities from which individual men and women choose different responses on varying occasions with different degrees of self-consciousness." For example, this view would suggest that women might be more nurturant when interact-ing with others who expect women to behave this way than when interacting with people having fewer gender expectations. Women might also behave in a more nurturant manner in social contexts where women have been traditionally defined as caretakers than when they are in social contexts where women have traditionally held other roles.

In this chapter, we examine three types of interactionist approaches. While they differ in important respects, they all view social categorization as essential to social interaction. **Social catego-rization** refers to the processes through which individuals classify others and themselves as members of particular groups. Virtually everyone agrees that sex category is an extremely important social category (Aries 1996). For some, as we will see, it is *the* most impor-tant social category. There are many other social categories, however, including those based on racial or ethnic distinctions, age, ability, etc. All of these social categories may be relevant for social interac-tion in particular situations and settings.

Social categorization is important because it sets into motion the production of gender differences and inequality. The three per-spectives examined below differ somewhat in their understanding of how and why that occurs, however. The first interactionist approach – "doing gender" – argues that social interaction is the vehicle through which people present themselves to others as women or men. Status characteristics theory takes a different view, emphasizing the ways in which sex categories become the basis for people's expectations about others' competence. The third interactionist perspective – what I call the homophily approach – emphasizes the consequences of people classifying others as similar or different from themselves. This perspective generally assumes that being different from or similar to others is more important in shaping interaction than *how* one differs or is similar.

Ethnomethodological views: "doing gender"

Sociologists influenced by the ethnomethodological tradition offer an interaction-based view known as "doing gender" (West and Zimmerman 1987, 2009; see also Deutsch 2007; Jurik and Siemsen 2009). These theorists disagree with those who see gender as a stable set of personality traits or internalized gender norms. Instead, from a **"doing gender"** perspective, gender – or, rather, the belief that the world is divided into two, mutually exclusive categories – is understood as an "accomplishment", a product of human effort.

Like the previous interactionist accounts, ethnomethodologists believe that sex categorization is a habitual, virtually automatic, and rarely questioned aspect of social interaction. Sex categorization both reflects and contributes to "the natural attitude" regarding gender (Garfinkel 1967; see also Chapter 1). Ethnomethodologists believe that sex categorization and the "natural attitude" are social constructions rather than biological or physical realities. Understanding how social interaction produces a gender-differentiated world is the central goal of these appproaches.

In later work, West and Fenstermaker (1995) extended this view: "Doing difference" is their attempt to describe the exercise of power and production of inequality more generally, not just in relation to gender. West and Fenstermaker argue that the same dynamics that "accomplish" gender in interaction also produce other forms of inequality and power differentials, such as those stemming from social class and race. This implies that not only gender, but race and social class as well, are products of social interaction, not essential characteristics of people. "Doing difference" is West and

Fenstermaker's way of explaining multiple types of inequality with a single analytic framework.

From an ethnomethodological perspective, gender is "done" in virtually all social situations. Ethnomethodologists claim that because sex categories are always present, they are always available as a basis for interpreting others' behavior. "In short," as West and Fenstermaker (1993, p. 157) explain, "persons engaged in virtually *any* activity can hold themselves accountable and be held accountable for their performance of that activity *as women* or *as men*" (emphasis in original). This claim – that gender is being "done" always and everywhere – distinguishes ethnomethodological approaches from the preceding interactionist accounts.

"Doing gender" has been highly influential in gender scholarship and credited with providing a powerful alternative to the "gendered person" approaches discussed in the previous chapter. As this perspective has gained popularity, however, some argue that it has been better at explaining "gender conformity" – how gender differences are maintained – than social interactions that challenge these differences (Deutsch 2007). A more longstanding criticism of this approach is that it goes too far in emphasizing the fluidity and variability of gender. For example, Thorne (1995) argues that ethnomethodologists' preoccupation with gender as a "performance" or as something that is "done" in social interaction underemphasizes the factors that shape or constrain people's ability to produce gender displays. Extending the metaphor of the performance, we could say that ethnomethodologists focus on each performance's unique details to the exclusion of how performances differ systematically and how these differences may be shaped by the theatre, the stage and the props that form its backdrop. To fully understand these influences, we turn to other interactionist accounts.

Status characteristics theory:
The importance of expectations

How does social interaction help produce gender distinctions and inequalities? Status characteristics theory (also referred to as the theory of "expectation states") offers a straightforward answer to this question: Because interaction requires that people orient themselves to one another, it is necessary to have some basis for categorizing others vis-à-vis oneself (Ridgeway 1997). In Risman's (1998, p. 33) words: "Gender is something we do in order to make social life more manageable."

Sex categorization serves this purpose better than any other categorization system, according to Ridgeway and other status characteristics theorists. Sex categorization activates gender stereotypes, and people learn to expect certain kinds of behaviors and responses from others based on their sex category. These expectations serve as cognitive reminders of how we are supposed to behave in any given situation. People thus respond to others based on what they believe is expected of them and assume that others will do likewise.

To explain why and how categorizing others by sex produces gender expectations and stereotypes, these theorists introduce the idea of a **status characteristic**. A status characteristic is "an attribute on which individuals vary that is associated in a society with widely held beliefs according greater esteem and worthiness to some states of the attribute (e.g., being male) than others (being female)" (Ridgeway 1993, p. 179). Gender is not the only basis on which people differentially assign power and status. Gender in most contemporary societies is clearly a status characteristic. Men are generally regarded more positively than women. Once a characteristic like sex category has status value, it begins to shape expectations and form the basis for stereotypes.

Status characteristics theory was developed to explain goal-oriented interaction, such as occurs in workplaces, classrooms, or in any group oriented toward a collective end. In these kinds of settings, the important expectations are those relating to performance. Group members assess how competent each is and how much value to attach to each other's contributions. Because multiple status characteristics may be activated in any situation, people form their expectations about others' competence by weighing each status characteristic in terms of its relevance to the task at hand.

This weighting process is not assumed to be conscious or precise; rather, expectation states theorists believe that people seek cues as to how others will perform in a particular situation and use status characteristics to assess this. These performance expectations tend to disadvantage those with lower status value (in the case of gender, women). Women are expected to be less competent than men and their contributions are expected to be less valuable.

Status characteristics theory recognizes that the effects of gender on social interaction may vary from situation to situation. This is why this theory provides a contextual account of gender: Gender is viewed as a "background identity" that may be more or less central to people's awareness in any particular encounter (Ridgeway and Correll 2004, p. 516). Ridgeway expects gender to be most influential when two conditions hold: the interactants are members of different sex categories, and when gender is relevant to the task or purpose of the interaction. As an example of these differences in the salience of gender, consider the high-tech science firms described in Box 3.1.

Box 3.1   Gender in innovative, high-tech firms.

My first example comes from studies of the small, science-focused start-up firms that have become a leading edge of the biotechnology and information technology (IT) industries. As Kjersten Whittington and Laurel Smith-Doerr (2008; Whittington 2007) describe, many of these high-tech firms have adopted a new organizational logic called the network form. Work in these firms is organized in terms of project teams that are often jointly constructed with a network of other firms. Scientists in a firm move flexibly among these project teams, and the hierarchies of control over their activities are relatively flat.

Is this informal, flexible structure advantageous or disadvantageous for women scientists who work in these high-tech

(Continued)

Box 3.1 *(Continued)*

firms? Whittington and Smith-Doerr's (2008; Whittington 2007) research suggests that the answer is quite different for biotech firms based in the life sciences than it is for firms based in engineering and the physical sciences, such as IT firms. To understand why the same organizational logic plays out so differently for women scientists in one context compared to the other, we need to take into account how the background frame of gender acts in each context.

The life sciences are not strongly gender-typed in contemporary culture. Women now constitute about a third of the PhDs in the area (Smith-Doerr 2004). Applying our framing account to this situation leads us to expect that because of the mixed gender composition of the workforce in this field, cultural beliefs about gender will be salient in biotech firms, but only diffusely so. Because the field is not strongly gender-typed, we expect these background gender beliefs to create only modest advantages for men in expected competence. Facing only modest biases, women scientists in biotech should have the basic credibility with their coworkers that they need to take effective advantage of the opportunities offered by the flexible structure of innovative firms. They should be able to press forward with their interests, work around "bad actors" if necessary, find projects that match their skills, and excel (Smith-Doerr 2004). As a result, in the biotech context, an informal, flexible organizational form could be more advantageous for women than would a more hierarchical structure.

In fact, Whittington and Smith-Doerr (2008) find women life scientists do better in these innovative biotech firms than they do in more traditionally hierarchical research organizations such as pharmaceutical firms. In comparison to more hierarchical firms, women in these flexible firms achieve more supervisory positions (Smith-Doerr 2004) and attain parity with men in the likelihood of having at least one patent to their name

Box 3.1 *(Continued)*

(Whittington and Smith-Doerr 2008). Even in these innovative firms, however, the total number of patents women acquire is less than that of comparable men, as it also is in traditional hierarchical firms. This remaining disadvantage is not surprising if we remember that background gender biases still modestly favor men, even in this innovative biotech context.

In contrast to the life sciences, engineering and the physical sciences are still strongly gender-typed in favor of men in our society. Thus, the background gender frame in the IT context is more powerfully relevant and creates stronger implicit biases against women's competence than in biotech settings. In this situation, the informality and flexibility of the innovative firm is unlikely to be an advantage for women scientists and may even be a disadvantage. Facing strong challenges to their credibility, it will be harder for women to take effective advantage of the flexible structure. Also, in the context of a masculine-typed gender frame, the informal work structure may lead to a "boys club" atmosphere in these innovative IT firms.

Consistent with the above analysis, Whittington (2007), in her study of patenting, found that women physical scientists and engineers were no better off in small, flexible, less hierarchical firms that they were in traditional, industrial research and development firms. In both contexts, they were less likely to patent at all and had fewer patents overall than did comparable men. In another study, McIllwee and Robinson (1992) found that women engineers actually did better in a traditional, rule-structured aerospace firm than in a more informal, flexible IT start-up because in the context of a disadvantaging background gender frame, formal rules leveled the playing field to some extent. This example suggests that we cannot understand the full implications of a particular organizational

(Continued)

> ## Box 3.1 (*Continued*)
>
> logic for the gender structure it will produce without consider-
> ing how that organizational logic interacts with the back-
> ground effects of the gender frame.
>
> *Source*: Cecilia L. Ridgeway. 2009. "Framed before we know it:
> How gender shapes social relations." *Gender & Society* 23: 145–160.

Many kinds of social interactions meet these conditions. For example, according to status characteristics theory, how women and men interact depends in part on the nature of their task. If the group works on a task that the larger culture strongly identifies with men (e.g., an engineering project), we would expect men to display inter-actional styles associated with power and competence (e.g., more talking, speaking longer, etc.). If the task is more closely associated with women, however, then women would be more likely than men to behave in these ways.

Contrast this interactionist approach with one focusing on gender socialization. A socialization account would emphasize how women and men learn to behave in dominant or assertive ways. The inter-action styles associated with dominance thus would be treated as personality characteristics, and these styles would undoubtedly be viewed as more typical among men than women. Status character-istics theory instead treats interaction styles as less a matter of individual personality and more a function of the setting, including the group's sex composition and task orientation. In this view, the fact that men may interact in dominant ways more often than women has less to do with men's personalities or socialization and more to do with the types of settings where women and men typi-cally encounter each other.

Like the ethnomethodological approach, status characteristics theory suggests that gender differences emerge out of more general processes that shape interaction. Their methods for studying social interaction differ considerably, however. Ethnomethodologists prefer fine-grained, qualitative studies of particular settings and tend to resist abstract theorizing. By contrast, status characteristics theorists have developed their ideas primarily through laboratory experiments. Further, these theorists aim to create a formal theory of status processes. Through these efforts, status characteristics theory is constantly being refined and expanded. Researchers work to better understand the kinds of situations that activate gender and other status characteristics (Ridgeway and Diekema 1992; Ridgeway 1993).

For status characteristics theorists, a group's sex composition helps to determine how gender will shape the group's interactions. The third interactionist approach focuses explicitly on the role of sex composition. From this perspective, the meaning and impact of one's own sex category depends on the sex composition of the group. A person's own sex category is less relevant to any particular interaction than the sex category memberships of those with whom he or she is interacting.

Opposites attract, or don't they?
Homophily and Gender

We are probably all familiar with the adage "opposites attract." Like many forms of conventional wisdom, however, this one is not accurate. In fact, a better description of social relations is "birds of a feather flock together." Similarity tends to be a much stronger source of interpersonal attraction than difference. Indeed, much research suggests that social ties of all types tend to be organized according to the homophily principle: Social ties tend to be between people who are similar on salient sociodemographic dimensions (Popielarz 1999).

There are at least two reasons why this occurs. Partly, it reflects people's preferences. **Homophily** is a term used to describe people's preference for interacting with those like themselves (Rothman 1998). In addition, however, the homophilous social ties experienced in everyday life are reinforced – and developed – in the groups to which people belong. Groups include such things as the neighborhoods where people live, the clubs and organizations they belong to, or their church membership. As McPherson, Popielarz, and Drobnic (1992, p. 168) explain, "We argue that most homophily occurs because ties are shaped by the opportunities presented to people in groups. We do not encounter people who are seriously different enough from us frequently enough for them to become social network contacts."

When sociologists say that similarity attracts, we mean that people are drawn to those whose attitudes, values, and beliefs are similar to themselves. People who share our views affirm us, thus positively reinforcing who we are and how we live. We may also feel that people like us in these ways are easier to communicate with than those who do not share our views. We may trust them more and feel a greater sense of kinship with them. Conversely, when people are different from us, we may feel threatened and find communication difficult. Trust may be lacking or simply be harder to achieve.

These ideas about the importance of similarity in social life have implications for understanding gender and the relations between women and men. To understand why, consider how it is that people decide who shares their views of the world and who does not. The best way to make this determination would be to get to know on a personal level each individual with whom we interacted. It takes time and effort to really learn about a person, though, and it is unrealistic to assume that we would ever be able to acquire this type of knowledge about all of the people in our daily lives. Moreover, would we even want to devote time and energy to this task, given other life priorities? Under these circumstances, most of us are much more selective. We may get to know some people in our lives very well, but will not expend so much energy on every single person. In the absence of information about people's attitudes and beliefs, we instead rely on a sort of "social shorthand": We infer information about them – and their degree of similarity to us – from characteristics that are easily visible and accessible. We use these visible and accessible characteristics as "proxies" for qualities that would be time-consuming to determine, such as values, attitudes, and beliefs.

Ascribed characteristics, such as sex, race, and age, are the kinds of proxies most often used to infer similarity (or dissimilarity) with another. Recall that ascribed characteristics are relatively immutable and not voluntarily chosen. Sex, race, and age are important ascribed characteristics in social life because they are so easily observed and difficult to hide. The power of these characteristics also derives from the fact that sex, race, and age are highly institutionalized statuses and, hence, each is laden with layers of social meaning. This increases their value as "proxies" for similarity and dissimilarity since they are believed to be reliably associated with particular characteristics.

The similarity-attraction hypothesis implies that being a member of a group containing all women (if you are a woman) or all men (if a man) would be preferable to being in a more sex-integrated group (other factors being equal). In other words, people should prefer to interact with others like themselves and feel uncomfortable, threatened, and less committed when they are in more heterogeneous groups. These issues have received significant attention from researchers and have been especially important in understanding women's and men's work experiences (see Part II).

For example, Tsui, Egan, and O'Reilly (1992) examined the consequences of "being different" for workers' attachment to their firms. They hypothesized that people who were more different from other members of their work groups would be less attached (e.g., less psychologically committed, more likely to be absent from work, and more likely to quit) than those who were more similar. Several forms of difference were examined, including sex, age, race, education, and tenure with the employer. Tsui, Egan, and O'Reilly found that being different from one's co-workers on ascribed characteristics (i.e., age, race, and sex) had negative consequences on attachment, while being different with respect to education or tenure with the employer did not have these consequences. Moreover, whites and men – that is, those who were members of the historically dominant categories – reacted more negatively to being different than non-whites and women. This research thus suggests that being different is difficult for people, especially when it involves difference on an ascribed characteristic, like sex.

While Tsui, Egan, and O'Reilly (1992) focus on the reactions of those who are different from others in the group, others look more broadly at group composition and dynamics. Allmendinger and Hackman's (1995) study of symphony orchestras provides one example. These researchers were interested in how the sex composition of a symphony orchestra affected its members' attitudes. They analyzed data collected from 78 orchestras in four geographical locations, including the U.S., the United Kingdom, the former East Germany, and the former West Germany. Historically, women have been only a small percentage of players in professional orchestras, and this is true worldwide. In this study, women were between 2 and 59 percent of each orchestra.

Allmendinger and Hackman's (1995) findings are generally consistent with the similarity-attraction hypothesis, though they show that it is more complicated than one might assume. For example, they found that while women were less satisfied when they were in orchestras dominated by men (i.e., 90 percent or more male) than those that were more balanced (i.e., between 40 and 60 percent women), they were especially dissatisfied in orchestras that contained between 10 percent and 40 percent women. Male orchestra members also were less satisfied when women were greater than 10 percent but less than 40 percent of members. These findings held true in all four countries, underscoring the power of group composition.

Allmendinger and Hackman suggest that once women become a significant minority (i.e., greater than 10 percent), they gain power and cannot be as easily overlooked by their male counterparts. In their words: "Together, these processes result in tightened identity group boundaries for both genders, increased cross-group stereotyping and conflict, less social support across gender boundaries, and heightened personal tension for everyone" (Allmendinger and Hackman 1995, p. 453). These issues are the focus of another research stream, which focuses on interactions between numerical minorities and majorities.

Box 3.2   Personal strategies for managing demographic differences.

The best place to begin is with each and every individual who finds the presence of dissimilar others to be an inevitable fact of life in today's world of work. It would be helpful for each individual to recognize that it is natural to be biased in favor of others similar to oneself and against others who are dissimilar to oneself. The most promising solution to the diversity problem is for every individual to make a commitment to address this issue. The best place to begin is not with others but with oneself.

Discovering the Primary Bases of Self-Identity

How should one begin this process of developing personal strategies to operate effectively in today's diverse world? A reasonable starting point is for all persons to understand what social categories they use to describe themselves. Each person can ask: On what basis do I categorize myself and others? From what sources do I derive my self-image and what about me makes me proud? How strong do I feel about my gender, my cultural ethnic background, my educational achievement, the kind of work I do, my religious belief, my age, where I was born and raised, where I live, and where I work? Who are my friends at work and outside of work and what is the primary social and demographic background of each? When I meet someone new for the first time, what am I most likely to notice first about the person and what am I most interested in finding out about that individual? The answers to these questions can provide some insight into the primary sources of one's own social identity and how one might react to others who do not share the primary social categories from which one's self-identity is based.

(Continued)

Box 3.2 (*Continued*)

This self-knowledge will not only help us understand how we react to others who are different from us, it also can reveal why we feel the way we do about ourselves when we are in the presence of dissimilar others. Both types of reactions (reactions about others and about ourselves) are natural outcomes of our basic need to have self-esteem. Our esteem is bolstered by accentuating the positive attributes of the social group to which we belong and exaggerating the negative attributes of the "other" groups to which we do not belong. Self-esteem is enhanced when we define ourselves as members of high-status social groups. Clearly, these reactions and associated behavior triggered by the social categorization process, while useful to oneself, do not necessarily contribute to positive and productive interactions among individuals in different social categories. However, such reactions are understandable. Since we are all victims of such social psychological processes, we are all in the same boat. Empathy toward each other is a helpful step toward mutual acceptance and support.

Remembering a Simple Statistical Rule

One simple statistical rule can help people counteract the tendency to stereotype others who are strangers. On most psychological or personality characteristics (e.g., attitudes, conscientiousness, mathematical ability, loyalty, assertiveness, dominance, diligence), people are normally distributed (i.e., the distribution of the attribute fits a normal curve). Though the average person from one social category, say Asians, may be higher on an attribute such as shyness than the average person of another category, say Americans, any one Asian could be higher or lower on this attribute than an American. In other words, for any meaningful psychological or personality characteristic, there is almost always an overlapping

Box 3.2 (*Continued*)

region—sometimes a large overlapping region—between any two social categories.

There is a second reason why this simple statistical rule can be useful. It provides us with a baseline to determine the likely behavior, attitudes, or tendencies of a specific individual. In other words, we can make an estimate of the probability of the person's true characteristics. Let us use an example to illustrate this point. From cross-cultural research, we know that people in collectivist cultures tend to cooperate while people in individualistic cultures tend to compete in interpersonal situations. In other words, the average person in the collectivist culture would be cooperative while the average person in the individualistic culture would be competitive. However, to assume that any single individual in a particular social group would be like the average member of that group would be an act of stereotyping. The simple statistical rule of the normal curve would remind us that we could be wrong. However, the statistical rule also suggests that chances are greater that an individual from a collectivist culture is more likely to be cooperative than an individual from an individualistic culture. The problem is not that we do not make this probable guess. The problem is that we do it too often or too well. Stereotyping an individual on a particular personality attribute or behavioral tendency based on his or her category membership is making a probable guess that the individual will be like an average individual in that group. Over 30% of the people in any particular group are, however, not the average. To avoid what is referred to as the Type I error (to assume it is when it is not), it is critical that we verify our inference (or probable guess) by observation of actual behavior of that individual. Since our perceptual process is such that we see what we believe, obtaining multiple observations of the individual and from multiple sources (if possible) would be desirable.

(*Continued*)

Box 3.2 (*Continued*)

Along the same vein, we often make Type II errors (to assume that it is not when it is) by the stereotypic response that an individual from a collectivist culture would not be individualistic. It is probable that any one individual from the collectivist culture would be as or perhaps more individualistic than an individual from an individualistic culture. Therefore, being a skeptic about one's ability to accurately judge and observe people is a critical skill of a responsible individual.

While having multiple interactions with others and receiving information from multiple sources enable one to guard against stereotyping, it is not always possible to do this. For example, workers who interact with customers in service encounters interact primarily with strangers, i.e., people with whom they have no prior interaction and with whom they do not intend to interact in the future. Under these circumstances it is particularly easy to apply stereotypes to these customers (and it is equally easy for the customers to stereotype service providers who are strangers to them). Therefore, it is especially important to be mindful of that possibility and retain a healthy skepticism about being able to judge these strangers accurately.

Assessing One's Vulnerability to Self-Stereotyping

It is also important to be aware of the extent to which one is vulnerable to self-stereotyping. To do so is especially detrimental to people who belong to a social category associated with negative attributes. (See Steele, 1997, for an overview of research on this topic.) For those who are in social categories that are positively stereotyped, self-stereotyping would provide an additional source of self-confidence. The intergroup dynamic associated with the self-enhancement of one group may, however, be costly to the well-being of the comparison group and make it difficult to form a productive rela-

Box 3.2 *(Continued)*

tionship between people from the two categories. Therefore, self-stereotyping should be avoided by members of any social category. It is probably always better to have an accurate assessment of one's traits and abilities. Gaining self-esteem at the expense of others and relationships with others is of debatable merit.

Most of the research on the performance impact of self-stereotyping assumes that the stereotypes are negative in nature, perhaps because negative stereotypes can do more damage than positive ones, including to those people who are most unlike the stereotype. For people who are sensitive to negative stereotypes associated with the social categories to which they belong, it is critical to develop an awareness of the extent to which they are vulnerable to self-stereotyping. Here is a list of questions that may help determine the extent to which one may be engaging in self-stereotyping on the basis of gender, race, religion, ethnicity, national origin, occupations, or educational background or level:

a. How often do I perceive myself as typical of other who share the same social category (demographic background) as myself?
b. Do I behave or perform differently when I am in a group consisting primarily of people like myself, and groups consisting primarily of people different from myself?
c. How often do I believe that others view me or judge me based on my membership in a particular group more than based on the characteristics unique to myself?
d. How often do I think people respond to me for what I really am rather than for my membership in my primary social category?

(Continued)

Box 3.2 (*Continued*)

e. How often do I think that, because of my demographic background, people around me play it safe and hold back from saying what is really on their mind?

f. How often do I wonder if people sometimes judge my ability based on stereotypes of my social group?

g. How often do I think, because of my demographic background, people put on an act of friendliness that does not match their true feelings toward me?

h. Is it easier for me to seek help from others who are similar to me on certain demographic dimensions than from people who are different?

i. Am I comfortable in entering situations where I am the sole member of my particular background?

j. When other members of my particular background embarrass themselves, do I worry about how their actions will reflect upon me?

A person who answers yes or often to many of these questions is likely to be a victim of self-stereotyping. A simple example is an Asian who believes that Asians are not assertive and is therefore reluctant to speak up in work setting. Others believing in such a stereotypic attribute of Asians would be reluctant to call upon the Asian for suggestions in a group setting. Sometimes this happens because others have the good intention of wanting to protect or respect the needs of the Asian person. Not being asked to contribute, the Asian becomes even more hesitant. Thus, the entire process becomes a self-fulfilling prophecy for everyone, and it reinforces the stereotype held by everyone (observers as well as the garget person) that Asians are not assertive and this particular Asian fits the stereotype. In reality, this particular Asian could be an extremely eloquent speaker in a social setting where such stereotyping is not applicable or is less salient, such as around the family dinner table or in a Asian church discussion group.

Box 3.2 (*Continued*)

The term "stereotype threat" (Steele, 1997), has been used to describe a situation where a negative stereotype about one's social category becomes relevant to interpreting oneself or one's behavior in an "identified-with" setting. The Asian in the example above might experience stereotype threat if he considers himself a particularly eloquent speaker, contrary to the stereotype of Asians, and is placed in a situation where others are expecting him to be reticent and quiet. Another example is an African-American who considers herself very good at math being placed in a competitive situation with others who expect African-Americans to perform poorly in math. In these types of situations, Steele (1997) and his colleagues have found that the stereotype-threatened perform less well than they do when they are not in that kind of situation.

What should those susceptible to self-stereotyping do? Once they become aware of this tendency, there are a number of possible actions. They can consciously begin to let their actions reflect their true selves. They can inform others of their true inclinations and solicit support from their friends at work. Self-regulation in the form of seeking feedback and help from others and adjusting one's behavior accordingly often results in positive impressions by others. These suggestions are obviously quite straightforward and may be too obvious to dwell upon. Nonetheless, self-awareness is an excellent starting point and self-regulation is an excellent process for increasing personal and professional effectiveness in the diverse work setting.

Taking Ownership of the Problem

Members of both the minority and the majority categories can feel frustrated by the diversity problem. Both can feel that members of the other category cause the problem and

(*Continued*)

Box 3.2 *(Continued)*

receive favored treatment by management. Management, by instituting diversity programs with most of the focus on structuring career paths for the historically disadvantaged groups and by providing training to supervisors on the diversity issue, essentially are taking ownership of the problem, leaving individuals waiting for something positive to happen to them. The relatively deprived ask, "When is management going to be serious about addressing this diversity problem?" The dominant majority wonders, "When will it be my turn to receive the benefits that I deserve?" The message here is that everyone believes "It is not my problem, it is yours!" It is worthwhile to reiterate that understanding differences is everyone's problem, and hence it is everyone's responsibility to address it. This means that every member should take ownership of the problem and take the initiative to resolve it.

This includes all employees (of any social category), the work group leader or supervisor, the middle manager leading the department or operating unit, and the top executive for the entire organization. For example, everyone can work to avoid placing anyone of any social category in a "stereotype threat" position. It is unfair to expect some people's work to reflect only on them and to expect other people's work to reflect on everyone in their social category. Knowing that a failure to speak eloquently will reflect on all Asians or that a failure to perform well at math will be interpreted as proof that women are not good at math puts undue pressure on people who themselves do not fit the negative stereotype.

Source: Anne S. Tsui and Barbara A. Gutek. 1999. *Demographic Differences in Organizations*. Lanham, MD: Lexington Books (pp. 146–153).

The power of proportions   Rosabeth Moss Kanter explored this topic in her 1977 classic, *Men and Women of the Corporation*. Kanter argued that the relative proportions of different "social types" in a group shape members' social relations. "As proportions shift," she suggests, "so do social experiences" (Kanter 1977, p. 207). Proportions have this effect because they influence how people perceive one another.

Kanter (1977, p. 208) was particularly interested in what she called, "skewed groups." In these groups, one social type is numerically dominant and the other is a very small numerical minority (e.g., 15 percent or less). Kanter's focus on this type of group stemmed from the fact that this is likely to be the situation experienced by "newcomers" to a social setting. Women who enter jobs or workplaces historically dominated by men, for example, are apt to enter as a minority of this type, as are people of color who enter jobs historically dominated by whites. Because it is unlikely that an employer would hire large numbers of women or people of color at one time, sex (and race) integration happens slowly, one or two people at a time. Members of the numerical minority in skewed groups are called **tokens**. For Kanter, the term "token" is a neutral label, referring to those whose "social type" constitutes 15 percent or less of a group.

Kanter argues that relations between tokens and dominants in skewed groups are shaped by three perceptual tendencies: **visibility**, **contrast**, and **assimilation**. First, tokens – because they are different from the majority – are easily noticed. In the organization she studied, Kanter (1977, p. 212) found that token women in high-level positions were "the subject of conversation, questioning, gossip, and careful scrutiny." Moreover, tokens' behavior was often attributed more to their social category membership than to their own individual characteristics. Thus, tokens carry an extra burden: they represent their entire social category (Kanter 1977). Tokens responded to these "performance pressures" in numerous ways. Some overachieved, while trying hard not to stick out too much, thus avoiding the resentment of dominants. Others enjoyed being the only woman and thus emphasized their uniqueness, while still others kept low profiles and tried to become socially invisible. In all cases, however, tokens were performing under very different conditions than dominants.

Contrast is the second perceptual tendency associated with tokenism. As Kanter (1977, pp. 221–2) notes, "The presence of a token or two makes dominants more aware of what they have in common at the same time that it threatens that commonality." Tokens are threatening to dominants because their presence creates uncertainty: norms, beliefs, and styles of communication that dominants take for granted may be challenged or misunderstood. At its most extreme, dominants' uncertainty and discomfort can be expressed in hostility toward tokens and result in efforts to isolate or exclude them from social interaction. More typical perhaps are dominants' attempts to exaggerate and affirm their differences from tokens, a set of behaviors Kanter (1977, p. 229) refers to as "boundary heightening."

The third perceptual tendency associated with tokenism is assimilation. Dominants see tokens less as individuals and more as representative members of their social category. Moreover, because the characteristics dominants associate with a token's social category are often overly simplified or inaccurate stereotypes, assimilation contributes to the dominants' misperceptions of the token. Kanter contends that these processes ultimately force tokens into highly restricted and caricatured roles. This "role encapsulation" may make dominants more comfortable in tokens' presence, but it can be detrimental to tokens. Because the roles that tokens are constrained to perform may inhibit rather than enhance job success, Kanter refers to these as "role traps."

Kanter's contention that how people experience work is shaped in part by how many of their social type are present is well-documented. Further, studies of women in token roles have identified many of the interactional dynamics she described. There is less consensus about the broader consequences of tokenism. Although some studies suggest that women in these roles experience negative consequences – such as lower pay and promotion opportunities – others fail to show this effect (Budig 2002; Roth 2004).

Although Kanter's research focused on female tokens, she believed that the processes associated with tokenism would operate regardless of whether tokens were male or female. However, most researchers who have examined this question have concluded that the dynamics of tokenism are not gender-neutral. Studies by Roth (2004) on women MBAs working on Wall Street and Williams (1989, 1995) on men employed in traditionally female fields illustrate some of the differences between tokens of different genders.

Roth (2004) argues that the effects of tokenism outlined by Kanter can be explained by people's preferences for homophily. She also draws on status characteristics theory in her study of women's experiences in the traditionally male world of Wall Street financial firms. Roth found that women working in the most male-dominated specializations, such as trading, were excluded from the social networks of their co-workers:

> Me and this other woman were total outcasts. They went so far as, there were, on our immediate desk, there were six of us. The rest of the group would play golf every weekend. They'd go out to dinners and whatnot. We were never invited once. It was pathetic. To tell you the truth, because of that we had absolutely no desire to be anything social with them, but they were like a boys' club and were just like the two chicks who didn't fit in. It was fun. They certainly didn't sit and talk to us on the desk and they ignored us at work, but socially they completely ignored us and it was obviously a little harder to fit in when somebody spends the whole weekend with the other three of them, playing golf and going on vacations together. Going to strip clubs together and stuff like that. It's kind of hard to fit in. (Roth 2004, p. 201)

Exclusion could be costly in this setting because it limited women's access to mentors and restricted their ability to form the kind of informal connections that would lead to good assignments and clients.

Roth also found that that status expectations were operating in these workplaces. Women's competence was suspect and closely scrutinized:

> When I started work, the person who ended up being my mentor came to me and said, "Can you amortize a loan?" Which is the most insulting question in my business. Can I amortize a loan? I should have been able to amortize a loan when I came out of high school. So he did this little test. I went and I amortized my little loan for him and everything and then he was fine. I thought that was insulting that they would have done that. I had interactions with people. ... I was once at a dinner when we were all in our training program and I was talking to someone and it was so insulting because this guy was in corporate finance so he was going to be some general relationship manager and I said, "I'm in asset backs." And he said to me, "Oh, are you comfortable with numbers?" (Roth (2004, pp. 204–5)

In addition to understanding women's experiences, Roth was interested in learning about the strategies successful women used to overcome the interactional dynamics of tokenism. Some used individual strategies, such as finding powerful mentors, developing experience in a critical area, or simply having a thick skin. Others sought out positions where their performance was most likely to be objectively evaluated.

Compare these experiences to those of the male tokens Williams (1992, 1995) studied. In her interviews with male nurses, elementary school teachers, librarians, and social workers, she found that many view their token status as an advantage. For example, when asked whether he found it difficult to be a male nurse in pediatrics, one of Williams's (1992, p. 255) interviewees responded: "No, no, none ... I've heard this from managers and supervisory-type people with men in pediatrics: 'It's nice to have a man because it's such a female-dominated profession.'" These men also reported having mostly positive working relationships with co-workers and supervisors, which included being invited to informal social gatherings.

While women in token roles may have their competence questioned, men in predominantly female jobs experience another type of pressure – the **glass escalator**. As Williams (1995, p. 12) explains: "Like being on an invisible 'up' escalator, men must struggle to remain in the lower (i.e., 'feminine') levels of their profession." These pressures help explain why other studies of men in traditionally female jobs (discussed in Chapter 6) find that men's pay and promotion chances are often greater in these fields than those of their female co-workers (Budig 2002).

Despite these advantages, male tokens remain – in the language of the "doing gender" perspective – "accountable" as men. For example, in their study of male clerical temporaries, Henson and Rogers (2001) ask: How do men "do masculinity" in a predominantly female job? The vast majority of clerical workers are women, and this is also true among those in temporary jobs. Henson and Rogers (2001) note that, prior to the 1960s, most temporary employers of clerical workers (e.g., Kelly Girl – later Kelly Services) did not even accept male applicants. Not surprisingly, then, men who become clerical temporaries are likely to face questions, surprise, and disapproval from their peers and co-workers. One man interviewed by Henson and Rogers (2001, p. 223) commented: "People are looking at me like, 'What are you doing here?' Like they're thinking, 'Gee, what's the deal? Shouldn't you be, I don't know, doing something else?' I mean it's sort of fine if you're just out of school. They kind of expect well, you're just doing this until you get a regular job."

In response, male clerical temporaries reasserted their masculinity using several strategies designed to set them apart from and superior to women. For example, they reframed the work, replacing the term "secretary" with more masculine or gender-neutral descriptions, such as bookkeeper or word processor (Henson and Rogers 2001). They used "cover stories" to create an alternative occupational identity, such as actor or writer, and minimized the significance of their temporary job. The male clerical temporaries in Henson and Rogers's (2001) study also asserted their masculinity by refusing to perform the deference (see

Chapter 6) typically required of subordinates – especially women (Pierce 1995).

Summary of interactionist views

The three interactionist perspectives agree that social categorization – particularly sex categorization – is an important social process. In addition, all three approaches emphasize the ways that gender emerges and is reproduced in social interaction. In this way, they diverge from individualist approaches, which see gender as residing primarily within individuals. Interactionist approaches are a useful counterpoint to individualist understandings of gender. While individualists see gender as a relatively stable property of people, interactionist approaches emphasize the ways that social context and social interaction influence the expression and significance of gender.

Gendered Organizations/Gendered Institutions

Much of social life is organized and routine, and many of our interactions take place within organizations. An **organization** is a social unit established to pursue particular goals. Organizations have boundaries, rules, procedures, and means of communication (Hall 2002). Because organizations are so much a part of daily life, the social practices associated with them play an especially important role in the production and reproduction of gender and gender inequality.

Institution is a somewhat more abstract and all-encompassing concept. Sociologists define an **institution** as those parts of social life that are complex, ongoing, and organized. They seem so regular and so permanent that they are often accepted as just "the way things are." Friedland and Alford (1991, p. 248) suggest that institutions each have "a central logic – a set of material practices and symbolic constructions. ..." These logics include structures, patterns and routines, and they include the belief systems that supply these with meaning. Lodged within these logics are roles, positions, and expectations for individuals. Institutions incorporate more of the social landscape than organizations.

Many institutions contain several different types of organizations. For example, education is a social institution not only comprised of teachers and students, but also includes schools, school boards, accrediting agencies, and professional organizations such as teachers' unions. Institutions can be even more all-encompassing and abstract. Capitalism can be considered an institution, for example, or even the global economy itself. Researchers applying an institutional framework to understand the social world are interested in identifying the patterns, roles, rules, and beliefs that constitute these systems. For purposes of discussion here, I refer to this view of gender as the gendered institutions approach, recognizing that it includes aspects of organizations as well.

Gendered institutions

Acker (1992) observes that many of the institutions that constitute the "rules of the game" in American society – and, indeed, most societies – embody aspects of gender. To say that an institution is gendered means

> that gender is present in the processes, practices, images and ideologies, and distributions of power in the various sectors of social life. Taken as more or less functioning wholes, the institutional structures of the United States and other societies are organized along the lines of gender. ... [These institutions] have been historically developed by men, currently dominated by men, and symbolically interpreted from the standpoint of men in leading positions, both in the present and historically. (Acker 1992, p. 567)

From this perspective, aspects of social life that are conventionally treated as "genderless" or gender-neutral are, in fact, expressions of gender. This way of thinking about gender directs attention to the organization, structure, and practices of social institutions, and it emphasizes the ways that these entrenched, powerful, and relatively taken-for-granted aspects of the social order produce and reproduce gender distinctions and inequality. An example may help you better understand these ideas.

Gendered institutions in everyday life: The case of sport   Sport is an institution of worldwide significance and reach. Competition, power, and domination are perhaps the values most central to this institution (Stempel 2006). Like other institutions, sport also involves organized activities that reach across a broad spectrum of social life. The participants include athletes, coaches, and fans, among others, as well as many types of organizations, both large and small. Millions of boys and girls are introduced to sports through clubs or in schools. Media, such as websites, magazines, and television, influence people's exposure to sports, teams, and athletes. Governing bodies, such as the International Olympics Committee (IOC) and Fédération Internationale de Football Association (FIFA), and large corporations, such as Adidas or Nike, also play powerful roles in shaping sports practices, policies, and beliefs.

Gender permeates virtually all of these aspects of sport. Sport is a gendered institution because of its roles in creating and reinforcing beliefs about gender inequalities and distinctions; differential opportunities for each gender to be involved in sport; and differential resources for women and men participating in this arena. These elements are intertwined.

Competition, power, and domination are the qualities most closely associated with sport, and these qualities are typically viewed as masculine characteristics (Stempel 2006). Although the belief that natural sex differences make women unsuited for sport competition has abated, sport today helps to perpetuate gender distinctions and inequalities in other ways. For example, studying youth sports in California, Messner (2009) found that women became "team moms," while coaches were almost entirely male.

Although the parents that he interviewed believed that participation in youth sports was beneficial for girls and boys, youth sports were organized in ways that tended to reinforce gender distinctions and inequalities.

Sport contributes to ideas about male and female bodies and their physical capabilities or limitations. Female athletes in many sports face pressures to avoid being perceived as too powerful or aggressive. Women who cross this line may be assumed to be lesbians, a label that might prevent some heterosexual women from participating in sport and lead lesbians in sport to hide their identity. Sports journalist Joan Ryan (1995) argues that the popularity of sports such as women's gymnastics and figure-skating stems in part from their highly feminized presentation. Elite female gymnasts are typically young and petite, and image and appearance figure highly in women's figure skating. As Ryan (1995, p. 129) explains: "Skaters don't show their muscles or their sweat. They wear makeup and sequins and even have a beauty consultant backstage at competitions. Skating offers the wholesomeness of sports without the aggression, the beauty of female athleticism without the hazy overtones of lesbianism. The athletes are starlets in blades, with agents and fans fluttering about them."

Their gender creates a different set of pressures for male figure skaters. Their challenge is to distinguish themselves from women – lest they be perceived as gay – and to present themselves as masculine. Male skaters use costume, music, and movement to achieve this. What counts as masculine differs by nationality, however. For example, male skaters from former Soviet-era states are more likely than those from the West to draw on classical ballet and opera (Kestnbaum 2003). Whereas these forms of cultural expression connote femininity in the West, they are expressions of national pride for skaters from former Soviet states.

Sports media play a key role in perpetuating gendered beliefs. While coverage of female athletes and women's sports has increased, sports involving women are treated very differently than those involving men (Kane and Lenskyj 1998). For example, Stone and Horne (2008) found gender differences in the media coverage of

Great Britain's Olympic skiing and snowboarding teams. Though receiving about the same amount of coverage, descriptions of male and female athletes diverged along traditional gender lines. Male athletes were described as active and aggressive: "Ben attacked with venom competing trick after trick," while female athletes were described in terms of their demeanor and appearance, using phrases such as "alpine angel" and "22-year-old model from Twickenham" (cited in Stone and Horne 2008, p. 103). Sports advertising and coverage related to so-called "alternative" or "extreme" sports relies on gendered depictions of athletes (Rinehart 2005).

This discussion reveals several important aspects of institutions. First, institutions are an important source of cultural beliefs about the social world, including beliefs about gender. Institutions provide scripts that become guides for action. For example, as we will see in Part II, gender has been a tremendously important element of the institutional logics governing work and family in the United States. These institutions are the source of many people's beliefs about how women and men are and should be. Beliefs about gender also feed back into these institutions, shaping their organization and practices. No one can really escape these institutional forces. Even those who may not share the logics that govern institutions must nevertheless respond to them as they organize their lives.

A second important feature of institutions revealed in the preceding example is that they tend to be self-perpetuating, almost taking on a life of their own. There need not be – and often is not – any conscious intent to create or reproduce gender differences and inequalities. Instead, beliefs are taken for granted and past practices continue unless and until a conscious and large-scale effort is made to change them. In the United States, it was not until 1972 and the passage of Title IX that sex discrimination in education became illegal and girls and women had equal access to organized sports in high school and college. The struggle for gender equity in sport and education continue to this day, underscoring the tremendous inertia that is built into the largest and most powerful social institutions.

A related feature of institutions is that, because they are taken for granted, they produce a socially shared "account" of their existence and purpose. The availability of these accounts helps explain why institutions are so rarely challenged or scrutinized: People believe that their purpose and functioning are self-evident. When I ask my students why Olympic gymnastics is a sport for petite, prepubescent young girls and strong, muscular men (and thus why there are few gymnastics opportunities for adult women and prepubescent boys), they offer a quick and ready answer: In my students' eyes, it is unremarkable and completely obvious that people would rather watch young girls and adult men than the alternative. The question of why this should be true is not something many have ever considered, underscoring the power of institutions to avoid scrutiny.

The gendered institutions approach directs researchers' attention away from individuals and interaction patterns to the study of social structure and culture. Gender thus is not viewed as something individuals possess but rather is conceived as an aspect of social organization. But are all organizational structures and practices "gendered"? Or is the "gendering" of institutions a matter of degree and form?

These are difficult questions that gender scholars continue to explore (Britton 2000). In the meantime, however, England (1998) provides one useful way to address these issues. She draws on legal doctrines to propose two ways to identify whether and how an organization (or practices and policies within an organization) are gendered. She suggests that practices, policies, or procedures that treat women and men differently represent a form of "**disparate treatment**," while practices, policies, or procedures that do not specify differential treatment, yet have a "**disparate impact**" on women and men, represent a second form of gendering. In England's view, either or both practices may be sufficient to identify an organization as gendered. As we will see in later chapters, proponents of a gendered institutions perspective have uncovered both forms of gendering in the key social institutions of modern industrial life.

Toward a Multilayered Conception of Gender

Interactionist approaches argue that students of gender should focus less on individuals and more on social interaction and social relations. For these theorists, gender emerges and is sustained within social interaction; hence, social context – the groups and settings where people gather – plays a much greater role in these views than in individualist approaches. Institutional perspectives capture the ways that gender is embedded within social structure and a part of the taken-for-granted reality in contemporary society. Both approaches can be contrasted with an individualist perspective, which treats gender as an attribute of people. None of these approaches alone is sufficient, however. Instead, gender is a multi-layered system of practices and relations that operates at all levels of the social world (Ridgeway and Smith-Lovin 1999; Risman 1998).

As a multilevel system affecting individuals' identities and characteristics, patterns of social interaction, and social institutions, the gender system shapes social life in crucial ways. In Part II, we will examine this system's operation in two key arenas: work and family. Each of the three frameworks introduced in this and the previous chapter will help us in this investigation.

No discussion of gender would be complete without attending to work and family. Both spheres directly affect the daily lives of adult women and men, and their children. Work, family, and gender have been intertwined historically. As the organization of work and family life have changed, so too, have women's and men's lives. In addition, beliefs about gender – about what men and women are and should be – are conditioned by these institutions.

Chapter Summary

This chapter examined interactionist and institutional approaches to gender. Interactionists focus on the social relations that produce gender distinctions and inequalities. The key perspectives within this tradition include ethnomethodology (i.e., "doing gender"), status characteristics theory, and theory and research on homophily. Though they differ in important respects, the process of social categorization is central to all three perspectives.

Institutional perspectives focus on gender as aspects of social structure and culture. Institutional perspectives thus direct attention to the practices and policies of organizations, and to the material and symbolic dimensions of large-scale social institutions, such as education, work, or family. Institutions are an important source of beliefs about gender. In addition, because they tend to be self-perpetuating, institutions play a central role in the perpetuation of gender distinctions and inequalities. The chapter concluded with a discussion of gender as a multilayered system, operating at the individual, interactional, and institutional levels.

Further Reading

Acker, Joan. 1992. "Gendered institutions." *Contemporary Sociology* 21: 565–569.

Kestnbaum, Ellyn. 2003. *Culture on Ice: Figure Skating and Cultural Meaning.* Middletown, CT: Wesleyan University Press.

Ridgeway, Cecilia L. 1997. "Interaction and the conservation of gender inequality." *American Sociological Review* 62: 218–235.

West, Candace and Zimmerman, Don H. 1991. "Doing gender," in Judith Lorber and Susan A. Farrell (eds.), *The Social Construction of Gender.* Newbury Park, CA: Sage.

Key Terms

Social categorization
"Doing gender"
Status characteristic
Homophily
Token
Visibility/contrast/assimilation
Glass escalator

Organization
Institution
Disparate treatment/disparate impact

Critical Thinking Questions

1 Discuss the claim that sex categorization is necessary for social interaction.
2 How do people "do gender"? In what ways is gender "performed"? Is gender best understood as a noun or as a verb?
3 Give examples of the ways that education, religion, and government can be considered "gendered institutions."

Part II

Gender in Context

Chapter 4

Work and Family as Gendered Institutions

Chapter Objectives

- Define and discuss the sexual division of labor.
- Explore the changing relations between gender, work, and family as these have developed historically.
- Describe the changes in work and family that occurred during the latter half of the twentieth century and the consequences of these changes for gender relations and inequalities.
- Examine how the institutions of work and family are shaped by national context.
- Identify trends affecting work, family, and gender in the twenty-first century.

Gender, work, and family are inextricably intertwined; changes in work and family give rise to changes in gender relations and changes in gender relations give rise to changes in family and work. As women's and men's lives have changed, so too have work and family. Work and family are gendered institutions. Understanding

The Sociology of Gender: An Introduction to Theory and Research, Second Edition. Amy S. Wharton.
© 2012 John Wiley & Sons Ltd. Published 2012 by John Wiley & Sons Ltd.

these relationships – where they come from and their consequences – is one goal of this chapter. We will also look closely at the structure and organization of work and family, paying particular attention to the ways these have evolved over the last few decades and their contemporary expression. This chapter sets the stage for a more in-depth look at family and work from individual and interactional perspectives (Chapters 5 and 6).

The Division of Labor

Throughout history and the world, divisions of labor have developed along the lines of sex. Hence, while work is an activity performed historically both by women and men, sex in virtually all societies has been an important basis of societal organization. The **sexual division of labor** thus refers to the process through which tasks are assigned on the basis of sex. This division of labor is one of the most fundamental ways that sex distinctions are expressed in social institutions. Many argue that sex, together with age, represent the oldest forms of the division of labor. Even at the dawn of the twenty-first century, however, sex continues to be a key basis on which tasks are divided.

There are many different views as to why societies differentiate labor on the basis of sex. Some locate the origins of the sexual division of labor in the fact that women historically have had primary responsibilities for the care of children. Children's dependence on their mothers' care shapes the type of labor women can perform (Collins et al. 1993). Conversely, men's greater average physical strength makes other activities more likely to be their responsibility. In hunting and gathering societies, for example, women were more likely to be gatherers and men to be hunters. While each set of tasks contributed to the group's survival by providing food that supplied necessary calories, women's labor provided most of the food supply (Lenski, Nolan, and Lenski 1995; Tanner and Zihlman 1976).

Over time, societies in many parts of the world adopted systems of agriculture based on the plow. Plow-based agriculture required greater physical strength than less intensive forms of food production, such as gathering or early horticulture, and thus was an activity performed most often by men (Boserup 1970; Lenksi, Nolan, and Lenski 1995). Hence, in these societies, men provided more of the necessary calories than women. More generally, evidence suggests that when women's labor is less vital to family survival than men's, their relative social status also declines (Guttentag and Secord 1983). Historical and geographical variations in female infanticide and resulting sex ratios thus can be correlated with the relative value of female labor.

These arguments suggest that the sexual division of labor whereby women and men specialize in different activities is also linked to the relative status of each sex. In particular, the relative contributions of women's and men's labor to survival influence the degree to which each sex is socially valued and hence the degree of sex inequality. Women and men are more equal in societies where the value of their labor is more similar.

Not everyone accepts this argument, however, and its relevance for understanding the sexual division of labor in today's society is quite limited. An alternative explanation for the sexual division of labor views it less as a response to women's and men's differing childcare responsibilities than as a cultural practice that justifies the devaluation of women. In this view, the sexual division of labor is rooted in gender, not sex. Moreover, these analysts question the relevance of attempts to explain the "origins" of the sexual division of labor, preferring instead to focus on how the sexual division of labor is reproduced in contemporary societies.

The first hunting and gathering societies emerged thousands of years ago. Yet, even at the beginning of the twenty-first century, women and men continue to do different kinds of work. Within families, the sexual division of labor is reflected most directly in women's and men's differential responsibilities for child-rearing. Women (and not men) give birth – a biological fact – but women in most societies have primary responsibility for children's care and rearing. Gender differences in the responsibility for children are an important component of family as a gendered institution, and shape many aspects of women's and men's work and family lives. In the paid labor force, the sexual division of labor is expressed in the sex segregation of employment at all levels. Although women's share of the paid labor force rose steadily during the last half of the twentieth century in most countries around the world, women and men are employed in different occupations, firms, and jobs (Reskin and Padavic 1994). Below, I discuss work and family, showing how these institutions are linked to one another and connected to broader entities, such as nation-states and political systems. Work and family are not separate or self-contained domains, and gender relations in one setting are intricately connected to those in the other.

Work, Family, and Gender in the Industrial Age

During the latter part of the nineteenth century, the economies of the West were primarily based on agriculture. Work and family were closely intertwined and the distinction between home and workplace was nonexistent. As Hodson and Sullivan (1990) note, the word "housework" was not introduced into the written English language until 1841, suggesting that the distinction between work performed at home and work performed elsewhere did not exist in previous eras. Pre-industrial family life in the U.S. and Europe has received much attention from historians and historical sociologists (Cowan 1983; Hareven 1990). These accounts describe the functioning of family economies within which wives, husbands, and children contributed their labor to the household and produced goods for sale in the market. Although tasks were divided on the basis of gender and age, neither women nor men experienced a separation between the worlds of family and work.

The twentieth century was a time of dramatic change in work and family life across most industrialized nations. The forces of industrialization were in full swing at the beginning of the century, but by the end, we were in the midst of what some call "the second industrial revolution" and the rise of the "global economy." As we will see in the next section, the changes occurring during the last half of the twentieth century are especially important for understanding the institutions of work and family today. To understand how things changed, however, we must first consider where we started.

Work and family transformed

Industrialization profoundly altered the nature of work and family life. With the creation of factories, goods production moved out of the home, and families began sending one or more of their members to work in these industrial settings. This occurred not only in North America and Europe, but also in parts of Asia and Latin America (Heymann and Earle 2010). Studies of the United States show that in some New England villages entire families went to work in local textile mills. This "family employment system," which often involved fathers paying wives, children, and other relatives out of their own wages, represented one way that work organizations in the early industrial era preserved familial influences.

The New England "mill girls" offer another example of the early industrial workplace. The "mill girls" were young women from rural backgrounds sent by their families to work in factories for a few years before their marriage (Hareven 1990). These women, whose labor was viewed as less necessary to the family farm than the labor of sons, contributed to their family's economic well-being by sending their wages home (Tilly and Scott 1978). Gradually, the "mill girls" were replaced by newly arriving European immigrants, who could be more cheaply employed. Immigrants were often recruited as families in a manner similar to the "family employment system" described above.

As industrialization unfolded, it was associated with other important societal changes, such as urbanization. For the growing middle class of managers and professionals, urbanization meant that work and family continued to grow apart, both geographically and symbolically. This separation was facilitated by zoning laws and various architectural arrangements that created clearly defined boundaries

101

between industrial and residential areas. These physical boundaries between work and family were further reinforced by a gender division of labor. Among the middle class, the workplace became men's domain, while families were seen as populated by women and children. Because middle-class wives cooked, cleaned, raised children, provided emotional support, entertained, and sacrificed their own ambitions for their husbands' careers, it was as if married, middle-class men brought two people to work, rather than one. Accordingly, despite the geographical separation of work and family, middle-class marriages and family lives during the industrial era were shaped by the demands of middle-class work.

Factory workers and others in the working class could not afford to relocate to the suburbs and hence lived much closer to the workplace than their middle-class counterparts. The cities thus became home to workers, who lived in densely populated areas not far from their workplaces. Unlike the middle class, where most women worked exclusively at home caring for their families, many working-class women combined their family responsibilities with a wage-earning job. Working-class men were employed in factories, while their wives worked in clerical or service positions. These gender-segregated work environments spilled over into the social lives and activities of the working class, which some have characterized as more gender-segregated than those of the middle class.

Many members of the working class are racial or ethnic minorities. Because racial and ethnic minorities of both genders have historically received lower earnings than the majority, two wage earners rather than one has been a typical pattern among minority families. Although the work and family configurations of these families are themselves diverse, minority men have generally been employed in factories or in agriculture. Minority women have found employment in these settings as well or as domestic servants in middle-class homes.

These descriptions of the industrial workplace illustrate the complex evolution of work and family arrangements over time, and they reveal the ways these relations were shaped by social class and race (as well as gender). The physical separation of work and family that accompanied industrialization had important impacts in the middle class, where work and family came to be seen as distinct domains inhabited by different genders. Middle-class men's roles were organized around the statuses of "worker" and "bread-winner," while the roles of "mother" and "homemaker" were assigned to middle-class women. Industrialization had different consequences for working-class families, who could often not afford a full-time homemaker and thus sent both women and men out to seek waged work.

Industrialization and the "Doctrine of separate spheres"

Industrialization's impact on work and households was intrinsically connected to its role in reshaping gender roles. Despite the fact that many working-class and minority women were employed for pay, the experiences of the middle class became the basis for cultural norms and employer practices that defined the workplace and workers as "male." As Reskin and Padavic observe:

> the sexual division of labor that assigned men to the labor force and women to the home encouraged employers to structure jobs on the assumptions that all permanent workers were men and that all men had stay-at-home wives. These assumptions freed workers (that is, male workers) from domestic responsibilities so they could work 12- to 14-hour days. These assumptions also bolstered the belief that domestic work was women's responsibility, even for women who were employed outside the home. (Reskin and Padavic 1994, p. 23)

One implication of these changes involved the emergence of what historians and sociologists have called "**the doctrine of separate spheres**" (Cancian 1987). This doctrine drew an association between the separation of home and work and the qualities deemed desirable in women and men. The paid workplace came to be seen as an arena of competition, rationality, and achievement – qualities that then became attached to men as the primary inhabitants of this sphere. Conversely, the home was portrayed as a "haven" from work and a realm characterized by domesticity, purity, and submissiveness. These characteristics, in turn, were ascribed to those who were seen to be primarily responsible for this domain – namely, women.

The doctrine of separate spheres was aimed as much at *prescription* as description, however. In other words, this doctrine supplied a cultural justification for men working for pay and women staying home to care for their family. The normative nature of this view is revealed in the treatment and views of those who deviated from its prescriptions. Men who were prevented from working altogether or whose work was too minimal to support their families were *denigrated not merely in their roles as workers, but as men*. Workers were men and, conversely, men were workers. Not working signaled being less than a man.

The late sociologist Jessie Bernard (1992, p. 207) referred to this association between manhood and paid work as the "**good-provider**" **role**: "To be a man one had to be not only a provider but a good provider. Success in the good-provider role came in time to define masculinity itself. The good provider had to achieve, to win, to succeed, to dominate. He was a bread*winner*" (emphasis in original). This view implied that men fulfill their obligations to their family through their paid work; men who could not accomplish this were deemed unfit husbands and fathers (Gerson 1993).

Women had different obligations to fulfill: "An ideal woman centered her life on love of husband and children, a love expressed mainly through emotions and piety, not through practical action" (Cancian 1989, p. 16). These qualities made women unsuited for paid work, however, just as the qualities required of paid workers make them unsuited for family caretaking. Moreover, just as the doctrine of separate spheres penalized men unable or unwilling to be good providers, it stigmatizes women who are unable or unwilling to be full-time family caretakers. As women, they are unsuited to be workers, while, as workers, they are unsuited to be women (or mothers).

The separation between home and workplace thus corresponded to changes in women's and men's lives. Men from all backgrounds gradually came to dominate factory work and other industrial jobs.

Those women who did work for pay tended to be young and unmarried, or poor. Married, middle-class women were likely to be at home caring for family and children. The social category of full-time homemaker thus emerged during this time period and became a way of life for some women.

Two points from this discussion are especially worth highlighting. First, men were not "naturally" or "automatically" the labor force of choice for early employers. Popular cultural conceptions of men as "workers" and "breadwinners" thus took time to emerge. Second, while rates of female labor force participation in the twentieth century have varied over time and place, women have always been a part of the paid labor force. What changed during the latter part of the twentieth century was not the fact of female labor force participation, but the composition and size of that labor force. By far, the biggest change in the female labor force in Europe and North America since the 1960s has been the entrance of married women with children (Goldscheider and Waite 1991; Heymann and Earle 2010).

In sum, the industrial era was extremely important in shaping our views of women, men, and work. We began to judge men by their work and judge workers according to whether they possess characteristics attributed to men. Because men were expected to achieve through work, their interest in and opportunities for participating in family life were constrained. Because workers were assumed to be men, women employed for pay were often forced to decide whether to be a woman or a worker. Success in one role, however, implied failing at the other. In addition, men who worked for pay were assumed to be fulfilling their family obligations through this act, while employed women were assumed to be abandoning their family responsibilities.

A Half-Century of Gender Change: Work, Education, and Gender Egalitarian Beliefs

During the past half-century, women's rates of labor force participation have been rising worldwide. Heymann and Earle (2010) report

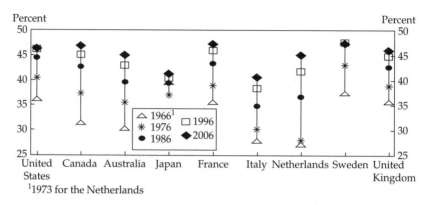

Figure 4.1 Women's share of the paid labor force in Europe, Australia, Canada, the United States, and Japan, 1966–2006.
Source: Jennifer L. Raynor. 2007. "Comparative civilian labor force statistics, 10 countries: A visual essay." *Monthly Labor Review* (December): 32–37.

that, between 1960 and 2006, women's share of the paid labor force rose not only in Western Europe and North America, but in Central America, the Caribbean, Northern and Southern Europe, Oceania (i.e., Australia, New Zealand, and the surrounding Pacific Islands), Central and Southeast Asia, and Southern Africa. Women's large-scale movement into paid work is "the single most influential change in the labor markets of industrialized countries in the postwar period" (Gornick, Meyers, and Ross 1998, p. 35). Figure 4.1 shows changes in women's share of the paid labor force in nine countries between 1966 and 2006. Women's share rose in all of these countries, with the lowest increases in Japan and the largest in the Netherlands.

In the United States, as Figure 4.2 shows, majorities of women and men worked for pay in 2008. Approximately 59.5 percent of women and just over 70 percent of men were in the labor force. Paid employment in the United States is typical for women and men of all racial and ethnic groups. Roughly three-quarters of African-American and white women, and two-thirds of Latinas, Asian-Americans, and Native American women worked for pay in 2005, as did majorities of men in each group (Lee and Mather 2008).

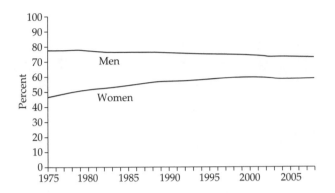

Figure 4.2 Labor force participation rates of U.S. women and men, 16 years and over, 1975–2008.
Source: TED: The Editor's Desk. U.S. Bureau of Labor Statistics (http://data.bls.gov/cgi-bin/print.pl/opub/ted/2009/ted_20091009.htm).

While U.S. women's rates of labor force participation rose during the last three decades of the twentieth century, U.S. men's labor force participation has inched slowly downward over the past 40 years, especially in the last two decades. Men's rates of labor force participation, even more than women's, have fluctuated in response to business cycles. In addition, men's rates have declined as the relative attractiveness and availability of alternatives to employment, such as school or retirement, have increased.

These changes in women's and men's rates of labor force participation can be traced to many interrelated economic, political, and social factors. Among them are the large-scale expansion of the service sector in the West and the corresponding decline of manufacturing employment. In the United States, manufacturing industries, such as auto, electronics, and steel, were the economic backbone of industrial society. These goods-producing industries expanded their share of employment until the 1950s, but have declined steadily since that time. The percentage of the U.S. population employed in agriculture has also been declining steadily; this sector now employs only about 2 percent of the labor force.

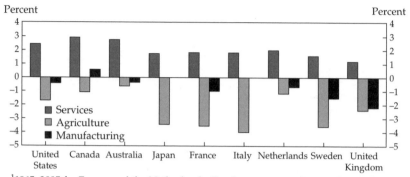

[1]1965–2005 for France and the Netherlands. Employment growth rates shown do not represent the total economy, because employment in mining and construction is excluded.

Figure 4.3 Average annual growth rates for employment by sector in Europe, Australia, Canada, the United States, and Japan, 1966–2006.
Source: Jennifer L. Raynor. 2007. "Comparative civilian labor force statistics, 10 countries: A visual essay." *Monthly Labor Review* (December): 32–37.

As Figure 4.3 shows, the growth of services and the decline of manufacturing and agriculture were not confined to the United States. The increase in service employment helped to create new job opportunities for women, while the decrease in manufacturing jobs reduced opportunities for men. These employment shifts are associated with a fundamental change in the world economy, characterized by the increasing flows of technology, resources, and information across borders and the emergence of an integrated global marketplace (Sweet and Meiksins 2008).

Changes in women's and men's rates of labor force participation in the latter half of the twentieth century are related to education as well. For example, examining World Bank and UNESCO data, Heymann and Earle (2010) show that girls' shares of enrollment in secondary school and university improved virtually worldwide between 1960 and 2004–5. This increase was greatest in industrialized economies, which have seen women become a majority of those earning a college degree (Charles and Bradley 2009; Shavit, Arum, Gamoran, and Menahem 2007).

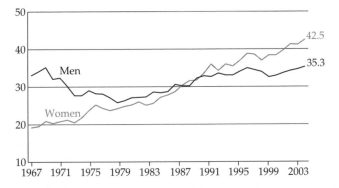

Figure 4.4 Proportion of 18–24-year old men and women enrolled in college, 1967–2005.
Source: U.S. Census Bureau.

In the United States, men's and women's rates of college enrollment have been rising since the 1970s, but women's have risen faster (Buchmann, DiPrete, and McDaniel 2008). U.S. women's rates of college enrollment have surpassed men's since 1991, with women earning 57 percent of all bachelor's degrees awarded in 2007–8 (U.S. Department of Education 2010; see Figure 4.4). Women's rates of enrollment were higher than men's among Blacks, Hispanics, and non-Hispanic Whites; Asian men's rates of college enrollment were slightly higher than Asian women's rates (62 vs. 59 percent). Rising education levels helped propel women into the labor force by enabling them to compete for a larger number of jobs. In 1970, only 11 percent of U.S. women between the ages of 25 and 64 working for pay held college degrees, while 36 percent of these women had college degrees in 2008 (http://data.bls.gov/cgi-bin/print.pl/cps/wlf-intro-2009.htm, retrieved 8/10/2010).

Gender, work, and parenthood

Prior to the 1960s, women throughout the industrialized world worked for pay only when they were compelled by circumstances such as poverty or divorce, or when they were young and

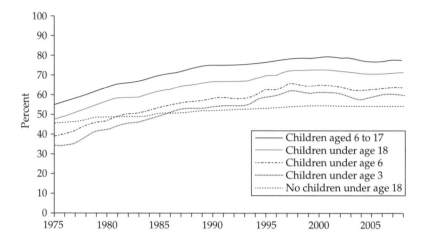

Figure 4.5 Labor force participation of U.S. women by presence and age of youngest child, 1975–2008.
Source: TED: The Editor's Desk. U.S. Bureau of Labor Statistics (http://data.bls.gov/cgi-bin/print.pl/opub/ted/2009/ted_20091009.htm).

unmarried. In 1948, for example, only 17 percent of married women in the United States were employed (Cohany and Sok 2007). Over the last half century, however, employment outside the home has become normative for all groups of women, including those who are married and have children. As Figure 4.5 shows, the labor force participation rates of married women in the United States, with and without children, have risen since the 1950s. Mothers' rates of labor force participation – regardless of marital status and age of child – have also increased. In 2005, 59 percent of mothers with children less than three years of age were employed (Mosisa and Hipple 2006). Rates of labor force participation for both sexes during the primary childbearing years (i.e., 25–45) are over 70 percent.

As with other employment trends we have discussed, increases in mothers' rates of employment occurred in most of Europe. Employment rates of women of primary childbearing age have increased over time, as has the percentage of women with young children (under age 6) in the labor market (Martin and Kats 2003). Overall, Heymann and Earle (2010) estimate that 340 million children under the age of six worldwide are being raised in households where all adults earn a living outside the home, and the numbers of school-age children in this situation are even larger.

The rise of gender egalitarian beliefs

New experiences and exposure to new ideas contribute to egalitarian beliefs (Davis and Greenstein 2009). As women (and men's) education levels rose and as women entered the labor force in large numbers, support for gender equality increased. As we have seen in earlier chapters, the second half of the twentieth century has been associated with growing public support for women's paid employment and for gender equality more generally. For example, in the 1950s and 1960s, majorities of U.S. women and men agreed that "It is much better for everyone involved if the man is the achiever outside the home and the woman takes care of the home and family," but these percentages have been declining almost continuously since (Farley 1996; Goldscheider and Waite 1991). Legislation such as the 1963 Equal Pay Act, Title VII of the 1964 Civil Rights Act, and the 1972 Education Amendments, as well as various Supreme Court decisions, provided a legal basis for gender equality in work and education.

Particularly significant for women's beliefs and experiences during the 1960s and early 1970s was the women's movement. Middle-class women, in particular, began to encounter gender egalitarian ideologies in college. Some gravitated to feminism as a direct result of their participation in the civil rights or anti-war movement, while others were attracted to the ideals of women's liberation itself. While many young white and middle-class women participated in the women's movement directly, other women (and men) were exposed indirectly to the movement's goals and philosophies. Economic independence and equal opportunity in the workplace were among the most important of these.

Studies of women who attended college during the late 1960s and early 1970s offer powerful evidence of the personal and cultural transformations brought about by the women's movement. In her study of female finance executives, Blair-Loy interviewed a woman who described the impact of feminism in this way:

> Most of the people in my age group were formed in college in the late 1960s. It shaped how we viewed life. Friedan, Steinem, Viet Nam, all of it. ... There was lots of social upheaval. It was the defining period of a whole generation of us. ... I started college in 1965. I was a good little sorority girl. I had to wear nylons and skirts. Then from 1965 to 1969, the whole world changed. It went to hell in a hand basket. (Blair-Loy 1999, pp. 16–17)

These changes also had implications for men's lives. Women's employment helped ease men's responsibilities as the sole bread-winner. Men's rates of labor force participation declined during the past few decades as alternatives to paid employment, such as education and retirement, became more viable. Although their paychecks continue to lag behind men's, women's salaries have helped considerably to ease the economic burdens on families. Indeed, households with two wage-earners earn considerably more than two-adult households with only one wage-earner.

These trends are not confined to the United States. As Figure 4.6 shows, majorities in all 22 countries surveyed by the Pew Research Center in 2010 agreed that women should be able to work outside the home, and most also agreed that marriages were more satisfying when both wives and husbands are employed (Pew Research Center 2010). These data also reveal a strong belief in gender equality overall, with majorities in almost all countries surveyed endorsing gender equality.

Changes in Gender, Family, and Caregiving

The family is perhaps the most taken-for-granted of all social institutions. In part, this is because the family is sometimes assumed to

	Women Should Be Able to Work Outside the Home		

	Agree %	Disagree %	DK %
U.S.	97	2	0
Britain	97	2	1
France	97	3	0
Germany	97	3	0
Spain	97	2	0
Poland	92	7	1
Russia	95	4	1
Turkey	95	4	1
Egypt	61	38	0
Jordan	58	40	2
Lebanon	96	4	1
China	97	3	0
India	95	4	0
Indonesia	88	12	0
Japan	94	5	1
Pakistan	69	29	2
S. Korea	96	3	0
Argentina	87	11	1
Brazil	96	5	0
Mexico	90	8	2
Kenya	87	12	0
Nigeria	84	16	1

Pew Research Center Q69b.

What Kind of Marriage Is More Satisfying?

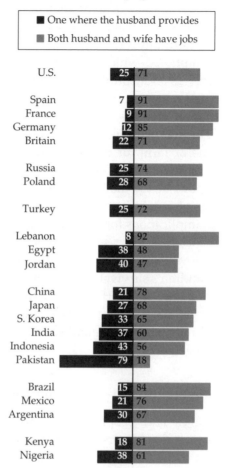

"What kind of marriage do you think is the more satisfying way of life: one where the husband provides for the family and the wife takes care of the house and children, or one where both have jobs and both take care of the house and children?" (Pew Research Center Q93)

Figure 4.6 Global gender beliefs.
Source: "Gender equality universally embraced, but inequalities acknowledged," July 1, 2010, the Pew Global Attitudes Project, a project of the Pew Research Center.

be natural, biological, or somehow "functional" for society, rather than a social construction whose configurations vary historically and culturally (Thorne 1982). People's uncritical faith in these assumptions, which reinforce the taken-for-grantedness of the family as an institution, have provoked (and continue to provoke) anxieties and concerns as the structure, composition, and meaning of family changes.

During the industrial era, families had to adjust as men left the home or farm for the paid workplace. In the post-industrial era, families were transformed again as both women and men worked for pay outside the household. This transformation affected many areas of family life, including marriages and relationships. It also had implications for childbearing and caring for children. In almost all societies, increases in women's access to education and paid employment are associated with overall declines in fertility, increases in children's survival, and lower risks of childhood poverty (Cooke and Baxter 2010; Heymann and Earle 2010). In addition, these changes have been accompanied by a rethinking of the meaning of family and an expanded range of family patterns and living arrangements.

Growing diversity of families and households

Families and people's living arrangements more broadly have become more diverse over time. To understand these changes, we need to first consider how those who track living arrangements define their terms. In the United States, the Census defines a family as "a group of two or more people who reside together and who are related by birth, marriage, or adoption" (https://ask.census.gov/cgi-bin/askcensus.cfg/php/enduser/prnt_adp.php?p_faqid=614&p_created=1091641666; retrieved 8/10/2010). This definition does not view adults who share a household but are not related legally through marriage as families. For example, gay and lesbian couples residing in states or countries where they are unable to legally marry are excluded from the Census definition, as are heterosexual cohabitors. When asked to identify members of their families, many middle-class Americans are likely to name members of their immediate family – parents, siblings, grandparents, children, and partner. Members of other social groups, both within the United States and outside it, may conceive of their families more broadly, including more distant relatives or even what Stack (1974) calls "fictive kin." Fictive kin are not related by blood, but rather assume the role of a family member.

Our own definitions of family are somewhat subjective, yet it is possible to identify at least one common element: Families cooperate in daily living. They pool resources and provide for one another. Family members' willingness, need, and ability to assume these obligations for others' well-being vary, of course, but the existence of these obligations indicates a family bond. Blood ties or ties formed by marriage or adoption are relevant as well; however, these ties do not exhaust the definition of family. This broad definition of family thus includes people legally prevented from marrying, such as gay and lesbian couples, and it includes various kinds of **fictive kin** – people who recognize obligations towards each other and contribute to each other's survival.

Although this definition of family does not map easily onto U.S. Census data or data collected by entities outside the U.S., we can use this information to look at changes in household composition over time. Table 4.1 reports changes in household type by country for roughly the last three decades. No single type of household dominated in 2008. For all countries shown, the percentage of households consisting of married couples with children has declined over time, with these households representing between one-quarter and one-third of all households in 2008. Roughly a third of all households contain married couples without children, a figure that has remained fairly stable over time. Remarkably, however, slightly more than a third of all households fall into other categories. That is, they include a single parent and children, people living alone, or other kinds of arrangements, such as cohabitation or group living. The increasing diversity of family and household composition reflects several other significant changes in family structure, marriage, and childbearing, which we will consider below.

Table 4.1 Percentage distribution of households by type and country.

Year	Total	Married-couple households[1]			Single parent[2]	One person	Other[3]
		Total	With children[2]	Without children[2]			
United States:							
1980	100.0	60.8	30.9	29.9	7.5	22.7	9.0
1990	100.0	56.0	26.3	29.8	8.3	24.6	11.0
1995	100.0	54.4	25.5	28.9	9.1	25.0	11.5
2000	100.0	52.8	24.1	28.7	8.9	25.5	12.7
2007	100.0	50.8	22.5	28.3	9.1	26.8	13.2
Canada:							
1981	100.0	66.8	36.3	30.5	5.3	20.3	7.6
1991	100.0	62.8	29.6	33.2	5.7	22.9	8.6
2001[4]	100.0	58.5	33.4	25.2	10.2	25.7	5.5
2006	100.0	57.4	31.4	26.1	10.3	26.8	5.5
Japan:							
1980	100.0	68.4	42.9	25.6	2.2	19.8	9.5
1990	100.0	65.2	33.1	32.1	2.3	23.1	9.4
1995	100.0	62.8	27.4	35.4	2.0	25.6	9.6
2000	100.0	60.3	23.6	36.7	2.1	27.6	10.0
2005	100.0	57.6	20.8	36.8	2.4	29.5	10.5
Denmark:[5]							
1980	100.0	50.3	25.0	25.3	3.9	44.9	1.0
1990	100.0	45.6	19.5	26.1	4.2	49.6	0.6

1995	100.0	44.9	18.2	26.6	4.2	50.4	0.5
2001	100.0	45.7	18.5	27.2	4.2	49.6	0.6
2008[4]	100.0	47.7	21.4	26.4	5.8	45.9	0.6
France:							
1982	100.0	67.5	39.8	27.7	4.5	24.6	3.4
1990	100.0	64.0	35.9	28.1	5.5	27.1	3.4
1999	100.0	59.3	29.9	29.4	6.3	31.0	3.4
2005[4]	100.0	56.4	27.2	29.2	6.7	32.8	4.1
Germany:							
1991	100.0	55.3	31.6	23.7	7.1	33.6	4.0
1995	100.0	53.3	29.2	24.0	6.8	34.9	5.1
2000[4]	100.0	56.8	28.0	28.8	6.0	36.1	1.2
2005	100.0	54.7	25.5	29.1	6.4	37.5	1.4
2007	100.0	53.4	24.3	29.1	6.5	38.7	1.4
Ireland:							
1981	100.0	(NA)	(NA)	(NA)	(NA)	16.9	(NA)
1991	100.0	61.6	47.9	13.7	10.6	20.2	7.6
1996	100.0	59.6	44.5	15.1	11.2	21.5	7.7
2002	100.0	59.2	41.4	17.7	11.7	21.6	7.6
2006	100.0	57.3	37.4	20.0	11.6	22.4	8.7

(Continued)

Table 4.1 *(Continued)*

Year	Total	Married-couple households[1]			Single parent[2]	One person	Other[3]
		Total	With children[2]	Without children[2]			
Netherlands:							
1988	100.0	64.7	37.3	27.4	5.4	28.7	1.2
1993	100.0	63.1	33.3	29.9	5.0	30.9	1.0
2000	100.0	60.2	30.6	29.6	5.6	33.4	0.7
2005	100.0	58.5	29.4	29.1	6.3	34.5	0.7
2007	100.0	57.7	28.7	28.9	6.4	35.3	0.7
2008	100.0	57.4	28.4	29.0	6.4	35.5	0.7
Sweden:							
1985	100.0	54.8	23.8	31.0	3.2	36.1	5.9
1990	100.0	52.1	21.9	30.2	3.9	39.6	4.4
1995[4]	100.0	50.7	21.2	29.4	4.6	42.3	2.4
2000	100.0	45.8	19.1	26.7	5.3	46.5	2.3
2006	100.0	45.6	18.8	26.9	5.0	46.5	2.9

United Kingdom: [6]

1981	100.0	65.0	31.0	34.0	5.0	22.0	8.0
1991	100.0	61.0	25.0	36.0	6.0	27.0	6.0
1994–95	100.0	58.0	25.0	33.0	7.0	27.0	8.0
2000	100.0	58.0	23.0	35.0	6.0	29.0	7.0
2008	100.0	56.0	21.0	35.0	7.0	30.0	7.0

NA Not available.

1 May include unmarried cohabitating couples. Such couples are explicitly included under married couples in Canada, Denmark, Ireland, France, the Netherlands, Sweden, and the United Kingdom. In Germany, cohabitants are grouped with married couples beginning in 2000. In other countries, some unmarried cohabitants are included as married couples, while some are classified under "other households."

2 Children are defined as unmarried children living at home according to the following age limits: under 18 years old in the United States, Canada (1981–96), Japan, Denmark (1980–2007), Sweden, and the United Kingdom, except that the United Kingdom includes 15-, 16-, and 17-year-olds in 1981 and 16- and 17-year-olds thereafter only if they are attending school full-time; under 25 years old in France and in Denmark in 2008; and children of all ages in Canada (2001 onward), Germany, Ireland, and the Netherlands.

3 Includes both family and nonfamily households not elsewhere classified. These households comprise, for example, siblings residing together, other households composed of relatives, and households made up of roommates. Some unmarried cohabitating couples may also be included in the "other" group. See footnote 1.

4 Break in series.

5 From family-based statistics. However, one person living alone constitutes a family in Denmark. In this respect, the Danish data are closer to household statistics.

6 Great Britain only (excludes Northern Ireland).

Source: U.S. Bureau of Labor Statistics, updated and revised from "Families and Work in Transition in 12 Countries, 1980–2001,"*Monthly Labor Review*, September 2003, with national sources, some of which may be unpublished.

Changes in marriage, divorce, and cohabitation

One important consequence of women's rising levels of education and labor force participation has been the age of marriage, which has been increasing for decades in the U.S. and across other industrialized economies (Cherlin 2010; Martin and Kats 2003). Marriages also became less stable during the latter part of the twentieth century. Divorce rates in the U.S. and other industrialized economies all rose steadily, especially in the United States. In fact, divorce rates in the U.S. have been much higher than in Europe and most Western countries, reaching their highest levels around 1980, after which they stabilized and declined somewhat (Casper and Bianchi 2002; Cherlin 2010).

Divorce rates are related to women's labor force participation. For example, a woman's divorce might necessitate a move into the paid labor force. Further, regardless of a person's own circumstances, as divorce becomes more common, it affects how young people – even those yet to marry – assess their options. In particular, women may be less willing to become economically dependent on men and instead make a greater commitment to work and career (Gerson 1985). Relations between divorce rates and women's employment are complex, however. Not only may higher divorce rates lead people to plan their futures differently, but paid employment itself may contribute to divorce. In their 1984 study of this issue, Booth et al. argued that, for the generation coming of age during the 1970s, wives' employment required a reorganization of family life for which neither gender's upbringing fully prepared them. This argument reminds us of the tremendous forces of social change that both produce and were produced by women's rising labor force participation.

Cohabitation – as an alternative or trial period prior to marriage – has also become significantly more common. Rates of premarital cohabitation, in particular, have increased in Northern and Western Europe and cohabitation in the U.S. is common among all educational groups. There is still much more to learn about cohabiting relationships, which are increasingly diverse in terms of couples' motivations for cohabiting and other characteristics of these house-holds (Cherlin 2010).

Same-sex marriage is another trend that is contributing to the redefinition of family. Same-sex marriage is currently legal in several countries and in six states within the U.S. Although data on same-sex unions are sparse, the 2000 U.S. Census counted just under 600,000 cohabiting same-sex couples. Other surveys show that les-bians are more likely to be in cohabiting relationships than men. Of those same-sex couples counted by the U.S. Census, roughly one-third of lesbian couples and one-quarter of male couples had chil-dren living with them (Cherlin 2010).

Changes in childbearing and caregiving

Childbearing and caregiving represent other areas of family life transformed during the last half century. An increase in the age at first marriage has been accompanied by an increase in age at first birth for women, rising from 21.4 in 1970 to 25 in 2000. As Smock and Greenland (2010, p. 579) explain, "Many women and men are waiting to be established economically before beginning family for-mation, and doing so typically requires not only extended educa-tion but several years of continuous commitment to employment." Childlessness, especially voluntary childlessness, has also increased over time. In the U.S., the proportion of childless women between the ages of 40 and 44 doubled during the last decades of the twen-tieth century (Smock and Greenland 2010). These trends – delayed childbearing and childlessness – are most heavily concentrated among highly educated women who are pursuing the most demand-ing careers.

Another significant change involves the rate of births to unmar-ried women. This includes women involved in cohabiting relation-ships and unpartnered women living alone. Most births in the United States occur among married couples, yet births to married couples make up a smaller share of all births than in the past (Smock and Greenland 2010). Fertility outside marriage is related to educa-tion, with less educated women more likely than those with higher levels of education to give birth outside of marriage. Race and ethnicity also matter: Births to unmarried women in 2007 were lowest among Asian/Pacific Islanders (17% of births) and non-Hispanic Whites (28% of births), and more common among Hispanics (51% of births), Native Americans/Alaska Natives (65% of births) and African-Americans (72% of births) (Smock and Greenland 2010).

Although not all nonmarital births are to single parents, a much higher percentage of children live in single-parent households now than in previous decades. The vast majority of single-parent households are headed by women, though the percentage of households headed by single men is growing. There are other ways to become a parent than through bearing a biological child and these methods – such as adoption – are also being used at least as frequently as in past decades.

Gender, Work, and Family: The Roles of Social Policy and the State

One benefit of a cross-national approach is that it enables us to examine how national policies and cultural patterns shape the organization of gender. The effects of these policies can clearly be seen when we consider work and family, and the lives of the women, men, and children who inhabit these institutions. As we have seen, many of the trends shaping work and family over the last half of the twentieth century have affected most of the industrialized world: Women's rates of labor force participation have increased and families have become more diversified. But those similarities are not the entire story. National governments have responded to changes in work and family in different ways, and these differences have shaped current work and family patterns.

How people allocate their time is an individual-level process, but we must also consider the larger context in which those decisions occur. One way to think about the influence of national context is to consider how laws and policies, in conjunction with cultural beliefs, can create incentives or disincentives for people to allocate their time in particular ways – such as working for pay vs. staying home to care for a child. Of particular interest here is behavior related to the amount of time women and men devote to employment, household work, and caregiving. Some researchers studying this topic employ a macro approach, identifying broad "policy regimes" or typologies that group similar types of countries together. Others pursue a country-by-country analysis, comparing women's and men's work and family activity across societies. I will focus on the former approach.

Work, family, and gender across welfare regimes

To understand differences across industrial societies, Esping-Andersen (1990) has identified three types of **welfare regime**s. The key difference among them is the degree to which states intervene in providing for the social welfare of the population. At one end of the spectrum are the English-speaking countries and Switzerland, which Esping-Andersen (1990) refers to as "liberal welfare regimes." These countries prefer to address social issues via the market, with little state intervention. Government support is reserved only for those unable to support themselves and is stigmatized.

In keeping with this philosophy, liberal welfare regimes view family and caregiving as individual responsibilities. Employers may provide family benefits, but this is not a societal expectation (van der Lippe and van Dijk 2002). With the exception of schooling, liberal welfare regimes provide little universal support to families and individuals. People are expected to provide for themselves and their families through paid work (Cooke and Baxter 2010). Because jobs are the vehicle through which people access health insurance and other benefits, and because caregiving responsibilities are left up to families and individuals, liberal welfare regimes reinforce a gender division of labor whereby men are primary breadwinners and women are caregivers.

The policies of liberal welfare regimes reflect what Misra, Moller, and Budig (2007, p. 808) call an "earner" role for women. Women are treated primarily as earners, not caregivers. Policies, such as

123

those promoting equal opportunity and nondiscrimination, encourage women's participation in the paid labor force, but there are few supports for caregiving or to encourage work–family balance.

The United States is an example of liberal welfare regime in the extreme. In the U.S., for example, employers, not the government, are the primary providers of health insurance and other benefits, and government regulation is often fiercely resisted. The United States is virtually unique with respect to its unregulated labor market. As Heymann and Earle observe:

> there is now an overwhelming global consensus regarding workers' rights to a weekly day of rest, paid annual leave, paid sick leave, and paid leave for new mothers, as well as large consensus on the right to breastfeeding breaks, there are some glaring geographical omissions – namely, the United States. ... The United States does not require employers to provide annual leave or a mandatory day of rest each week, nor does it limit the duration of the workweek or mandatory overtime. Only unpaid leave for serious illnesses is provided through the Family and Medical Leave Act, legislation that covers only half of all workers in the country (only employees who have worked at least 1250 hours for a firm employing over fifty people). (Heymann and Earle 2010, p. 116)

A second type of welfare regime is the corporatist-conservative approach. This regime, which characterizes continental Europe, more explicitly reinforces a male breadwinner/female caregiver model. Religious beliefs – more so than the market – are the primary influence on social welfare policies. Although these countries may offer more universal types of benefits than liberal welfare regimes, these benefits are directed in ways that reinforce a traditional gender division of labor (Cooke and Baxter 2010). Although these countries offer support for caregiving, this support is designed to encourage women to provide care in the family.

The social-democratic regime exemplified by the Nordic countries is the third regime type in Esping-Andersen's (1990) typology. These countries rely on high taxes and full employment to provide generous social welfare benefits to most sectors of the population.

To help insure full employment, social-democratic regimes offer support for dual-earner couples, such as public childcare and parental leave policies available to both women and men. These countries also place a greater emphasis than the other two welfare regimes on limiting wage inequality. Misra, Moller, and Budig (2007) argue that these policies contribute to an "earner-carer" role for women and men.

The lessons of comparative research

Cross-national research is important in showing how societal-level policies and laws can shape women's and men's work and family activities. Although women's labor force participation rate has risen throughout the industrialized world, the form and consequences of women's paid employment differ across policy regimes. For example, women (and mothers) are most likely to be employed in social-democratic and liberal regimes and least likely in corporatist-conservative countries. Despite relative similarity in the rates of female employment, however, the gender pay gap is larger in liberal regimes than in those that are social-democratic. In fact, wage inequality between women and men, as well as *among* men and *among* women, is greater in liberal than in social-democratic regimes. (We will look closely at the gender pay gap in Chapter 6.) Women in all types of regimes are more likely than men to work part-time, but women's rates of part-time employment are highest in countries where the male breadwinner model applies (Cooke and Baxter 2010).

National context also shapes women's and men's roles in caring for children and unpaid domestic work, and it shapes the policies states may provide to help with family caregiving. Although women in all welfare regimes do more housework and childcare than men, the gender gap is smallest in social-democratic regimes and largest in corporatist-conservative countries. Social-democratic regimes, especially the Scandinavian countries, provide numerous family policies. However, even in these countries, where parental leave is available to both genders, women are more likely than men to take advantage of this policy. (We will return to the topics of housework and care for children in the next chapter when we look at gender distinctions and inequalities inside families.)

As we conclude this discussion, there are a couple points to keep in mind. First, as Cooke and Baxter (2010, p. 529) observe: "neither the market nor policy has managed to close the gender gap in paid or unpaid labor." Gender inequalities can be found in all three of the welfare regimes discussed above, though how and where these inequalities are expressed may differ. In addition, remember that no typology can capture all societal-level variations in work and family. The organization of these institutions reflects the interplay of multiple factors too numerous to be fully accounted for by a single classification scheme. For example, Misra, Moller, and Budig (2007) argue that France and Belgium represent countries with an "ambivalent" view of women's work and family roles and thus do not fit neatly into any of the three welfare regimes. Policies in these countries reinforce neither women's caregiving or earning roles, but rather a mix of both. Finally, Esping-Andersen's (1990) model does not include non-Western countries. A more global, country-by-country approach is also needed, as Map 4.1 shows.

Gender, Work, and Family in the Twenty-First Century: Looking Ahead

The last half of the twentieth century was a period of dramatic change in women's and men's work and family lives. The most fundamental change involved the large-scale movement of mothers into the paid labor force. This trend seems to be slowing down, however. For example, U.S. women's overall rates of labor force participation have leveled off in the past few years and even declined somewhat from their peak in 1999. The labor force participation rates of married mothers, especially those with infants, have also stopped increasing. These rates declined in the late 1990s and have been relatively stable since (Cohany and Sok 2007). While most believe the leveling off of women's rates of labor force participation is related to the weakening economy (Lee and Mather 2008; Boushey

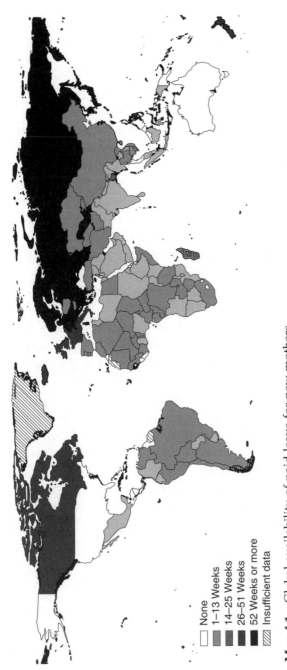

Map 4.1 Global availability of paid leave for new mothers.
Source: Jody Heymann and Alison Earle. 2010. *Raising the Global Floor: Dismantling the Myth that We Can't Afford Good Working Conditions for Everyone.* Stanford: Stanford University Press (map 5.6).

127

2005), others wonder if work–family conflict is partly to blame. As we will see in a later section, robust work–family policies do seem to make a difference in women's opportunity and interest in working for pay.

Regarding family life, Cherlin (2010) predicts that the current diversification of family forms, living arrangements, and relationships will continue. He notes that social scientists who study families have moved away from "the framework of a conventional, uniform family life cycle" (Cherlin 2010, p. 403). One troubling aspect of this trend, from his perspective, is the increasing divergence in family forms by income and education. This pattern may be related to changes in the workplace, particularly the widening gap in the employment opportunities and earnings for those with and without higher education. Immigration, the aging of the labor force, and the continued growth of the global economy are other trends reshaping both work and family life (Cherlin 2010; Lee and Mather 2008).

While the social changes of the twentieth century have been dramatic, it is important to remember that change is always uneven. As Moen and Roehling (2005, p. 189) observe, people's "real-life experiences" are often out of sync with social policies and taken-for-granted societal beliefs about major institutions, such as work, family, education, religion, and so on. Women's and men's adult lives today are significantly different than those of their parents and grandparents, but Moen and Roehling (2005) argue that many old assumptions about work and family still linger.

For example, family diversity is a social fact, but when people refer to "the family," they are likely to have in mind a wife, husband, and their biological children all living together. When imagining the "ideal worker," many would think about a person who begins a job after finishing school, works full-time until retiring, and makes work a central life priority. These images of "the family" and the "ideal worker" do not reflect reality, however. In addition to our earlier discussion about family change, consider that, in the U.S., 5.8 million grandparents reported living with their grandchildren in 2000 and, of those grandparents, 42 percent were primary caretakers (Cherlin 2010). Because of high rates of divorce and the dissolution of cohabiting relationships, many children in industrialized economies have a parent who does not live with them. Similarly, the image of the "ideal worker" is at odds with the lives of people who have both work and family responsibilities. These are just a couple of examples of the "disconnect" between lived reality and taken-for-granted beliefs. More broadly, they represent an instance of **structural lag**, which refers to the fact that "the policies and practices of governments, corporations, and other institutions typically change at a far slower pace than demographic, economic, technological, and other social transformations" (Moen and Roehling 2005, p. 190).

The persistence of gender

I began this chapter with a consideration of the sexual division of labor – the differential assignment of tasks and responsibilities to each gender. Although the chapter has focused on change, it is important to conclude with a reminder about those elements that have persisted over time. One is the sexual division of labor itself: Women and men are not randomly distributed across the various activities that comprise social life. And these differences shape their experiences, as well as societal expectations regarding how they should behave and what qualities are ascribed to them.

Eagly's (1987) social role theory argues that people form expectations of one another based on the roles they typically occupy in the social structure. Because the care of children worldwide remains largely women's responsibility, women are expected to behave in **communal** ways – emotionally expressive and generally concerned with others' welfare. Men's occupational roles are the basis for gender role expectations involving **agentic** behaviors (i.e., stressing competence and independence). These expectations grow out of and help to reinforce the gendered institutions of work and family. They form the backdrop against which people make life choices, and even those who reject these expectations are held accountable to them.

In addition to the persistence of gendered expectations about women and men is a continuing belief in gender distinctions themselves. A belief in gender equality is stronger in the twenty-first century than ever before. Despite the rise over time in gender egalitarian beliefs, however, Charles and Bradley (2009, p. 925) argue that **"gender essentialist ideology** persists." This ideology, which involves a belief in "fundamental and innate gender differences," is particularly strong in Western cultures, which emphasize individual achievement and self-expression (Charles and Bradley 2009, p. 925). For example, while women continue to increase their enrollment in higher education, Charles and Bradley (2009) show that this has not produced a "degendering" of educational institutions. Analyzing data on fields of study from colleges and universities in forty-four countries, they find that sex-typing by field of study is greater in advanced industrial societies than in those that are less developed. In particular, advanced economies show a gap in female and male students' pursuit of scientific and technical fields that is less pronounced in other countries. These results provide a further reminder that gender remains entrenched in our institutions and culture. While change is ongoing, it would be a mistake to downplay the ways in which gender permeates the organization of the social world.

Chapter Summary

Women and men have always worked, but the nature of their work has changed over time. Prior to industrialization, women and men both worked at home. In this agriculture-based economy, women and men each contributed to the tasks essential for survival, such as raising food. Industrialization dramatically changed the ways that people lived and worked. Men became the primary breadwinners for their families and women were expected to have lives revolving around the care of children and family.

During the years since the end of World War II, married women and women with children have entered the labor forces of developed economies in large numbers. This change coincided with the emergence of a service economy, the expansion of women's and girls' educational opportunities, and growing support for gender equality.

These changes in the economic realm transformed family life. People postponed marriage, divorce rates rose, and many couples began to cohabit – either prior to or as an alternative to marriage. Same-sex marriage was legalized in several coun tries and U.S. states. Overall, families and households became more diverse.

National context plays an important role in shaping work and family. Laws and policies of nation-states can shape women's and men's work and family lives by creating incentives or disin-centives for certain type of activities. Esping-Andersen (1990) identified three types of welfare state regimes characterized by differing levels of state investment in social programs. These regimes are also associated with different levels of female involve-ment in the paid labor force and public investment in family caregiving.

As the twenty-first century unfolds, work and family continue to change. Social change is always uneven, however. Although peo-ple's work and family lives today are very different from those of their parents and grandparents, people's taken-for-granted beliefs about these institutions have not changed as quickly. In addition, the practices and policies of employers and government have not adapted to the changes in peoples' daily realities. Overcoming structural lag is a challenge for the years ahead.

Work–family relations have been intertwined historically with conceptions of gender. A belief that work and family were "separate worlds" corresponded with a belief that women and men had distinct, nonoverlapping responsibilities and roles. Accordingly, women's move into the paid labor force has been accompanied by a recognition that work and family are not separate, but rather they intersect in complex ways. As relations between women and men continue to change, relations between work and family are likely to be redefined as well. Work and family are not static, unchanging

131

institutions, but reflect and adapt to developments in the wider society.

Further Reading

Charles, Maria and Bradley, Karen. 2009. "Indulging our gendered selves: Sex segregation by field of study in 44 countries." *American Journal of Sociology* 114: 924–976.

Esping-Andersen, Gosta. 1990. *The Three Worlds of Welfare Capitalism.* Princeton, NJ: Princeton University Press.

Heymann, Jody and Earle, Alison. 2010. *Raising the Global Floor: Dismantling the Myth that We Can't Afford Good Working Conditions for Everyone.* Stanford: Stanford University Press.

Moen, Phyllis Moen and Roehling, Patricia. 2005. *The Career Mystique: Cracks in the American Dream.* Lanham, MD: Rowman & Littlefield Publishers, Inc.

Key Terms

Sexual division of labor
Doctrine of separate spheres
"Good-provider" role
Fictive kin
Welfare regime
Structural lag
Agentic/communal
Gender essentialist ideology

Critical Thinking Questions

1   What is your definition of "family"? How does it compare with those discussed in this chapter?
2   Women's rates of college enrollment have surpassed men's in many industrial societies, but women and men continue to

pursue different fields of study. What factors might explain this pattern?

3 How would you describe the characteristics of the "ideal worker"? How well do these characteristics correspond to characteristics people associate with mothers, fathers, women, or men?

Chapter 5

Gender, Childhood, and Family Life

Chapter Objectives

- Discuss the research on parental preferences for and treatment of girls and boys.
- Explain how children learn to apply gender stereotypes to themselves and others.
- Discuss the research on the household division of labor.
- Explore the differences between "his and her" marriage and the ways that gay and lesbian relationships differ from heterosexual marriages.

The multilayered conception of gender developed in previous chapters will help us as we make sense of the vast amount of research on children, family, and households. For example, researchers often focus on gender differences in the experiences associated with family life – such as childhood socialization practices, marriage or cohabitation, parenting, and household work. Some of this research

The Sociology of Gender: An Introduction to Theory and Research, Second Edition. Amy S. Wharton.
© 2012 John Wiley & Sons Ltd. Published 2012 by John Wiley & Sons Ltd.

embraces a strictly individualist perspective, but much examines how gender emerges through social interaction – between children and their peers or partners in a relationship, for example. The gendered institutions approach will also make an appearance, especially as we consider how issues affecting families and children vary cross-nationally.

Parents' Preferences for Children's Sex

Research on India and China has shown that parents in these cultures are more likely to prefer sons to daughters. A preference for sons stems from their perceived economic usefulness (especially in agricultural societies) and their role in providing support for parents and carrying on the family name (Mills and Begall 2010). Numerous studies have examined the consequences of son preference for individuals, families, and society (e.g., Park and Cho 1995; Song and Burgard 2008).

A different pattern has been found in the West. Research on parents in the United States, Europe, and Australia generally finds a preference for having a child of each sex (Mills and Begall 2010; Raley and Bianchi 2006). For example, families with one or two children of the same sex typically express a preference for having a second or third child of a different sex. Parents having two children of the same sex transition faster to a third child than those with a boy and a girl. Studies that compare preferences of women and men, however, find that men seem to have a stronger preference than women for the sex of their children and men express a greater preference for sons (Raley and Bianchi 2006). Although women do express some preference for daughters, this preference is small in comparison to men's preference for sons. In their study of European parents' preferences for the sex of their children, Mills and Begall (2010) find that preferences for sons are greater in countries lower in gender equity than in those with higher levels.

These studies show how gender at both the societal and individual levels shapes parents' preferences and behavior regarding fertility. At the societal level, son preference is related to the relative status of women and men and their societal roles vis-à-vis the economy and the family. At the individual level, parents' gender shapes their preferences for the sex of their children. Although families in the West generally want children of both sexes, fathers' preferences for sons are much greater than women's preferences for daughters. In the following discussion we will see more examples of the ways that mothers' and fathers' views and behavior diverge, as well as consider some explanations for this pattern.

"Is it a Boy or a Girl?": Gender Construction in Families

Once a baby is born (or, as is increasingly the case, during pregnancy), one of the first questions asked is whether the baby is a boy or a girl. One reason why this question matters to people is that a child's gender gives us important clues about him or her. Specifically, a child's gender conveys to us information, expectations of behavior and personality, and offers some guidelines for interaction. The fact that people rely on gender – even in a newborn – to provide these clues reaffirms once more the power of gender as an important social category. Of course, simply because people rely on gender as a source of information does not mean that it is a *reliable* source. What matters is that we take for granted gender's ability to provide information about people and thus rely on it almost unconsciously. What is important, then, is that people *act as if* gender is a reliable source of information and behave accordingly. The Thomas theorem, associated with W. I. Thomas (1966, p. 301 [1931]), is relevant here: "Situations defined as real become real in their consequences."

Once a person is categorized as female or male, gender is used to organize and interpret additional information about that person and to shape expectations of behavior. This starts at birth or even earlier. Recall that in Chapter 1 I discussed how gender is assigned to a child at birth. Normally, this is done by inspecting the child's

---

Box 5.1 Supporting boys or girls when the line isn't clear.

OAKLAND, Calif., Dec. 1 – Until recently, many children who did not conform to gender norms in their clothing or behavior and identified intensely with the opposite sex were steered to psychoanalysis or behavior modification.

But as advocates gain ground for what they call gender-identity rights, evidenced most recently by New York City's decision to let people alter the sex listed on their birth certificates, a major change is taking place among schools and families. Children as young as 5 who display predispositions to dress like the opposite sex are being supported by a growing number of young parents, educators and *mental health* professionals.

Doctors, some of them from the top pediatric hospitals, have begun to advise families to let these children be "who they are" to foster a sense of security and self-esteem. They are motivated, in part, by the high incidence of *depression*, suicidal feelings and self-mutilation that has been common in past generations of transgender children. Legal trends suggest that schools are now required to respect parents' decisions.

"First we became sensitive to two mommies and two daddies," said Reynaldo Almeida, the director of the Aurora School, a progressive private school in Oakland. "Now it's kids who come to school who aren't gender typical."

The supportive attitudes are far easier to find in traditionally tolerant areas of the country like San Francisco than in other parts, but even in those places there is fierce debate over how best to handle the children.

Cassandra Reese, a first-grade teacher outside Boston, recalled that fellow teachers were unnerved when a young boy showed up in a skirt. "They said, 'This is not normal,' and, 'It's the parents' fault,'" Ms. Reese said. "They didn't see children as sophisticated enough to verbalize their feelings."

Box 5.1 *(Continued)*

As their children head into adolescence, some parents are choosing to block puberty medically to buy time for them to figure out who they are – raising a host of ethical questions.

While these children are still relatively rare, doctors say the number of referrals is rising across the nation. Massachusetts, Minnesota, California, New Jersey and the District of Columbia have laws protecting the rights of transgender students, and some schools are engaged in a steep learning curve to dismantle gender stereotypes.

At the Park Day School in Oakland, teachers are taught a gender-neutral vocabulary and are urged to line up students by sneaker color rather than by gender. "We are careful not to create a situation where students are being boxed in," said Tom Little, the school's director. "We allow them to move back and forth until something feels right."

For families, it can be a long, emotional adjustment. Shortly after her son's third birthday, Pam B. and her husband, Joel, began a parental journey for which there was no map. It started when their son, J., began wearing oversized T-shirts and wrapping a towel around his head to emulate long, flowing hair. Then came his mother's silky undershirts. Half a year into preschool, J. started becoming agitated when asked to wear boys' clothing.

En route to a mall with her son, Ms. B. had an epiphany: "It just clicked in me. I said, 'You really want to wear a dress, don't you?'"

Thus began what the B.'s, who asked their full names not be used to protect their son's privacy, call "the reluctant path," a behind-closed-doors struggle to come to terms with a gender-variant child – a spirited 5-year-old boy who, at least for now, strongly identifies as a girl, requests to be called "she" and asks to wear pigtails and pink jumpers to school.

(Continued)

139

Box 5.1   (*Continued*)

Ms. B., 41, a lawyer, accepted the way her son defined himself after she and her husband consulted with a psychologist and observed his newfound comfort with his choice. But she feels the precarious nature of the day-to-day reality. "It's hard to convey the relentlessness of it, she said, "every social encounter, every time you go out to eat, every day feeling like a balance between your kid's self-esteem and protecting him from the hostile outside world."

The prospect of cross-dressing kindergartners has sparked a deep philosophical divide among professionals over how best to counsel families. Is it healthier for families to follow the child's lead, or to spare children potential humiliation and isolation by steering them toward accepting their biological gender until they are older?

Both sides in the debate underscore their concern for the profound vulnerability of such youngsters, symbolized by occurrences like the murder in 2002 of Gwen Araujo, a transgender teenager born as Eddie, southeast of Oakland.

"Parents now are looking for advice on how to make life reasonable for their kids – whether to allow cross-dressing in public, and how to protect them from the savagery of other children," said Dr. Herbert Schreier, a psychiatrist with Children's Hospital and Research Center in Oakland.

Dr. Schreier is one of a growing number of professionals who have begun to think of gender variance as a naturally occurring phenomenon rather than a disorder. "These kids are becoming more aware of how it is to be themselves," he said.

In past generations, so-called sissy boys and tomboy girls were made to conform, based on the belief that their behaviors were largely products of dysfunctional homes.

Among the revisionists is Dr. Edgardo Menvielle, a child-adolescent psychiatrist at the Children's National Medical Center in Washington who started a national outreach group for parents of gender-variant children in 1998 that now has

Box 5.1 *(Continued)*

more than 200 participants. "We know that sexually marginalized children have a higher rate of depression and *suicide* attempts," Dr. Menvielle said. "The goal is for the child to be well adjusted, healthy and have good self-esteem. What's not important is molding their gender."

The literature on adults who are transgender was hardly consoling to one parent, a 42-year-old software consultant in Massachusetts and the father of a gender-variant third grader. "You're trudging through this tragic, horrible stuff and realizing not a single person was accepted and understood as a child," he said. "You read it and think, O.K., best to avoid that. But as a parent you're in this complete terra incognita."

The biological underpinnings of gender identity, much like sexual orientation, remain something of a mystery, though many researchers suspect it is linked with hormone exposure in the developing fetus.

Studies suggest that most boys with gender variance early in childhood grow up to be gay, and about a quarter heterosexual, Dr. Menvielle said. Only a small fraction grow up to identify as transgender.

Girls with gender-variant behavior, who have been studied less, voice extreme unhappiness about being a girl and talk about wanting to have male anatomy. But research has thus far suggested that most wind up as heterosexual women.

Although many children role-play involving gender, Dr. Menvielle said, "the key question is how intense and persistent the behavior is," especially if they show extreme distress.

Dr. Robin Dea, the director of regional mental health for Kaiser Permanente in Northern California, said: "Our gender identity is something we feel in our soul. But it is also a continuum, and it evolves."

Dr. Dea works with four or five children under the age of 15 who are essentially living as the opposite sex. "They are

(Continued)

Box 5.1 *(Continued)*

much happier, and their grades are up," she said. "I'm waiting for the study that says supporting these children is negative."

But Dr. Kenneth Zucker, a psychologist and head of the gender-identity service at the Center for Addiction and Mental Health in Toronto, disagrees with the "free to be" approach with young children and cross-dressing in public. Over the past 30 years, Dr. Zucker has treated about 500 preadolescent gender-variant children. In his studies, 80 percent grow out of the behavior, but 15 percent to 20 percent continue to be distressed about their gender and may ultimately change their sex.

Dr. Zucker tries to "help these kids be more content in their biological gender" until they are older and can determine their sexual identity – accomplished, he said, by encouraging same sex friendships and activities like board games that move beyond strict gender roles.

Though she has not encountered such a situation, Jennifer Schwartz, assistant principal of Chatham Elementary School outside Springfield, Ill., said that allowing a child to express gender differences "would be very difficult to pull off" there.

Ms. Schwartz added: "I'm not sure it's worth the damage it could cause the child, with all the prejudices and parents possibly protesting. I'm not sure a child that age is ready to make that kind of decision."

The B.'s thought long and hard about what they had observed in their son. They have carefully choreographed his life, monitoring new playmates, selecting a compatible school, finding sympathetic parents in a babysitting co-op. Nevertheless, Ms. B. said, "there is still the stomach-clenching fear for your kid."

It is indeed heartbreaking to hear a child say, as J. did recently, "It feels like a nightmare I'm a boy."

Box 5.1 *(Continued)*

The adjustment has been gradual for Mr. B., a 43-year-old public school administrator who is trying to stop calling J. "our little man." He thinks of his son as a positive, resilient person, and his love and admiration show. "The truth is, is any parent going to choose this for their kid?" he said. "It's who your kid is."

Families are caught in the undertow of conflicting approaches. One suburban Chicago mother, who did not want to be identified, said in a telephone interview that she was drawing the line on dress and trying to provide "boy opportunities" for her 6-year-old son. "But we can't make everything a power struggle," she said. "It gets exhausting."

She worries about him becoming a social outcast. "Why does your brother like girl things?" friends of her 10-year-old ask. The answer is always, "I don't know."

Nila Marrone, a retired linguistics professor at the *University of Connecticut* who consults with parents and schools, recalled an incident last year at a Bronx elementary school in which an 8-year-old boy perceived as effeminate was thrown into a large trash bin by a group of boys. The principal, she said, "suggested to the mother that she was to blame, for not having taught her son how to be tough enough."

But the tide is turning.

The Los Angeles Unified School District, for instance, requires that students be addressed with "a name and pronoun that corresponds to the gender identity." It also asks schools to provide a locker room or changing area that corresponds to a student's chosen gender.

One of the most controversial issues concerns the use of "blockers," *hormones* used to delay the onset of puberty in cases where it could be psychologically devastating (for instance, a girl who identifies as a boy might slice her wrists when she gets her period). Some doctors disapprove of block-

(Continued)

Box 5.1 *(Continued)*

ers, arguing that only at puberty does an individual fully appreciate their gender identity.

Catherine Tuerk, a nurse-psychotherapist at the children's hospital in Washington and the mother of a gender-variant child in the 1970s, says parents are still left to find their own way. She recalls how therapists urged her to steer her son into psychoanalysis and "hypermasculine activities" like karate. She said she and her husband became "gender cops."

"It was always, 'You're not kicking the ball hard enough,'" she said.

Ms. Tuerk's son, now 30, is gay and a father, and her own thinking has evolved since she was a young parent. "People are beginning to understand this seems to be something that happens," she said. "But there was a whole lifetime of feeling we could never leave him alone."

Source: Patricia Leigh Brown, "Supporting Boys or Girls When the Line Isn't Clear," *New York Times*, December 2, 2006.

genitals. In those rare cases where genitals are ambiguous, doctors and parents almost always attempt to assign the child to a sex category and construct appropriate genitalia (Kessler 1990). Most cultures adhere strongly to the belief that a child must be *either* male or female. Consequently, infants who cannot be easily categorized are normally subjected to complicated and extensive medical procedures to "correct" their ambiguous genitalia.

Assigning a child to a gender category, however, is just the beginning. Assignment sets into motion many other processes that all help to produce a gendered individual. For example, when expecting parents learn they are going to have a girl, they may decorate the nursery in pink or yellow rather than blue, or in pastel colors rather than colors that are bolder. Girls' rooms tend to be painted in a wider variety of colors than the rooms of boys, which are mostly blue (Pomerleau, Bolduc, Malcuit, and Cossette 1990). Parents' knowledge of their child's gender will also shape the kinds of clothes and toys they purchase: Clothes for infant girls tend to be soft, pink, and decorated with lace or bows, while clothes for male infants may be made of more rugged fabrics, such as denim, and decorated with sports imagery. Girls are more likely than boys to receive dolls from parents, while parents buy more sports equipment, tools, and vehicles for boys (Pomerleau, Bolduc, Malcuit and Cossette 1990). Not all toys are so strongly gender-differentiated, however: Toys such as animals, balls and balloons, books, musical and talking toys, and even kitchen appliances and utensils for children are as likely to be purchased for girls as boys (Pomerleau, Bolduc, Malcuit and Cossette 1990).

Even as infants, children live in a gendered social world and these experiences shape their development as females and males. Though infants and very young children have not yet developed a gender identity, the foundations of their gender schemas are being established. As Coltrane observes:

> Infants enter the world much more prepared to extract information from their environments than social scientists once thought. ... By the age of seven months, infants can discriminate between men's and women's voices and generalize this to strangers. Infants less than a year old can also discriminate individual male and female faces. Even before they are verbal, young children are developing gender categories and making generalizations about people and objects in their environments ... (Coltrane (1998, p. 125)

This ability to categorize others on the basis of gender is not just a human trait, but also extends to other species (Maccoby 1998).

Do parents treat girls and boys differently?

From an individualist perspective, parental socialization is the primary source of most gender differences in traits and personality dispositions. To gain support for this view, researchers design

145

studies to examine whether and in what areas parents relate differently to their daughters and sons. Demonstrating that parents treat their male and female infants and very young children differently, however, is more difficult than it seems.

A classic 1974 study aimed to uncover these differences by asking mothers and fathers of newborns to describe their infants (Rubin, Provenzano, and Luria 1974). Parents were given a list of adjectives, presented as pairs on an eleven-point scale, and were asked to choose how closely each described their baby. Eighteen pairs were provided, such as firm/soft, large featured/fine featured, strong/weak, hardy/delicate, etc. While infants as a group were generally described in positive terms (e.g., strong, friendly, alert, cheerful, easy-going), daughters were rated as softer, finer-featured, littler, and more inattentive than sons. Although the infants had been selected to be similar in weight, length, and muscle tone, parents of daughters described their children very differently to parents of sons.

Because the infants were physically very similar, the researchers concluded that parents were not reacting to real differences between children as much as they were applying gender stereotypes that could possibly result in differential treatment of their male and female children. For example, those who saw their child as delicate may be less likely to engage in physical play than those who saw their child as strong and coordinated. While their child's gender is not the only thing that new parents attend to, of course, it is very important – a "distinctive," "definitive," and "normative" characteristic (Rubin, Provenzano, and Luria 1974, p. 517). This is because parents and newborns are just getting acquainted and parents at this stage have very little additional knowledge about their child. In general, people seem to rely on gender to "fill in the gaps" in their assessments of others, and this is especially true when little else is known about a person (Stern and Karraker 1989).

Although studies such as the one described above are useful in showing that parents have different expectations for males and females, this research does not directly address the question of whether (and under what conditions) these expectations shape how parents behave toward their young daughters and sons. Studies exploring this latter issue have yielded some fairly consistent findings. Researchers from Maccoby and Jacklin (1974) to Lytton and Romney (1991) have concluded that in many areas of behavior parents *do not* differentiate between their infant daughters and sons. The results of Lytton and Romney's (1991) meta-analysis of 172 published studies of parental treatment of boys and girls showed few significant differences in treatment for most areas of socialization. Lytton and Romney (1991) also found little evidence that parental treatment of boys and girls has become significantly less sex-differentiated since the 1950s, nor did they find any strong effects of social class and education on parental behavior. This research thus suggests that boys and girls, on average, receive the same amount of nurturance, warmth, responsiveness, encouragement, and attention from parents.

Along with these similarities, however, are some differences in the ways parents relate to children. One important area of difference concerns toys, games, and childhood activities. Research by Maccoby and colleagues (Maccoby 1998; Maccoby, Snow, and Jacklin 1984; see also Lytton and Romney 1991) showed that, when given a choice, parents offered girls and boys different types of toys, such as dolls for girls and footballs for boys. Moreover, the kind of toys chosen for children shaped the way that parents and children interacted during play. Because boys were more likely than girls to be offered activity-oriented toys, such as balls, parents' play with boys tended to be rougher and more physical than play with girls. Maccoby (1998, p. 125) notes that: "The father–son dyad displayed the highest levels of roughhousing: three times as much rough play occurred between fathers and sons as between mothers and daughters."

Punishment and parental responses to misbehavior are other widely researched topics in the area of gender socialization. In general, research conducted in Western countries suggests that boys are more likely than girls to receive physical punishment, though this varies somewhat across samples (Lytton and Romney 1991). Some believe that these differences in exposure to physical punishment contribute to sex differences in aggression by indirectly encouraging physicality in boys. In general, however, there is little direct evidence that parents *encourage* aggressive behavior in their children – regardless of sex. Rather, it appears that parents attempt to discourage aggression in their children, though they may be somewhat more likely to tolerate it in their sons than in their daughters (Lytton and Romney 1991; Maccoby 1998). Focusing only on punishment, however, may obscure a more complicated pattern of parental involvement in children's lives. Maccoby (1998) argues that mothers may be more assertive with their daughters than their sons and give girls less autonomy in their behavior.

As children get older, they are often assigned household chores. Raley and Bianchi (2006) report that, while parents say they assign chores equally to their sons and daughters, time diaries – daily recordings of what children actually do – show that girls do more household chores than boys. Girls are more likely to do female-typed tasks, such as cooking and cleaning, while boys are assigned more male-typed tasks, such as outdoor work.

Parents may not only treat their sons and daughters differently, but families with sons may differ from families with daughters in other respects as well. Raley and Bianchi (2006) cite literature showing that parents of sons may have somewhat more traditional views of gender roles than those of daughters. Moreover, "fathers with sons may have a slight tendency to focus more on the conventional paternal breadwinning role than those with daughters, and mothers may be focused on fulfilling the conventional maternal caregiving role when they have sons rather than daughters" (Raley and Bianchi 2006, p. 407). It is not clear what might account for these differences. Are parents' views of appropriate gender roles shaped by the behavior of their sons and daughters? Or, do parents believe a more traditional family division of labor is especially beneficial for sons? Regardless of why these differences might exist, they underscore how salient children's gender is in shaping parental responses and family life more generally.

Mothers and fathers

Until now, I have referred mainly to *parents'* role in the socialization process rather than to the roles of *mothers* and *fathers*. However, if boys and girls are treated differently from birth, we might expect that, upon becoming parents, fathers and mothers might relate differently to their male and female children. In fact, studies suggest that fathers and mothers differ regarding the amount of time spent with their male and female children and the way they interact with sons and daughters.

No mother's or father's experience is exactly the same, of course. Parenthood brings joy and stress, good times and frustration. The qualities of their children also play a role in parents' experiences. Despite the fact that parents and children are unique in some important ways, motherhood and fatherhood are socially organized; people in similar kinds of circumstances often report similar kinds of feelings and experiences.

Overall, research indicates that mothers spend about the same amount of time with their daughters as with their sons. Fathers' time is more gender-differentiated, however (Raley and Bianchi 2006). For example, among married fathers, the presence of sons in a family increases the amount of time they spend in family leisure activities, and both daughters and sons receive more attention from married fathers when there are sons in the family (Harris, Furstenberg, and Marmer 1998; Harris and Morgan 1991). In families containing only boys, fathers spend more time interacting individually with their sons and do a larger share of childcare (Barnett and Baruch 1987). Stepfathers' behavior toward their male and female stepchildren is even more gender-differentiated than the behavior of biological fathers, and unmarried and divorced fathers remain more connected to sons over time than to daughters (Raley and Bianchi 2006).

To understand these differences regarding the amount of time spent with their sons and daughters, keep in mind that mothers generally spend more time with children overall than fathers (especially during infancy) and typically are more involved in children's daily care. Because these day-to-day caregiving responsibilities are not particularly gender-specific (all children need to be fed, clothed, bathed and so on), the roles of *parent* and *child* may be more significant to mothers than the roles of mother and daughter or son (Raley and Bianchi 2006). In addition, parents may feel that the father–son bond is special and should be encouraged or fathers may perceive themselves as having more shared interests with their sons than their daughters.

Mothers' and fathers' interactions with daughters and sons   In addition to time spent with their children, other research examines the ways that mothers and fathers interact with their sons and daughters. Summarizing 39 studies that compared fathers' and mothers' treatment of daughters and sons, Siegal (1987) concluded that fathers socialized their sons and daughters somewhat differently than mothers. Fathers were most likely to differentiate between sons and daughters in the areas of physical punishment and discipline. Specifically, numerous researchers have found that fathers react more negatively than mothers to sons engaging in cross-gender-typed play (i.e., playing games or using toys considered more appropriate for the other gender) (Lytton and Romney 1991). Young boys appear to understand their fathers' preferences: In a study of preschoolers, Raag and Rackliff (1998) found that many more boys than girls believed their fathers would react negatively to them engaging in cross-gender play. In fact, in this study, boys believed that fathers more than any other familiar person (e.g., mother, daycare worker or babysitter, sibling, best friend) would have a negative reaction to their cross-gender play.

Fagot and Hagan (1991) report other differences in mothers' and fathers' interactions with children; Fathers of children of eighteen months of age reacted less positively to sons playing with female-typed toys, while mothers' reactions to sons were not influenced by their toy choice. In addition, these authors found that fathers had more positive interactions (as compared to instructional or negative interactions) with children than mothers, but engaged in more physical play with their sons (Ross and Taylor 1989). Fathers also seem to expect their sons to be both physically and emotionally tougher than their daughters, an expectation that can be expressed in the form of emotional distance between father and son and in fathers' rejection of sons' dependence. In areas such as affection and everyday speech with infants and toddlers, however, research has revealed few differences in mothers' and fathers' interactions with their children (Siegal 1987).

Bem's gender schema perspective (discussed in Chapter 2) offers one way to explain fathers' more negative reactions than mothers to sons' cross-gender play. Because gender schemas tend to be highly androcentric, her approach predicts that males have stronger motives to avoid all that is associated with females and femininity than females have to avoid all that is associated with males and masculinity. Fathers would be expected to encourage this orientation in their sons and be more concerned than mothers that their sons display masculine characteristics. Psychoanalytic theory (also discussed in Chapter 2) offers a somewhat similar explanation. Recall that this perspective views male gender identity as less firmly established than female gender identity. Because males experience a painful psychological separation from their mothers in the course of establishing their gender identity as males, they learn to reject femininity and all that which they associate with females. Psychoanalytic theorists suggest that fathers (and men in general) would have a stronger psychic motive than mothers (and women in general) to reinforce gender distinctions in their children. Are there other factors that may account for these differences between mothers and fathers?

Before concluding this section, it is important to place these findings in a broader context. As we have seen, gender egalitarianism regarding preferences for children is the norm for parents in the West, and this norm has been getting stronger over time – in almost all areas of life. Although a close look at fathers' and mothers' investments in their children shows that sons may be favored in certain respects, these differences are not large. (Recall our discussion in Chapter 2 about the magnitude of differences between women and men.) In addition, as Raley and Bianchi (2006) observe, gender differences tend to receive more attention from researchers than similarities. The differences discussed above thus must be understood alongside the recognition that parental involvement with their children is gender-neutral in more areas than it is differentiated.

Turning the focus to children: learning gender

Although parents play a critical role in shaping their children's experience of gender, children themselves become increasingly skilled at decoding gender messages in the world around them. While this "self-socialization" starts in infancy, once they acquire gender identity, children become even more active participants in the socialization process. By the time they are three, most children can correctly identify themselves as female or male and can identify others as the same or different with respect to gender (Maccoby 1998). As we saw in Chapter 2, this ability to self-identify as female or male signifies the formation of a **gender identity**. Children's ability to self-identify as female or male influences their preferences for playmates, with children who are aware of their gender more likely than those whose gender identity is not developed to prefer same-sex playmates and gender-typed toys.

Children also learn to apply the labels "male" and "female" to others, using characteristics such as clothing and hairstyle (Coltrane 1998), and they learn **gender stereotype**s. Gender stereotypes can refer to characteristics associated with each gender, such as the belief that girls are soft, and they include beliefs about gender-appropriate activities, such as the belief that trucks are for boys. Beginning as early as age three, for example, "children will sort pictures of such items as a hammer, baseball, shirt and tie, razor and shaving cream, into a box for men and pictures of a dress, vacuum cleaner, cooking pot, cosmetics, handbag, into a box for women" (Maccoby 1998, p. 165). Once children assign gender labels to objects and activities, they use these labels to guide their preferences and their expectations of others. Martin, Eisenbud, and Rose (1995, p. 1454) explain this process, "a girl will reason that a doll is something girls usually like, I am a girl, therefore I will probably like to play with the doll.

In some situations, this kind of reasoning may become so well learned that it is done virtually automatically."

Young children do not associate every object, activity, or characteristic with a particular gender, of course. However, once these associations have been made, what Martin, Eisenbud, and Rose (1995, p. 1468) call **gender-centric reasoning** (i.e., what one gender likes the other does not; what a person of one gender likes, others of the same gender will also like) is likely to be employed, especially by younger children. Children from similar backgrounds who are exposed to similar cultural messages tend to agree on the content of those gender associations that do exist and use that information to organize their social worlds. Children are aware of the expectations their society attaches to gender and can associate these expectations with a wide variety of cultural objects and activities.

Gender stereotypes seem to be most entrenched among children aged five to eight – a period Maccoby (1998, p. 169) refers to as "the most 'sexist' period of life" and a time when "deviations from [gender stereotypes are seen as] positively *wrong*, not just misguided" (emphasis in original). Of course, children in this age group are not really sexist in any intentional way. Rather, they are actively applying the gender stereotypes they have absorbed from their cultural surroundings and using gender to organize information about people and things. Children's ability to do these things is rather remarkable, since many of the gender associations they acquire are learned not through direct observation, but rather through inference and reasoning. As Fagot, Leinbach, and O'Boyle (1992, p. 229) ask, how else could we explain why it is that children will associate a "fierce-looking bear" with boys and a "fluffy cat" with girls? Children's ability and willingness to make these associations signifies that they have in fact learned some of their culture's messages about gender; that is, they have been gender socialized. Over time, as children continue to mature, their ideas about gender-appropriate activities and behavior grow more sophisticated and they are less inclined to believe gender stereotypes must always be adhered to.

One final point about gender labeling and stereotyping among children is worth noting: There is some evidence that children's ability to assign gender labels and the degree to which they embrace gender stereotypes are influenced by their parents' behaviors. Fagot, Leinbach, and O'Boyle (1992, p. 229) found that children they call "early labelers" were more likely than others to come from households where mothers encouraged more gender-typed play and embraced more gender-traditional attitudes. This finding suggests that children's ability and inclination to use gender as a basis for making choices and organizing information varies to some extent based on parents' characteristics. Not surprisingly, children who grow up in homes where gender assumes an important role in daily life may rely on it more in their own lives than children for whom gender is less salient to everyday life. This may explain why at least some studies have found that white children – especially those from higher socioeconomic backgrounds – express more gender-stereotyped views than African-American children and those from lower socioeconomic backgrounds (Bardwell, Cochran, and Walker 1986). Members of the dominant social group may be more likely to embrace traditional societal values and norms than members of other social categories.

Childhood and the Importance of Same-Gender Peers

Another important aspect of children's experience of gender is the involvement of peers. As children move out of infancy and into their preschool and school-age years, a greater proportion of their play and interactions involve other children, such as siblings or peers. Parents are still important, of course, as they influence their children's choice of playmates, but their direct roles in the socialization process become somewhat less important.

One of the most widely studied aspects of children's relations with peers is their gender-segregated nature. Studies of gender segregation sometimes rely on an individualist framework, as they attempt to understand why girls and boys prefer same-gender playmates. More often, however, this research embraces a more interactionist approach; the focus is on the social relations of childhood groups and the nature of interaction within those groups.

By about age three, both girls and boys prefer same-gender playmates, though girls' preferences are the first to emerge (Fagot and Leinbach 1991). This preference for same-gender peers continues when children enter school, generally lasting until adolescence: "In fact, in nearly every study of school situations where kids from age three through junior high are given the opportunity to choose companions of the same age, girls have shown a strong preference to be with girls, and boys with boys" (Thorne 1993, p. 46). Gender segregation in childhood intrigues researchers in part because it is spontaneous and reflects the preferences of both girls and boys (Thorne 1993). Gender segregation among children is more likely to be found in settings where few adults are present than ones where adults are in charge (e.g., in the playground rather than in the classroom). A preference for same-gender peers has been found among children in many societies, including nonindustrial societies (Maccoby 1998).

The segregation of children's peer groups adds another layer of complexity to our understanding of the socialization process, and it challenges us to consider the broader set of social relations within which children are embedded. Because of gender segregation, much of what children learn from peers is acquired in a same-gender context. Boys are socialized by and with other boys, while girls' socialization is by and with other girls. This implies that the *content* of what is learned also varies by gender. One consequence of this is that girls and boys relate to one another as "familiar strangers," people "who are in repeated physical proximity and recognize one another, but have little real knowledge of what one another are like" (Thorne 1993, p. 47). Although gender segregation in childhood is by no means total, and boys and girls do have opportunities to interact with each other, their friendships and closest bonds are with same-gender peers.

Why children prefer same-gender peers has been explained in several ways. Perhaps these choices reflect gender differences in play styles, with children choosing to interact with those whose styles of play are more similar to their own. Research does suggest that groups of boys play differently than groups of girls (Maccoby 1998) and these differences in play style may partly explain children's preferences for same-gender peers. Cognitive theories of gender socialization provide an alternative explanation, as they suggest that children's preference for same-gender peers is related to a more general tendency to prefer and more highly value those labeled as having a similar gender to oneself, regardless of play style.

Alexander and Hines (1994) conclude that both explanations of children's same-gender playmate preferences have some validity. These researchers interviewed children ranging in age from four to eight about their preferences for imaginary playmates. They found that play style was more strongly related to boys' preferences for playmates than the preferences of girls: boys of all ages were more likely to choose to play with girls who displayed a masculine play style than boys displaying a feminine play style. By contrast, the factors shaping girls' preferences changed with age. Consistent with cognitive theoretical accounts, younger girls chose imaginary playmates based on gender rather than play style, while play style had a stronger influence on the preferences of older girls. This study suggests that no single theory can account for children's preferences for same-gender playmates.

Crossing gender boundaries

Think back one more time to your own early childhood. Do you fit the patterns described here? If you are female, were your close friends mostly girls? Did you play with dolls more than with trucks? If you are male, do your memories of early childhood friendships mostly contain boys, with whom you played games such as baseball or other sports? Some of you will answer "yes" to these questions and will have seen your childhood experiences reflected in the previous pages. For others, however, the general patterns uncovered by sociologists will be at odds with your childhood memories. Moreover, regardless of our own experiences, we probably all remember some childhood peers who preferred to play with the other gender and who had little interest in what were considered gender-appropriate activities.

The experiences of children who routinely cross gender boundaries have been of special interest to researchers. When Thorne conducted research on elementary school children in the early 1990s, she found that several girls in her study crossed gender boundaries on the playground and in other school settings; they regularly played games with boys and sat with them in the cafeteria, although they moved just as easily among the girls. Moreover, Thorne found that girls were more likely than boys to want to join the other gender's activities. By contrast, playing with the girls was unambiguously negative for boys, who mostly avoided joining girls' games. Moreover, when they did attempt to participate in girls' activities, boys often did so disruptively, rather than as a serious participant.

Sex differences in crossing gender boundaries are consistent with other material presented in this chapter. Girls seem to face less pressure than boys to conform to gender stereotypes, are more likely than boys to cross gender boundaries, and girls receive less negative attention than boys when they do participate in activities or games with the other gender. The gender socialization that occurs during childhood thus appears to be more restrictive for boys than girls. Boys' behavior and activities are more closely monitored for their gender appropriateness by parents (especially fathers) and peers than the behavior and activities of girls. Hence, although both genders experience socialization, girls seem to have a wider range of options for behavior than boys.

Are these differences universal?

Most of the research discussed in the preceding sections was conducted in North America among samples that were predominantly (though not exclusively) white. Given this, can the findings and patterns reported here be generalized to other cultures? The answer to this question is not a simple "yes" or "no." In fact, a comprehensive, in-depth study of children in six cultures (India, Okinawa, Philippines, Mexico, Kenya, and the U.S.) found some similarities in patterns of gendered behavior across societies, but concluded that "the differences are not consistent nor so great as the studies of American and Western European children would suggest" (Whiting and Edwards 1988, p. 296).

In general, these researchers found that girls displayed more nurturing behaviors than boys, while boys' play was more aggressive (e.g., "rough and tumble) and dominance-seeking than girls. Whiting and Edwards conclude that these universal gender differences reflect some similarities in *socialization contexts* – that is, in learning environments – across cultures. In general, girls tend to interact much more than boys with infants and younger children, while boys spend more time than girls interacting with older children. Because each type of interaction tends to require different kinds of skills and abilities, boys and girls are socialized somewhat differently and acquire somewhat different preferences and styles of interaction. Consistent with this argument, Whiting and Edwards (1988) found that in societies where boys are expected to participate in domestic tasks, including caring for infants, there are fewer differences between girls and boys. Although there are some broad similarities in gender socialization across cultures, societies vary in the size of gender differences in behavior. These differences tend to be *smaller*, on average, than studies focusing solely on North America have suggested.

Gender Socialization in Childhood Reconsidered

Socialization is never completely consistent, nor is it total or all-encompassing. These inconsistencies and disruptions in the socialization process stem from many factors. For example, children may receive different kinds of messages from different agents of socialization in their lives. Saturday morning cartoons may present children with different images of how girls or boys are supposed to behave than a parent. In addition, children are not blank slates; temperament – which many believe is partially shaped by genetic factors – shapes what children learn and how they interpret gender messages. More important, as we have seen, how children are socialized, as well as the content of the gender messages they receive, varies because of a number of factors such as race and ethnicity, social class, religion, etc., so it is doubtful than any two people have been socialized in exactly the same way. For all of these reasons, we should not expect that the kinds of patterns uncovered in sociological research would ever fully capture all of the variation and complexity in males' and females' experience of childhood.

The Household Division of Labor and the Family

Child-rearing is just one of many activities that take place in families. Maintaining a household also requires that adults perform many other tasks. The division of labor in the family (or, as it is also called, the **household division of labor**) is among the topics most often studied by sociologists interested in gender and family life and is essential to understanding the changes in work and family described in the previous chapter. We know that increases in women's labor force participation have fundamentally altered family structure and formation. But how has this change affected the kinds of activities engaged in by women and men at home and what factors shape each gender's involvement in these activities?

Time spent in housework and childcare

In order to study the division of household work, researchers must decide what activities count as housework. Should we count only activities involving physical labor, such as cooking or cleaning, or should the "emotion work" of providing support and showing care for others also count? Is childcare a form of housework or should it be considered something else? While what counts as housework varies somewhat across studies, most researchers define it as

159

"unpaid work done to maintain family members and/or a home" (Shelton and John 1996, p. 299).

Social scientists examining trends in people's daily activities use time diaries to collect information on all of the ways that people spend their time in a 24-hour day. This methodology results in more accurate information about how much time people spend in various activities than surveys in which people are asked to recall past events. Diaries also enable researchers to collect information about time engaged in very specific activities, such as watching television or eating, rather than performing broad categories of behavior (e.g., leisure). One limitation of time diaries, however, is that they only capture "primary" activities and not the multitasking that is typical of many parents (i.e., cooking dinner while keeping an eye on the children).

There have been some significant changes in both women's and men's household work over the last few decades, though women continue to perform more household chores than men. The amount of time women spend doing housework has decreased over time, while men's involvement has risen. Table 5.1 shows the average amount of time women and men spent on a range of paid and unpaid activities over four decades, averaged across 16 countries (Gauthier, Smeeding, and Furstenberg 2004). In the 1960s, married (or cohabiting) men employed full-time spent about an hour and a half per day performing housework and just over eight hours per day in their paid job. Women employed full-time worked fewer hours for pay than men (about two and a half hours less) and devoted over three hours more to housework. By the 1990s, men were doing over two hours of housework per day, while women spent just under three and a half hours per day engaged in this activity.

More recent data, collected in the United States, appear in Figure 5.1. This table reports on time use for married mothers and fathers between the ages of 25 and 54 who are employed full-time. Compared to married women, married men spend about an hour longer per day in paid work (9.1 hours vs. 8.1 hours) and about a half hour per day engaged in leisure activities (2.3 hours vs. 2.9 hours). Women spend more hours than men performing

Table 5.1 Mean time spent on selected activities (in hours per day) for married or cohabiting parents, aged 20–49 years old, with at least one child under age five, by sex, employment status, and decade, averaged across selected countries.

Sex and employment status[a,b]	Decade[c]	PAID	EDUC	HOUSE	CCARE	TV	FREE	SLEEP	EAT	PERS	TOTAL[d]
Men											
Full-time	1960s	8.06	0.21	1.54	0.50	1.23	2.49	8.07	1.15	0.74	24.0
	1970s	6.84	0.18	1.59	0.49	1.67	2.86	8.06	1.24	0.86	24.0
	1980s	6.68	0.08	1.84	0.75	1.76	3.08	6.96	1.01	1.71	24.0
	1990s	6.69	0.09	2.13	1.16	1.73	2.69	7.77	1.08	0.65	24.0
Women											
Full-time	1960s	5.66	0.10	4.67	1.40	0.79	1.71	7.83	1.06	0.78	24.0
	1970s	4.71	0.14	3.90	1.31	1.07	2.43	8.16	1.13	0.97	24.0
	1980s	4.08	0.06	3.85	1.90	1.22	2.85	6.88	0.97	2.04	24.0
	1990s	4.81	0.11	3.44	2.20	1.14	2.41	7.98	1.09	0.80	24.0
Nonemployed	1960s	0.19	0.01	7.21	2.36	1.16	2.26	8.59	1.47	0.74	24.0
	1970s	0.21	0.10	5.76	2.26	1.72	3.09	8.40	1.39	0.91	24.0
	1980s	0.27	0.15	5.13	2.77	1.63	3.48	7.43	1.15	1.83	24.0
	1990s	0.29	0.15	4.96	3.36	1.58	3.29	8.27	1.27	0.79	24.0

(Continued)

161

Table 5.1 (*Continued*)

Sex and employment status[a,b]	Decade[c]	PAID	EDUC	HOUSE	CCARE	TV	FREE	SLEEP	EAT	PERS	TOTAL[d]
All	1960s	1.81	0.05	6.36	2.08	1.10	2.14	8.35	1.36	0.76	24.0
employment	1970s	1.43	0.10	5.21	1.97	1.58	2.99	8.29	1.33	0.93	24.0
statuses	1980s	1.85	0.10	4.62	2.38	1.49	3.18	7.35	1.10	1.78	24.0
	1990s	2.12	0.12	4.44	2.80	1.39	2.94	8.19	1.18	0.78	24.0

NOTE: Paid work includes time spent on first and second jobs including overtime, breaks, and travel to/from work.
PAID = paid work; EDUC = Education; HOUSE = Housework; CCARE = Childcare; TV = Television; FREE = Other leisure; SLEEP = sleep and naps; EAT = Meals and snacks at home; PERS = other personal care activities (bathing, dressing, receiving medical care).
[a]Average across the seven days of the week. The average was not adjusted to take into account the size of the sample in each survey.
[b]Full-time employment refers to persons working 30 or more hours per week. The employment status was coded from a question about the respondent's main activity during the week preceding the survey. Although some people may reply that they were not employed, they may have devoted time to paid work on the diary day.
[c]The 1990s surveys also include UK 2000.
[d]The total may not add to 24 hours because of a small number of activities that could not be classified and were placed in a "miscellaneous" category (not reported here).

Source: Anne Gauthier, Timothy M. Smeeding, and Frank F. Furstenberg, Jr. 2004. "Are parents investing less time in children? Trends in selected industrialized countries."*Population and Development Review* 30: 647–671 (table 1, p. 658).

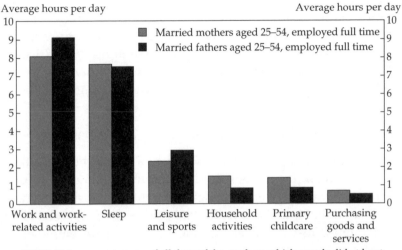

NOTE: Data are an average of all days of the week on which people did at least some work. All activity categories except for sleep include associated travel. Data refer to parents with biological, step, or adopted children aged 17 or younger living in the household.

Figure 5.1 Comparison of average hours spent per day on selected activities for married mothers and married fathers.
Source: Mary Dorinda Allard and Marianne Janes. 2008. "Time use of working parents: A visual essay." *Monthly Labor Review* 131: 3–14 (p. 7).

household activities, primary childcare, and purchasing goods and services.

These declines in women's hours of household work do not extend to childcare. Both women and men are devoting more hours to children than in the past, and this is true even for women employed full-time. Parents have made more time for children by decreasing the amount of time they spend doing other activities, including leisure and personal activities (Gauthier, Smeeding, and Furstenberg 2004). Returning again to Table 5.1, we can see that men employed full-time have increased the involvement in childcare by just over one-half hour, while full-time employed women's time with children increased by just under an hour per day. Even non-employed women's time with children rose between the 1960s and

1990s, according to these data. These findings are consistent with within-country studies. For example, research conducted in the United States shows that children in two-parent families are spending more time with their parents today than in the 1980s (Bianchi 2000; Sandberg and Hofferth 2001), with similar patterns found for the United Kingdom (Fisher, McCulloch, and Gershuny 1999).

The household division of labor: caring and repairing

Earlier in this chapter, we learned that sons and daughters are likely to be assigned different household chores. It should not be surprising that this pattern of each gender doing different tasks extends to adults as well. Household work, like paid work, is divided along gender lines. Just as allocating one's time to paid employment versus unpaid work at home can be seen as a form of specialization, so too can the allocation of time at home to one type of activity (e.g., cooking) versus another (e.g., repairing the car). In the household, women and men specialize in different activities, with each performing tasks typically associated with their gender (e.g., men perform outdoor tasks, such as mowing the lawn or working on the car, while women do cleaning and care for children) (Berk 1985; Blair and Lichter 1991). The tasks typically performed by women and men diverge in other respects as well. Household tasks performed by men involve greater personal discretion than those women perform, are more likely to have a fixed beginning and end, and are more likely to involve a leisure component (Coltrane 2000; Hochschild 1989).

Although both parents' time spent with children has increased over time, women continue to provide more childcare than men. The amount of care provided by mothers and fathers evens out somewhat as children age, but even mothers of teenagers have more caregiving responsibilities than fathers of children in this age group (Allard and Janes 2008). Caring for children involves routine activities, such as preparing meals, washing clothes, bathing, etc. and it involves play and interaction. Women and men engage in both types of activities, but a smaller share of women's childcare involves

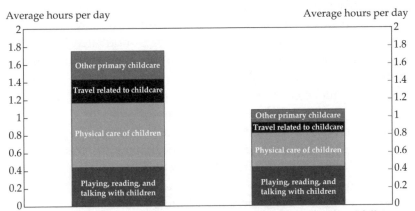

Average hours per day   Average hours per day

Mothers, aged 25–54, employed full time   Fathers, aged 25–54, employed full time

NOTE: Data refer to married parents with biological, step-, or adopted children aged 12 or younger living in the household. Data are averages of all days of the week.

Figure 5.2   Comparison of average hours spent per day on childcare activities for married mothers and married fathers.
Source: Mary Dorinda Allard and Marianne Janes. 2008. "Time use of working parents: A visual essay." *Monthly Labor Review* 131: 3–14 (p. 13).

the nonroutine elements. Breakdowns of U.S. women's and men's childcare activities are shown in Figure 5.2.

Explaining Women's and Men's Involvement in Household Work and Childcare

Our examination of the household division of labor has revealed both change and continuity over time. The changes involve men's increasing levels of involvement in both housework and care for children. Women's behavior has also changed; they do less household work now than in the past, but spend more time with children. Less change has occurred in the degree of task specialization within the household. Women continue to do most of the childcare, especially the physical tasks involved in caring for children.

Researchers seeking to explain these patterns have been especially interested in the conditions associated with more egalitarian household divisions of labor. This interest is motivated by at least three factors. First, researchers want to understand how (and if) the trend toward gender egalitarianism more generally in industrial societies is reflected in women's and men's household activities. Second, they are interested in the consequences of the shift in women's roles from caregivers to earners (or earner-caregivers) for men's family roles. A third motivation concerns the well-being of women and men, and children. As Hook (2010, pp. 1480–1) explains: "Men's and women's mix of housework and paid work not only determines their daily experience of life but also affects their economic standing and social relationships. Increased specialization by sex associated with marriage and parenthood puts women at economic risk and men at social risk. Women's responsibility for the home limits employment and advancement, and men's responsibility for breadwinning limits relationships with children" (Goldscheider 2000).

There are several theories that might explain the relative amount of time women and men devote to household work. The **time constraints approach** has received the most attention. This perspective argues that women and men allocate their time to household work based on their respective ability to do so, given other time demands (Hook 2006). This view predicts that, as women spend more time in paid employment, they will spend less time involved in housework. In fact, women who work for pay perform fewer hours of household work than full-time homemakers, and women employed part-time do less household work than those with full-time jobs. The number of hours men spend doing household work is also dependent on the time demands of their paid job: Men who work longer hours for pay tend to spend less time doing household work than other men (Moen and Roehling 2005). Overall, studies suggest that the hours both spouses spend performing housework are influenced by the hours each spends in paid employment and having children, especially younger children. Children increase the hours women spend performing housework much more than men's housework hours, however (Bianchi, Milkie, Sayer, and Robinson 2000). As a result, some suggest that time constraints are "gendered"; Women's household work time is more affected than men's time by the presence of children in the home.

A time constraints perspective can be used to understand how tasks are allocated within households, as well as the changes in women's and men's household work over time. Consistent with this perspective, increases in women's labor force participation have been accompanied by decreases in the time they spend performing household work and increases in men's involvement in these tasks. While men's involvement in household work has risen over time, this has not fully compensated for the amount of time that women have devoted to paid work. Hence, a gender gap in women's and men's unpaid work time remains.

Another way to explain differences in the amount of time women and men devote to household work requires us to consider the **relative resources** of husband and wife (Brines 1994; England and Farkas 1986). Because earnings are one important resource in relationships, this perspective suggests that husbands' performance of household work should respond to changes in wives' relative wages. Studies have found some support for this argument. Wives do less housework and men do more as the proportion of family income contributed by the wife increases (Casper and Bianchi 2002). Similarly, when wives are the same age as their husbands, they do less housework and husbands do more than when wives are two or more years younger than their spouse. Regarding the overall gender gap in women's and men's household work, this perspective would expect that, as women's relative earnings increase, this gap would shrink.

To illustrate how time constraints and relative resources may operate simultaneously, consider white and African-American husbands' involvement in household work. Historically, financial need often compelled African-American wives and mothers in the United States to work for pay. These women faced less disapproval for working from friends and families than white women, and were often encouraged to work by their husbands (Landry 2000). This

167

legacy of labor force participation and supportive families among African-Americans has been used to account for African-American husbands' greater involvement than white husbands in household work (Landry 2000).

In addition to these factors, the household division of labor is shaped by factors such as marital status and family type. For example, according to studies cited by Shelton and John (1996), married women perform more household work than cohabiting women, other factors being equal, though there are no differences between married and cohabiting men. A 22-country study of pre-marital cohabitation and housework found that, while women did more household work than men in all countries, household work was divided more equally among married couples that had cohab-ited prior to marriage than in those that had not cohabited before marrying (Batalova and Cohen 2002). The authors suggest that cohabitation in general attracts those with more egalitarian views of relationships and this set of beliefs persists when they marry. Studies of gay and lesbian households suggest that these couples are somewhat more egalitarian in their sharing of household tasks than heterosexual couples (Blumstein and Schwartz 1983).

Other attempts to account for differences in women's and men's household work emphasize the role of **gender ideologies**. These studies explore how women's and, to a lesser extent, men's gender attitudes influence the type and amount of household work each performs. The results of this research at the individual level are mixed. Although some conclude that gender ideologies are unre-lated to husbands' and wives' performance of household work, others find greater support for this argument (England and Farkas 1986). Hochschild (1989) offers a more complex perspective of the relations between gender ideologies and the household division of labor. She suggests that, while gender ideologies shape women's and men's conceptions of their family roles and the "gender strate-gies" they pursue to enact those roles, there may be an inconsis-tency between the form each spouse believes the division of labor "should" take and its actual expression. Couples may develop what she calls "family myths" to manage this tension between their gender ideologies and the realities of the household division of labor.

The meanings of housework: an interactionist perspective on the household division of labor

Other research on the household division of labor draws from an interactionist view of gender. These researchers argue that to truly understand housework and childcare, we must explore the meanings people give to these activities and the ways these meanings develop within social interaction (Ferree 1990). From an interactionist perspective, the performance of household work results in both the production of goods and services (e.g., meals, clean laundry, etc.) *and* the production of gender (Berk 1985; West and Fenstermaker 1993). In West and Fenstermaker's (1993, p. 162) words: "Our claim is not simply that household labor is regarded as women's work, but that for a woman to do it and a man not to do it draws on and affirms what people conceive to be the essential nature of each."

In her study of "feeding the family," DeVault (1991) draws on these ideas to explore how family caregiving activities, such as cooking and preparing family meals, are understood by those who perform them. DeVault explains that it was difficult for some people in her study to describe their experiences:

> They talked about feeding as something other than work in the conventional sense, trying to explain how their activities are embedded in family relations. Some, for example, talked of this work in terms of family ties. They described feeding as part of being a parent: "I feel like, you know, when I decided to have children it was a commitment, and raising them included feeding them." Or as part of being a wife: "I like to cook for him. That's what a wife is for, right?" (DeVault 1991, p. 10)

For DeVault, the vocabulary of paid work is insufficient to describe how people doing family work think about their activities.

On a more general level, Coltrane (1989, p. 473) explores how women's and men's performance of household labor "provides the

169

opportunity for expressing, confirming, and sometimes transforming the meaning of gender." He shows that parents in families where household work and childcare are shared are more likely to view women and men as similar than those in households with less equitable arrangements. For Coltrane (1989), however, family members' conceptions of gender are the product, rather than the source, of the household division of labor. In other words, participation in the everyday activities associated with household work produces family members' beliefs about women and men.

Interactionist perspectives have also been useful in understanding "counter-normative situations (for example, the wife is the primary breadwinner)" (Hook 2006, p. 642). Most theories predict that in couples where women are primary breadwinners – working longer hours and earning more money than men – men should do more household work than women. This is true only to a point, however. When wives earn substantially more than husbands, some studies find that men's contributions to housework decrease and women's rise (Brines 1994). If work and home responsibilities provide opportunities for women and men to "do gender," a reversal of women's and men's typical economic roles represents a form of "gender deviance" (Bittman, England, Folbre, Sayer, and Matheson 2003, p. 192). Men (and women) neutralize this deviance by adopting a more traditional household division of labor.

Cross-national perspectives on variation and change in the household division of labor

Social scientists seeking to understand the factors affecting women's and men's involvement in unpaid work find cross-national data particularly useful for this purpose. Instead of focusing only on the individual-level factors that might explain the amount of time devoted to a particular activity, cross-national data enable researchers to consider both individual- and societal-level factors, and the ways that both may have changed over time. This research has given us greater insight into the ways that the policies and practices of nation-states, as well as those of welfare regimes (see Chapter 4), shape the household division of labor. Through their laws, policies, norms, and practices, countries can reinforce a model of gender equality, characterized by support for men and women as earner-caregivers. Alternatively, they can reinforce a more gender-differentiated arrangement which emphasizes women as caregivers and men as earners.

Hook's (2006) longitudinal study of men's unpaid work in 16 countries (including North America and most of Europe) illustrates how a country's parental leave policies shape men's participation in household work. Focusing on the period between 1965 and 2003, Hook (2006) found that married, employed fathers have increased the amount of time they spend doing unpaid work by about 6 hours, but these increases have not kept pace with women's involvement in paid employment. Hook (2006) argues that parental leave policies that favor women are an important part of the explanation for this pattern. By enabling women to assume caregiver roles when their children are born, fathers are freed up from doing more unpaid work at home. Hence, men's contributions to household work were greater in those countries where men as well as women were eligible to take parental leave.

In a second study, Hook (2010) examines differences over time across 19 countries in the degree to which men and women specialize in different types of household work. This study examines the effects of several different aspects of national context, including "working-time regimes" (or the degree to which long standard work weeks are normatively and legally enforced); reliance on part-time work as a strategy to enable women to combine work and home responsibilities; parental leave policies and their availability to men as well as to women; and public childcare. Hook finds that specialization – the tendency for women to perform certain tasks and men to perform others – has decreased over time. Nevertheless, what she calls "time-inflexible family work" (i.e., cooking meals and cleaning up) continues to be women's responsibility (Hook 2010, p. 1509).

Hook (2010) argues that parental leaves for women – especially those lasting up to a year – contribute to greater gender inequality in household work. Long parental leaves for women increase the amount of time they spend on cooking, as well as housework more generally. When men take parental leave, however, women do less cooking, but men do not do significantly more. Among the broader conclusions of this study, however, is her finding that the least specialization in household tasks occurred in contexts involving "short average workweeks, high employment for women with low rates of part-time work, modest parental leaves with leave reserved for men, and high provision of child care" (Hook 2010, p. 1512). These conditions may be most likely found in Scandinavian countries but are not present in their entirety in any industrial society.

Welfare regimes, as discussed in Chapter 4, can also influence women's and men's household behavior. For example, Sayer, Gauthier, and Furstenberg (2004) analyzed time diaries to examine educational differences in parental time with children in four countries (Canada, Germany, Norway, and Italy), each representing a different type of welfare regime. They found that mothers devote more time to childcare than men in all four countries, with gender differences smaller in liberal (Canada) and social-democratic (Norway) regimes than in corporatist (Germany and to a lesser extent, Italy) regimes. Welfare regimes were less important in explaining educational differences in mothers' time with children than fathers' time, however. More educated mothers in all four countries spent more time with children than those less educated. Educated mothers thus seemed to view time with children as an important investment, regardless of the level of state support for families. For fathers, the education gap in time spent with children was smaller in countries that provided family support. Such support made possible greater father involvement with children in those countries, especially fathers with lower education levels. As Sullivan, Coltrane, McAnnally, and Altintas (2009, p. 236) observe: "Just as states facilitated and even encouraged women to become workers through different political processes and social policies, they can also facilitate and encourage men to become caregivers."

In addition to their findings regarding the effects of particular national policies, cross-national research is important for reminding us that even behaviors that take place inside the family, such as deciding who should cook, clean or pick up the children, are affected by the larger societal context. This context shapes not only what is legally permissible, but also shapes what is normatively accepted. By reinforcing some practices versus others, the context shapes the choices people make and the way alternatives may be evaluated. For example, countries in which women mostly work part-time for pay and men work full-time reinforce a view of women as primary caregivers of children. In these countries, part-time work for women comes to be seen as a more acceptable and viable strategy for families seeking to combine work and parenthood than other strategies that are not as socially sanctioned. Societal-level beliefs about women's and men's roles are also important in and of themselves. For example, several studies have shown that men do a greater share of household work when gender attitudes are more egalitarian or when women have greater economic and political power in the society (Baxter 1997; Fuwa 2004; Stier and Lewin-Epstein 2003).

Even more important are beliefs about motherhood. In advanced industrial societies, motherhood is sometimes said to be "compulsory" for women. **Compulsory motherhood** refers to a set of cultural beliefs prescribing that "women should find total fulfillment in having children and taking care of them" (Coltrane 1998, p. 91). Of course, the reality may be quite different. For example, women find their opportunities to be mothers and care for their children restricted by social policies (such as welfare laws that reduce or limit benefits when additional children are born, or laws that make it difficult for gay and lesbian parents to adopt) or poverty. Further, although many women do have children and find it fulfilling, motherhood is demanding and not always as intensely satisfying as the ideology of compulsory motherhood suggests. In addition, as we saw in the previous chapter, most mothers – even mothers of infants – are employed for pay at least some hours during the week.

Despite this reality, motherhood remains laden culturally with meanings that still resonate with women, regardless of social class, sexual orientation, or employment status. The ideology of compulsory motherhood helps to explain why women in almost all industrial societies continue to do more childcare than men and why women's time with children has increased, even for those employed full-time. Though women who become mothers may not even be conscious of their impact, women draw on these taken-for-granted meanings to make sense of their experiences and gain a feminized sense of themselves as mature adults. This process of drawing on deeply ingrained cultural beliefs about mothers and motherhood illustrates how gendered institutions shape people's lives and sense of self.

Lesbian and Gay Families Rewriting Family Life

Research on lesbian and gay parents offers another way to understand families as gendered institutions and see the power of gender in shaping people's experiences of themselves as mothers and fathers. Lesbian and gay couples can become parents by giving birth themselves (in the case of lesbians), adoption, or through a previous heterosexual relationship. Regardless of how children join lesbian or gay households, only in some countries and U.S. states does the law automatically recognize both partners as parents, as it does in the case of married, heterosexual couples who give birth or adopt. Instead, in many settings, the law recognizes one person as the mother or father (biological or adoptive) and the partner must petition the court to be granted co-parenting status. Thus, for lesbian and gay couples, becoming a two-parent family requires that they work around the dominant cultural understanding of the family as a heterosexual unit.

In heterosexual families, the duties, expectations, and obligations associated with parenting are strongly gendered, and these, in turn, are closely linked to sex category: Women become mothers and men become fathers. What happens in gay and lesbian households with two co-parenting women or men? Dalton and Bielby's (2000) research on lesbian families shows that these households are not immune from the gendered expectations attached to mothering. Instead, in lesbian families, mothering is likely to be shared, with both partners embracing the duties and responsibilities of this highly gendered role. By adhering to conventional gender expectations regarding mothering, lesbian parents reinforced traditional cultural understandings of motherhood.

In many other respects, of course, lesbian families challenged what Dalton and Bielby (2000, p. 57) call "heteronormative conceptions of the family." For example, while marriage signifies heterosexual couples' commitment to family, lesbians and gays are legally prevented from taking this step. Several of the lesbian couples in Dalton and Bielby's study participated in commitment ceremonies to publicly identify themselves as families. On one hand, these ceremonies acknowledge the role of marriage as a means of demonstrating commitment to family. On the other hand, these same efforts challenge those forces that restrict the link between marriage and family to heterosexuals.

As this discussion shows, the power of a social institution like the family extends both to those who conform to traditional understandings and those who do not conform. This underscores the power of institutions and the necessity of looking beyond individuals when seeking to understand gender's role in social life.

Marriage, Families, and Their Consequences for Women and Men

The organization of family life has important consequences for women's and men's lives both within and outside of the family. These consequences have been explored in depth by researchers. First, we consider how marriage and the household division of labor affect women's and men's experiences in the labor market. In her 1977 classic, *Men and Women of the Corporation*, Rosabeth Moss Kanter cited what used to be and perhaps still is a common belief about the effects of marriage on men's and women's value as employees: "Married men bring two people to the job, while married women bring less than one." This suggests that married men are more productive employees than married women. Married men are assumed to benefit at work from the fact that they have a spouse.

The spouse's efforts on behalf of the family and, in particular, the husband, are assumed to enhance his work performance. Because she cleans, cooks, and runs the household, he can devote his time and energies to work. The situation is different for married women. Marriage – and the household responsibilities it entails – is assumed to interfere with married women's abilities to be successful in the job. Because they have responsibilities at home, they have less time and energy to commit to the paid workplace. A married woman is seen as less than one "full" worker.

Consistent with this view, Williams (2000) suggests that the ideal worker in the eyes of most employers is one who does not have any nonwork responsibilities. Because women typically have more responsibilities than men for housework and child care, this is not a gender-neutral preference. As a result, men rather than women embody the ideal worker. Work organizations reflect this preference as well. They contain "built-in advantages for men that are often unnoticed; indeed, they seem like natural or inevitable characteristics of all organizations" (Williams 2000, p. 9).

Current research suggests that marriage is a different kind of "signal" to employers for men than it is for women. By "signal," I am referring to marriage as an indicator of a person's qualities and responsibilities. Marriage, for men, signals many positive qualities to employers, such as maturity and responsibility. In addition, married men may be seen as having a helpmate at home, a source of emotional support and a person to perform household chores. Marriage for women, on the other hand, may send employers a different kind of signal. Rather than being seen as more committed, they may be viewed as a greater risk for an employer, especially in jobs that require extensive training and those where workers are costly to replace.

The male marriage wage premium

Do employers actually hold such views of married men and women? Is there any evidence that marriage differentially affects men's and women's job performance and orientation to work? The first question is best answered somewhat indirectly since many people – employers included – would hesitate to directly express the kinds of attitudes described above. Given this, another way to assess how married women and men are viewed in the labor market is to examine whether marriage "pays" for each sex, and whether it pays differently for women and men. Marriage pays if it can be shown that being married results in a net economic benefit, such as a higher salary, for married people as compared to the unmarried.

In fact, there is evidence that men in the United States receive a **marriage wage premium**. In a 1992 study of almost 4,000 male college professors, Bellas (1992) found that never-married men had the lowest salaries, followed by men with employed wives; the highest salaries were found among men with nonemployed wives. Differences between each group of men in terms of job characteristics and achievement levels (e.g., educational degree, rank, and productivity) partly explained these salary differences. Married men with nonemployed wives had the highest salaries and achievement levels. Nevertheless, even when these job and achievement characteristics were held constant (i.e., when comparing men with roughly equivalent levels of achievement and similar employment characteristics), Bellas (1992) found that men with employed wives earned about $1,000 a year more than never-married men, and men with nonemployed wives earned approximately $2,000 a year more than men who never married. This study suggests that marriage – especially to a nonemployed spouse – has an economic pay-off for this group of male workers. Marriage for men may "signal" positive qualities to employers and, as Bellas's (1992) research suggests, wives – especially those who are nonemployed – may contribute to their husbands' careers. For example, by caring for children and the home, nonemployed wives may make it possible for their husbands to devote more time and energy to work. Wives may be an important source of social and emotional support as well, or may perform other tasks such as entertaining that may help their husbands' career advancement.

If married men receive a premium from marriage, do married women suffer a wage penalty at work, as compared to unmarried

women? The answer to this question appears to be that employed women are not penalized for marriage and may even derive
a wage advantage, relative to other women, all else equal (Budig
and England 2001). The finding that employed women overall are
not economically penalized by marriage must be qualified in one,
important respect, however: Mothers – regardless of marital status
– earn less than non-mothers. Budig and England (2001) estimate
that U.S. mothers experience a wage penalty of about 7 percent per
child. The **motherhood wage penalty** is not confined to the United
States, however, but has been reported in cross-national studies
including Canada, Australia, and several European countries
(Harkness and Waldfogel 1999; Misra, Budig, and Moller 2007).

A wage penalty for mothers could be caused by several factors.
First, because women have primary responsibility for children –
especially young children – women may lose work experience and
seniority when they become mothers. The birth of a child may lead
some women to change jobs or decrease the time they spend at work,
both of which are associated with lower wages. Perhaps mothers
continue to work for pay, but become less productive and devote less
effort to their jobs, relative to non-mothers. This, too, would reduce
their wages. The motherhood wage penalty may also reflect mothers'
tendency to seek employment in "mother-friendly" jobs, such as
those with flexible schedules, on-site childcare, or reduced work
hours. Some economists would argue that the "mother-friendliness"
of these jobs compensates for the job's lower wages. In this view,
mothers trade off higher wages for the opportunity to have a job
that can be combined with their childcare responsibilities.

Finally, it may be that employers discriminate against mothers
by restricting them to lower-paying jobs. Just as marriage for men
may "signal" positive qualities to employers, motherhood for
women may send negative signals. Regardless of how mothers
actually perform relative to non-mothers, employers may *believe*
that mothers will perform less well. Employers who act on these
beliefs by refusing to promote mothers or hire them into high-
paying jobs are engaging in discrimination – differential treatment
of a group on the basis of motherhood.

Which explanation is correct? In a sophisticated statistical analysis of these arguments, Budig and England (2001) concluded that about one-third of the 7 percent motherhood wage penalty could be explained by mothers having less work experience and seniority than non-mothers. When women become mothers, their involvement in the paid work force lessens somewhat, and this partly explains their decreased earnings. Nevertheless, two-thirds of the motherhood wage penalty remains even after accounting for differences in work experience and seniority: Among women with similar levels of experience and seniority, mothers earn roughly 4 percent less than non-mothers. This may reflect differences between the productivity levels of the two groups, or it may indicate that employers are discriminating against mothers. In any case, as Budig and England (2001) observe, the wage costs of motherhood are born primarily by mothers themselves.

Motherhood as a status characteristic

Correll, Benard, and Paik (2007) drew on status characteristics theory (see Chapter 2) to examine the degree to which employers may be biased against mothers. Recall that status characteristics are distinctions among people that become salient in particular situations and are used to assess competence, worth, and performance. Correll and her colleagues argued that motherhood is an important status characteristic in the workplace as a result of the conflict between cultural understandings of mothers and "ideal worker" norms. While the "ideal worker" is expected to be committed, fully available, and devoted to the job, mothers are expected to be child-centered and thus less reliable and committed workers.

Correll, Benard, and Paik (2007) tested this argument in two ways. First, they conducted a laboratory experiment in which undergraduate students were asked to rate fictitious job applicants. The applicants were similar except for their parenthood status. They found that mothers were judged to be less competent and committed than women without children, were offered a lower starting salary, and regarded as less promotable to a management position.

179

Fathers were not regarded any differently than non-fathers on most measures, and were more favorably evaluated in some respects. In particular, fathers were offered higher starting salaries than non-fathers. These findings were similar regardless of whether the fictitious job applicant was identified as African-American or white, and regardless of whether women or men were making the evaluations. One unanticipated finding was that women without children were viewed more favorably than childless men in some areas.

To examine whether these results would be the same outside the laboratory, Correll and colleagues mailed out fictitious applications containing cover letters and résumés to real employers. The applications differed only in terms of the gender and parenthood status of the applicant. The authors sought to determine how these characteristics would affect the likelihood that an applicant was "called back" for an interview or other follow up by an employer. The results were similar to those found in the laboratory experiment: Mothers were called back only about half as often as non-mothers; fathers experienced no disadvantage relative to non-fathers. Because most employed women and men have children at some point during their work lives, this study has broad implications for gender inequality in the workplace.

"His" marriage and "her" marriage

The employment effects of marriage and parenthood are only part of the story. It is also important to examine how marriage affects women's and men's psychological health and well-being. To address these questions, we start with the classic work of sociologist Jesse Bernard. In her 1973 book, *The Future of Marriage*, Bernard argued that researchers had overlooked an important point about marriage; they had ignored the fact that marriage was gendered. In Bernard's view, marriage had to be understood from the perspective of "his" and "hers." Women and men, she argued, experienced marriage differently, in part due to their differing life situations prior to marriage and in part due to their roles and responsibilities in marriage.

Bernard (1973b, p. 41) explained these differences with what she called a "**shock theory of marriage**." Specifically, Bernard claimed that marriage was a greater "shock" for women than men. As a result, she argued that married women were generally more psychologically distressed than single women and married men. Although married life is a change for all involved, Bernard believed that married women had to make greater adjustments than their partners. One of the most obvious ways that this occurs is if a woman takes her husband's name at marriage and gives up her own. This may signal a loss of independence for a woman, who is now identified in terms of her relationship to her husband. As we have seen, married women may find themselves having to take on more of the household work – even when both wife and husband are employed. Regardless of whether both are employed or only the husband is employed, it is likely that his job will have the greatest influence on the couple's lifestyle, including where they live and how often they move (Moen and Roehling 2005).

The differential adjustments each gender makes to marriage reflect a larger truth about relationships – even intimate relationships: Those with greater resources tend to have more power in the relationship. Unequal resources imply unequal power and dependence. Because men's economic contribution to the family is greater than women's, on average, men typically have more power in the household. By this logic, full-time homemakers are most dependent on their spouses and have the least amount of power in the relationship. When Bernard proposed the shock theory of marriage, she was thinking most about the situation of the full-time homemaker.

Marriage reassessed

Is Bernard's (1973b) description of marriage still accurate today? We know that much has changed. Throughout the industrialized world, fewer people are marrying and alternatives to marriage are flourishing. Fincham and Beach (2010, p. 630) argue that "marriage as a social institution is less dominant in the United States than at any time in history." Within marriage, there are far fewer full-time homemakers today than in the 1970s, and women's economic dependence on men in marriage has lessened. Fewer women than ever take their husband's name at marriage and some men take their wife's name, or adopt a combination of both. In addition, Bernard may have overlooked some of the positive effects of marriage for women and may have understated some of the negative effects of paid employment.

Waite and Gallagher (2000) argue that marriage is overwhelmingly positive for women. Married women, they contend, are happier with their lives, report fewer mental health problems, have more satisfying sexual relations, are less likely to be victims of domestic abuse, and are better off financially than their unmarried or cohabiting counterparts. Despite these apparent benefits, the health benefits of marriage nevertheless seem to be greater for men than women (Waite and Gallagher 2000). This is because single men, in general, are much worse off than single women. For example, single men are more likely than single women *and* married men to engage in risky and unhealthy behaviors, such as excessive drinking. Single women are more likely to care for their health than single men; Married men receive this care and attention from their wives. Single women also have closer ties to family and friends and this lesser social isolation improves their health relative to single men.

Despite these findings, it is not easy to make an overall assessment of the relative benefits of marriage for women and men (England 2001). Clearly, marriage can provide both partners with important social and financial resources. At the same time, this arrangement works out somewhat differently for women and men. In this respect, Bernard's contention that marriage should be understood in terms of "his" and "her" marriage continues to capture an important aspect of this gendered institution.

Lesbian and gay relationships

Although most studies on families and marriage focus on heterosexual couples, gay and lesbian couples are receiving more attention from social scientists. In an early study of this topic, Blumstein and Schwartz (1983) compared gay and lesbian couples to hetero-sexual couples with respect to issues such as the household division of labor, compatibility, and sexual satisfaction. These researchers not only found some differences between heterosexual and non-heterosexual couples, but they also found that gay and lesbian couples differ in some important ways. For example, gay and lesbian couples tended to spend more time together and share more interests than heterosexual couples. Later research, reported by Kurdek (1995), found that gay and lesbian couples were more likely than heterosexual couples to relate to each other as best friends and aspire to an egalitarian relationship. Research also suggests that the household division of labor in gay and lesbian households tends to be more egalitarian than in heterosexual households; Blumstein and Schwartz (1983) found that lesbian couples were most likely to share tasks equally. These differences between heterosexual and gay and lesbian couples are not the whole story, however, as research has found some significant differences between gay and lesbian couples. The majority of lesbian and heterosexual couples in Blumstein and Schwartz's sample, for example, tended to be monogamous, while gay men tended to prefer more sexually open relationships (see also Kurdek 1995).

As these authors suggest, these patterns can be best understood by thinking about *gender* and *gender roles*, not *sexual orientation* (Stacey 1996). In other words, people's expectations about and behavior in relationships depend more on their gender than their sexual orientation. Similarly, what people expect of their partner depends more on the partner's gender than his or her sexual orientation. As we have seen in earlier chapters, those with an individu-alist orientation to gender emphasize the ways that gender shapes people and the choices they make. This is especially true with respect to people's choices and behavior in relationships as both are influenced by growing up male or female.

Returning to the household division of labor may help to illus-trate this point about the importance of gender in both heterosexual and gay and lesbian couples. As Blumstein and Schwartz (1983, p. 324) note, "An extremely important effect of having one male and one female in heterosexual couples is that each gender is automatically assigned certain duties and privileges.... For heterosexual couples, gender provides a shortcut and avoids the decision-making process.... Same-sex couples cannot, obviously, rely on gender to guide their decisions about who will do what in the relationship." Heterosexual couples may find themselves conforming to a household division of labor like that described earlier – women do routine, day-to-day tasks, while men are likely to do tasks involving more discretion. These patterns stem less from conscious choices as from people's reliance on tradition, social norms, and personal experiences growing up. Same-sex couples cannot rely on these clues about how to behave and are likely to rely more on trial and error as a basis for organizing and dividing household work. The household division of labor is more "scripted" for heterosexual couples and may be more difficult to alter or challenge than for same-sex couples. At the same time, same-sex couples may have more flexibility in organizing their lives as a couple, but lack the traditions and models that guide heterosexual couples.

This discussion of gay and lesbian couples is not meant to suggest that these relationships are free of conflict and inequality. Some of the problems faced by gay and lesbian couples are similar to those found in any intimate relationship, regardless of sexual orientation. For example, both kinds of couples confront issues associated with balancing the demands of work with personal and family life (Dunne 1998).

Other issues may be more unique to gay and lesbian couples, just as heterosexual couples may face challenges that are unique for them. Blumstein and Schwartz (1983, p. 330) observed that: "Gay [and lesbian] couples face problems that arise from 'sameness of gender'; these give us an indication of where it might be wise for partners to be different. Heterosexuals face problems that arise from their 'differentness'; these give us guidance about where it might be better for two partners to be more alike." Differentness, for example, may be a liability for heterosexual couples interested in creating an egalitarian household division of labor. Men and women may have distinct preferences and skills, and different expectations regarding roles and responsibilities. At the same time, similarity may create problems for gay and lesbian couples. As Blumstein and Schwartz (1983, p. 305) explain, "Same-sex couples understand each other better and share similar sexual goals, but roadblocks may arise when neither partner wants to take on behavior that seems inappropriate to his or her gender."

Gay and lesbian couples also confront several other obstacles to maintaining close relationships and building families. These couples are legally able to marry only in some settings which limits the rights and obligations of many gay and lesbian family members. Many states explicitly prohibit same-sex marriage and in 1996 Congress passed the "Defense of Marriage Act," a federal prohibition against same-sex marriage. The issue of same-sex marriage is hotly debated among gays and lesbians. While believing that the opportunity to marry is a civil right denied them as a result of sex discrimination and homophobia, some gays and lesbians do not wish to model their relationships on the heterosexual standard. They prefer the freedom and flexibility to form intimate relationships and families without having to conform to the norms, laws, and institutions that govern heterosexual marriage (Stacey 1996). Others feel differently and have agitated strongly for the legal right to marry, arguing that this right would strengthen families, encourage long-term, committed relationships, and protect the children of gay and lesbian parents.

Chapter Summary

Socialization is the process through which people become gendered. They learn what is expected of them because they are female or male and how to display these characteristics. Gender socialization has an especially central role to play in individualist understandings of gender, as these approaches emphasize the ways that gender is embodied in people. Parents (especially fathers) do seem to have different levels of involvement with their male and female children, but these differences in parental treatment coexist alongside parental beliefs in gender egalitarianism with respect to children. Children are actively involved in the socialization process, learning to apply gender stereotypes to themselves and others. Peers are also an important source of gender-related information, especially as children get older.

While socialization is important, many sociologists have criticized research that relies exclusively on socialization as an explanation for gender differences. Critics argue that this type of explanation falsely creates a view of women and men as homogenous groups, possessing internally consistent and unchanging motives, behavioral dispositions, etc. (Gerson 1985, 1993; see also Epstein 1988). In the section on peer groups, I showed how an interactionist approach that takes into account features of the social context can help us understand the creation of gender distinctions.

Like other areas of gender research, studies of the household division of labor draw upon diverse conceptions of gender and pursue different objectives. While some examine gender differences in the type and amount of women's and men's household work, others want to uncover the meanings associated with these activities and the ways these meanings are produced. The former topics generally reflect an individualist view of gender, while the latter derive from an interactionist approach. Although men are performing more chores around the house than they used to, researchers still find that women have primary responsibility for housework and childcare. From an interactionist perspective, "doing" household work and caring for children are not merely activities one performs; rather, these activities help to create people's gendered sense of themselves. Cross-national research has contributed to our understanding of the factors that can explain changes in the household division of labor over time, and differences in women's and men's contributions to household work.

Marriage has different consequences for women and for men. Economically speaking, being married "pays off" for men. Employers seem to view married men as more responsible and productive workers. Women are not economically penalized by marriage, but married women – especially those with children – are assumed to be less committed to their jobs than women without family obligations and suffer a "motherhood wage penalty" in the workplace. The psychological rewards of marriage also differ for women and men. Bernard's "shock theory of marriage" posits that marriage requires women to accommodate more to men than vice versa, although evidence suggests that this may have changed somewhat. Lesbian and gay families are on the rise. These couples face some of the same issues faced by heterosexual couples, but also confront unique challenges.

Further Reading

Correll, Shelley J., Benard, Stephan, and Paik, In. 2007. "Getting a job: Is there a motherhood penalty?" *American Journal of Sociology* 112: 1297–1338.

Maccoby, Eleanor E. 1998. *The Two Sexes: Growing Up Apart, Coming Together*. Cambridge, MA: Harvard University Press.

Williams, Joan. 2000. *Unbending Gender: Why Work and Family Conflict and What to Do About it*. New York: Oxford University Press.

Key Terms

Gender identity
Gender stereotype
Gender-centric reasoning
Household division of labor
Time constraints approach
Relative resources
Gender ideologies
Compulsory motherhood
Marriage wage premium
Motherhood wage penalty
Shock theory of marriage

Critical Thinking Questions

1 Despite a general trend toward more gender-egalitarian beliefs and practices, fathers interact with their sons differently than their daughters, and families with sons differ in some respects from families with daughters. How would you explain these differences?
2 Both women and men spend more time with their children than in previous decades, even in families where both genders are in the paid labor force. How would you explain this change?
3 Discuss the differences between how mothers, fathers, and childless women and men are perceived by employers. How might the motherhood wage penalty be eliminated?

Chapter 6

Gendered Jobs and Gendered Workers

Chapter Objectives

- Define sex segregation, explain how it is measured, and discuss variations across time and place.
- Discuss the ways that jobs, hierarchies, and work relations are gender-typed.
- Explain how wages are determined and how gender enters into the wage-setting process.

Classical sociologists Karl Marx and Max Weber had much to say about the industrial capitalist workplace. For Marx, capitalist means of production unleashed tremendous productivity, but the social relations of work were exploitative and alienating for workers. Weber called attention to the forces of bureaucratization that were

The Sociology of Gender: An Introduction to Theory and Research, Second Edition. Amy S. Wharton.
© 2012 John Wiley & Sons Ltd. Published 2012 by John Wiley & Sons Ltd.

transforming all institutions, including the institution of work. Marx and Weber's observations have long served as the foundation for sociological analyses of the workplace.

Neither theorist, however, had much to say about gender. Rather, both seemed to suggest that the processes they described were gender-neutral, meaning that they were somehow generic and general, unaffected by and separate from gender meanings and distinctions. Many have critiqued these understandings of work for their assumption of gender neutrality and suggested that gender is embedded in, not separate from, organizational processes.

This chapter considers three ways in which gender may be incorporated into the workings of employment. First, gender shapes the social organization of work, expressed primarily in the sex segregation of occupations, jobs, and firms. Second, gender shapes the meanings people assign to particular occupations, jobs, and work activities, leading us to see some as more appropriate for women and some as more appropriate for men. Third, gender shapes the "worth" of jobs, leading some jobs to be more valued and paid more than other jobs. As we explore these issues, we will be drawing from individualist, interactionist, and institutional perspectives.

Sex Segregation and the Division of Labor in Paid Work

In the previous chapter, we examined the household division of labor and saw that women and men do different amounts and kinds of household work. Here, we turn our attention to the paid labor force, where similar patterns are found. Women and men are not randomly distributed across occupations. **Sex segregation** – the concentration of women and men into different occupations, firms, and jobs – is a pervasive feature of the workplace in most societies, yet it is one that is often overlooked by the casual observer. A trip to a U.S. doctor's office, for example, is unlikely to prompt reflection on why all of the nurses happen to be women. This reflection might only be prompted by the presence of male nurse – an exception to the dominant pattern. What we expect and are used to, however, rarely attracts our attention. A second reason why sex segregation may be invisible to the casual observer stems from the forms segregation often assumes. For example, walking into an office you may observe both women and men at work. Only by looking more closely at their job assignments and titles, however, would it become clear that women and men are, in fact, performing different jobs.

On a broader level, however, sex segregation in the workplace is easily spotted. Many people know, for example, that nursing is a predominantly female occupation, while engineering (in the United States) is dominated by men. Many would be surprised to encounter a childcare worker, a receptionist, or an elementary school teacher who was not female, just as they would be to meet an auto mechanic, a surgeon, or a plumber who was not male. Sex segregation is a taken-for-granted feature of the workplace.

Types and amounts of sex segregation

Sex segregation can occur at the job, occupation, or firm levels. Occupational sex segregation refers to the concentration of women and men in different occupations. Due to the large amount of contemporary and historical data on occupations, most studies focus on this form of segregation. In recent years, however, more data have become available on the sex composition of jobs and firms (Huffman, Cohen, and Pearlman 2010; Tomaskovic-Devey, Zimmer, Stainback, Robinson, Taylor, and McTague 2006). This has enabled researchers to examine the degree to which women and men are segregated into different jobs both within and across firms. In the U.S. labor force, occupations, jobs and work establishments are segregated not only by sex, but also by race and ethnicity (Reskin 1999; Reskin and Padavic 1994; Tomaskovic-Devey 1993).

Three general conclusions have emerged from sex segregation research. First, sex segregation at the job level is more extensive than sex segregation at the level of occupation. By focusing only on occupational sex segregation, researchers underestimate the degree to which women and men work in different jobs and firms.

191

A second conclusion is that women and men hardly ever truly work together. Women and men are not distributed evenly across occupations, and, when they are members of the same occupation, they are likely to work in different jobs and firms. Third, overall levels of sex segregation have declined over time in all industrial societies.

Measuring sex segregation

The most widely used measure of sex segregation is the **index of dissimilarity** (also referred to as the index of segregation). The index of segregation ranges from 0 to 100. A score of 100 indicates that there is complete segregation in the entity being measured: This means that the units (e.g., occupations, jobs, etc.) comprising that entity (e.g., labor force, firm, etc.) are all either 100 percent female or 100 percent male. A score of 0 indicates complete integration of the entity being measured: This means that every unit (e.g., occupations, jobs, etc.) comprising the entity has the same proportion of women and men in it as the entity as a whole. The value of this index can be interpreted as the percentage of either sex who would have to change occupations in order for the sex composition of every occupation to be the same as the sex composition of the labor force as a whole. For example, a score of 35 means that roughly a third of either women or men would have to move to another occupation in order to bring about an occupationally sex-integrated labor force.

Trends in occupational sex and race segregation

Although problems with the comparability of occupational categories over time do complicate matters, researchers have examined trends in occupational sex segregation from the turn-of-the-century to the present. These studies show that occupational sex segregation was relatively stable during most of the twentieth century, then began to decline in the 1970s. The relative stability of segregation levels during the first three-quarters of the twentieth century is

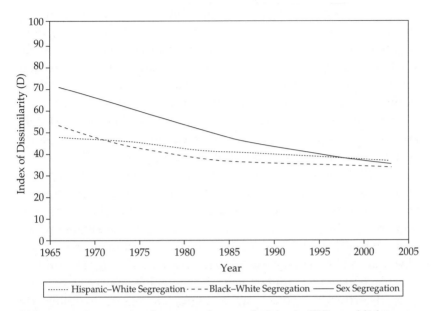

Figure 6.1 Segregation by sex and race-ethnicity in U.S. establishments, 1966–2003.

Source: Donald Tomaskovic-Devey, Catherine Zimmer, Kevin Stainback, Corre Robinson, Tiffany Taylor and Tricia McTague. 2006. "Documenting desegregation: Segregation in American workplaces by race, ethnicity, and sex, 1966–2003." *American Sociological Review* 71(4): 565–588 (figure 2, p. 572).

remarkable in light of all of the other social, economic, and cultural changes that occurred during this period.

Researchers have been particularly interested in sex and race segregation trends over the past few decades. The results of one such analysis, by Tomaskovic-Devey et al. (2006), appear in Figure 6.1. Shown are establishment-level segregation indices for a sample of U.S. private-sector firms. These data indicate that both sex and race segregation have declined since the mid-1960s. Sex segregation declined from a high of 70 (as measured by the index of dissimilarity) to 35 in 2003, with the rate of decline somewhat higher prior to 1980. Black–white segregation in establishments has also declined, though most of the decline in black–white segregation came in the two decades between 1965 and 1985. Hispanic–white segregation, which was lower than the other two forms of segregation in the 1960s, has declined as well. Overall, this figure shows that levels of sex and race segregation in U.S. firms are roughly equivalent, but declines in sex segregation have been much more consistent.

In more detailed analyses of these trends, Tomaskovic-Devey and his colleagues found that that declines in sex segregation occurred across almost all labor market sectors and in all regions of the United States. The shift to a service economy (see Chapter 4) also contributed because this shift involved a decrease in many predominantly male industrial jobs and an expansion of less sex-segregated jobs in the service sector. Levels of race segregation vary more by sector and region than sex segregation. For example, Hispanic–white segregation in areas such as agriculture, mining, construction, and manufacturing has remained fairly stable over time. The trends in black–white segregation seem to follow the passage and enforcement of U.S. civil rights legislation. As Figure 6.1 shows, black–white segregation declined after the passage of the U.S. Civil Rights Act in 1964, but slowed as enforcement of this legislation weakened in the 1980s.

From an historical perspective, an important aspect of occupational sex segregation is the way that occupations can change their sex composition over time. Librarians, clerical workers, teachers, and bank tellers are examples of occupations in the United States that used to be mostly filled by men, but are now dominated heavily by women. The feminization of occupations – the movement of women into fields dominated by men – is primarily responsible for the decline in aggregate levels of occupational sex segregation that occurred during the 1970s (Reskin and Roos 1990). During this time period, women's representation increased markedly in fields such as public relations, systems analysis, bartending, advertising, and insurance adjusting. The feminization of occupations continues. For example, while women students were rare in U.S. schools of veterinary medicine in the 1960s, they are now in the majority (Gose 1998). The number of female veterinarians has doubled since 1991, while the number of male veterinarians has fallen by 15 percent.

There are far fewer examples of occupations that have shifted in the other direction – from mostly female to mostly male. For example, while Reskin and Roos (1990) identified 33 occupations that feminized in the 1970s, they could find only three (cooks, food-preparation kitchen workers, and maids and housemen) where the percentage of men significantly increased. The processes that create and maintain a sex-segregated occupational structure are ongoing, and the sexual division of labor is maintained even as particular occupations experience changes in their sex composition.

Cross-national pattern of sex segregation

The enduring aspects of segregation can be seen even more clearly when we look at trends and patterns cross-nationally. Researchers have used the index of dissimilarity, as well as other statistical techniques, to compare levels of occupational sex segregation across societies. Although this can be challenging given the tremendous variability across countries in the quality and availability of occupational data, these studies have yielded useful information. Most important, they show that occupational sex segregation is a persistent feature of all industrial societies. In general, a country's level of occupational sex segregation depends upon a variety of economic, social, and cultural factors. Women generally have greater access to predominantly male occupations in countries with low birth rates and strong egalitarian belief systems, while sex segregation is increased when countries have large service sectors (Charles 1992). Governmental policies relating to gender also play a role in shaping a country's level and pattern of occupational sex segregation.

A central question for researchers studying cross-national patterns is whether the gender egalitarian pressures witnessed in many other areas of life in advanced industrial societies are reflected in these countries' occupational structures. There is not a simple answer to this question. In the United States, for example, sex segregation has declined over time, but it has not changed as much as the gap in women's and men's rates of labor force participation, women's levels of educational attainment relative to men, and both genders' endorsement of egalitarian beliefs about gender roles (Charles and Grusky 2004). Similar patterns can be observed in other industrial societies. Moreover, studies find that countries considered highly gender egalitarian, such as Sweden and Norway, have more highly segregated occupational structures than some less gender egalitarian countries, such as Italy and Japan.

In order to explain this finding, as well as the slow pace of change in sex segregation relative to other areas of gender change, Charles and Grusky (2004) argue that sex segregation has both a vertical and a horizontal dimension. **Vertical segregation** refers to a process whereby men occupy the most desirable occupations (e.g., most prestigious, high paying, most powerful, etc.). This form of segregation has not disappeared, but gotten considerably weaker over time. This is because vertical segregation in its most overt forms is difficult to sustain in an era of egalitarian norms and legal principles regarding equal rights of women and men. **Horizontal segregation** has been much slower to change and is reflected in the distribution of women and men across occupations in ways that reaffirm gender stereotypes. According to Charles and Grusky (2004, p. 298), horizontal segregation is reproduced through "a logic of gender essentialism," whereby women are presumed to excel in personal service, nurturance, and social interaction and men in more instrumental or physical tasks. Sex segregation in advanced industrial societies tends to reflect this "different but equal" model. And in the case of Sweden, this model is especially strong. From this perspective, overall levels of sex segregation in any particular society then reflect a mixture of both its vertical and horizontal expressions.

Occupational distributions of women and men

We can see these patterns of vertical and horizontal segregation more clearly if we look at the occupational distributions of women

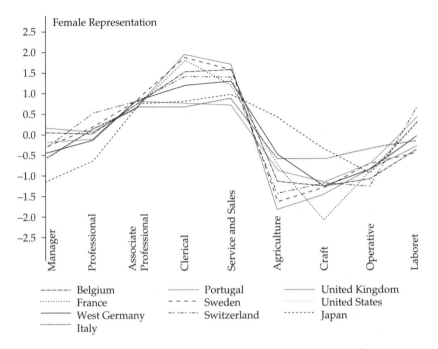

Figure 6.2 Female representation in major occupational groups by country. *Source*: Maria Charles and David B. Grusky. 2004. *Occupational Ghettos: The Worldwide Segregation of Women and Men*. Stanford: Stanford University Press (p. 80).

and men. In general, women are more likely than men to be in nonmanual occupations and, within the nonmanual area, to work in sales, service, and clerical positions. This pattern is shown in Figure 6.2, which shows the degree to which women are over- or underrepresented among major occupational categories in ten countries. Table 6.1 lists the top twenty occupations for women in the United States in 2009. These occupations are almost exclusively in the service sector.

Women and men work in different jobs, and jobs themselves often come to be understood as "male" or "female." This process

Table 6.1 The top twenty occupations for U.S. women in 2009.

1. Secretaries and administrative assistants
2. Registered nurses
3. Elementary and middle school teachers
4. Cashiers
5. Nursing, psychiatric, and home health aides
6. Retail salespersons
7. First-line supervisors/managers of retails sales workers
8. Waiters and waitresses
9. Maids and housekeeping cleaners
10. Customer service representatives
11. Child care workers
12. Bookkeeping, accounting, and auditing clerks
13. Receptionists and information clerks
14. First-line supervisors/managers of office and administrative support workers
15. Managers, all other
16. Accountants and auditors
17. Teacher assistants
18. Cooks
19. Office clerks, general
20. Personal and home care aides

Source: U.S. Department of Labor, Bureau of Labor Statistics.

underlies both vertical and horizontal forms of segregation, as described earlier. Next, we look at some of the factors that might explain how women and men end up in different jobs. Then we examine the gender typing of jobs and tasks, and the gender meanings attached to different kinds of work.

Explaining Sex Segregation

To understand why men and women work in different jobs, we will consider two sets of factors. First, some argue that we must consider the characteristics of workers themselves, particularly their early socialization and preferences for certain kinds of jobs. The second focuses on processes operating inside the workplace and involve the ways that people are hired and jobs are assigned.

Gendered workers and gendered jobs

As we know from Chapter 2, socialization is one process through which men and women may develop different traits, abilities, values, and skills. If each gender comes to possess different "bundles" of work-related characteristics, they may choose and be best suited for different kinds of jobs. This is a more difficult issue to examine than it may seem. Although women and men do have job preferences and make employment choices, whether these choices are truly external to the opportunity structure women and men face is not easily determined.

For example, while children's occupational aspirations are highly gender-typed, these differences get smaller as children age and enter adulthood, and women's preferences have changed over time. Marini and Shu (1998) found that younger women were less likely than older women to aspire to predominantly female occupations and were more likely to aspire to occupations with higher earnings' potential. These changes occurred among all social classes and racial groups, to some extent, though were particularly strong among women from higher socioeconomic backgrounds. Men's occupational aspirations remained relatively stable across the birth cohorts in Marini and Shu's study.

Research by sociologist Kathleen Gerson (1985, 1993) on how people's childhood experiences shape their work and family decisions found that childhood plans and experiences, while not insignificant, explained very little about people's adult lives. As she explains:

> Among the men whose life paths we will trace, some recreated the patterns of their childhood environment but most did not. Over time, these men had experiences that led them to reassess the meaning of

199

their parents' lives and their own early outlooks. Childhood experiences neither prepared them for the obstacles and challenges of adulthood in a rapidly changing world nor determined how they would react. The childhood context simply provided them with a point of departure. (Gerson 1993, p. 61)

Gender, choice, and constraint   The influence of early gender socialization on women's and men's occupational choices continues to be debated. Although socialization is important, people's occupational choices are formed in significant ways by the circumstances of adulthood. Women and men respond to opportunities and constraints, and adjust and change their aspirations as new opportunities present themselves and others are closed off.

One of the most consequential influences on women's occupational choices in adulthood involves children. Ferriman, Lubinski, and Benbow (2009) examined the work and life preferences of top math/science graduate students at ages 25 and 35. Tested first in their mid-twenties, these high-achieving students showed few gender differences in their values, career interests, lifestyle preferences, or academic abilities. Ten years later, many similarities between women and men remained and, to the extent that changes did occur, women and men changed in similar ways on several measures. For example, both women and men came to place more importance on leadership opportunities and merit-based pay, and less emphasis on the social aspects of work.

Although these women and men shared many of the same career goals and values, the presence of children ten years later significantly altered women's views. Men and women in their twenties viewed flexible schedules and control over work hours in similar ways, but mothers in their thirties saw these as much more important than fathers or childless women and men did. Mothers but not fathers were endorsing career trajectories that they perceived as more accommodating to family life. These patterns do not stem from differences in women's and men's intellectual capacities, motivation for work, or work commitment, but instead are ways that mothers begin to shape their career preferences around the realities of household and childcare responsibilities. Inevitably, these decisions will likely steer mothers into different types of jobs within science than fathers, childless men, or childless women.

The women and men in Ferriman, Lubinski, and Benbow's (2009) study were highly educated, with the ability and the opportunity to pursue high-level scientific careers. These patterns have also been found among other groups of women in the U.S. who are attempting to balance motherhood with work obligations. The problem, as Webber and Williams (2008, pp. 772–3) observe, is that "mothers confront a labor market divided into 'good' jobs, which confer many privileges but do not accommodate motherhood, and 'bad' jobs, which accommodate mothering responsibilities but without adequate or just compensation." By using "the language of choice" to make sense of their circumstances, women in both "good" and "bad" jobs draw attention away from the ways that the organization of work imposes structural constraints on employment options.

Employers and the gendered opportunity structure

Workers' choices do not occur in a vacuum but rather are shaped by the opportunity structure of work. Employers' roles are central here and help to maintain sex segregation through the hiring process, the assignment of workers to jobs, and promotions (Fernandez and Sosa 2005). These situations create opportunities for **"allocative discrimination,"** which involves assigning women and men to different (and differently compensated) jobs (Petersen and Saporta 2004).

At the point of hire, employers screen workers and assess their skills. This process creates a potential for **statistical discrimination,** which occurs when a job applicant is treated as if he or she possesses the qualities and characteristics "typical" of his or her gender. When employers statistically discriminate, they are assumed to be *correctly* assigning group averages to individuals. This distinguishes statistical discrimination from discrimination resulting from employers' use of incorrect, exaggerated, or unsubstantiated stereotypes to hire or assign jobs to workers. The issue of whether or not employers' views are accurate is important. Consider this example, which relates to racial differences, but can easily be applied to gender differences as well:

> Suppose a bank has found over the years that its black tellers make slightly more mistakes than its white tellers. Suppose that when all else is equal blacks with four years of college perform as well as whites with two years of college, while blacks with two years of college perform as well as white high-school graduates. If this were the bank's experience, an economically rational policy would be to hire blacks only if they had at least two more years of schooling than otherwise similar whites. Statistical discrimination of this kind would be illegal, but it might nonetheless make economic sense from the bank's viewpoint. (Jencks 1992, pp. 42–3)

Employers sometimes discover on their own, or learn about from other sources, the existence of average group differences in performance or other job-related characteristics. This information can then be used to make hiring decisions. In this way, group characteristics such as gender serve as screening devices for employers to identify qualified workers and to exclude less qualified. For instance, the bank in the above example could decide to exclude all men from teller positions and hire only women.

Research suggests that women are most likely to be excluded from jobs that require a large employer investment in on-the-job training. Employers hiring for these positions may correctly conclude that women are more likely than men to have primary responsibility for childcare, to take parental leave, and to leave their job when a spouse's job requires a move. They may therefore conclude that women will be more costly to employ in these positions than men, and thus may exclude all or most women from such jobs. Of course, any individual woman may or may not be different from any individual man regarding intent to remain with the employer for an extended time. Employers who fail to determine this on an individual basis are engaging in gender discrimination.

Research on job searches lends strong support to the conventional wisdom that people get jobs based in large part on who they know (Granovetter 1974). Because men's and women's social networks are likely to be distinct, however, job information is exchanged between people of the same gender. If people learn about jobs from people like themselves, they are likely to get jobs where similar people predominate. This process in compounded by employers' behavior (Fernandez and Sosa 2005). Employers often rely on employee referrals. While current employees are quite reliable sources for these referrals, they are likely to refer people like themselves. If men exchange job information with other men and women rely on other women for this information, jobs are likely to be filled by people similar to those already employed.

Sex segregation may also be maintained by practices built into the formal structure of work organizations. For example, **internal labor market**s refer to structured opportunities for advancement that are made available to those already employed. While entry-level positions may be filled from the external labor market, competition for promotions after hiring is restricted to those already employed. Internal labor markets are often very complicated, however, governed by seniority systems and other complex rules for promotion. These factors may make it difficult for people who begin their careers in a sex-segregated entry-level job to move to a less-segregated position later. In this way, internal labor markets can institutionalize sex segregation within a firm.

Gender Typing of Jobs, Hierarchies, and Workplace Expectations

We turn now to the "gendering" of jobs – that is, how particular jobs come to be understood as "male" or "female." A **gender-typed job** or occupation thus is one that is seen to require distinctly feminine or distinctly masculine characteristics. Examples of gender-typed occupations are everywhere. For instance, when asked to describe the qualifications for being a nurse, many would list characteristics assumed to be much more typical of women than men, such as nurturance and caretaking ability. Similarly, many would assume that jobs presumed to require aggression and competitiveness, such as prosecutor, are more appropriate for men than women.

One way in which jobs and occupations become gendered is as a result of their sex composition. In other words, jobs take on the characteristics of those who typically perform them. Nursing in the United States is an example of that process. As it came to be filled disproportionately by women, it was viewed as an occupation that demanded "feminine" qualities, such as empathy. This assumption, in turn, helped perpetuate the traditional sex composition of nursing since it implied that women as a group are inherently better suited than men for this occupation. Hence, a job's sex composition will shape its gender type and its gender type will perpetuate its sex composition.

That jobs dominated by a particular sex come to be seen as most appropriate for that sex may seem unproblematic and inevitable, but this association is produced through a complex process of social construction. As Reskin and Roos (1990, p. 51) note, virtually any occupation can be understood as being more appropriate for one sex or another "because most jobs contain both stereotypical male and stereotypical female elements." Hence, the creation of a link between an occupation's sex composition and its gender type necessarily involves processes of selection and deselection. Certain aspects of occupations may be emphasized as particularly important or essential, while others may be downplayed. Nursing, for example, requires workers to be skilled in the use of complex medical technologies. Emphasizing the caring aspects of this occupation, however, allows it to be cast as an occupation particularly appropriate for women.

Most jobs and occupations contain enough different kinds of characteristics that they can be construed as appropriate for *either* women or men. The gender type of an occupation thus can be altered relatively easily, as occurred in the United States during World War II. As Milkman (1987, p. 50) notes, jobs "that had previously been viewed as quintessentially masculine were suddenly endowed with femininity and glamour for the duration. The war mobilization era not only illustrates the resilience of job segregation by sex, but also graphically demonstrates how idioms of sex-typing can be flexibly applied to whatever jobs women and men happen to be doing." Hence, "masculine" jobs that had been filled by men prior to the war were relabeled as appropriate for women during wartime when female workers were in demand.

Gender and emotional labor

Another way in which jobs become gender typed is through the kinds of **emotional labor** they require. Service economies produce many jobs that require workers to interact directly with clients or customers. Employers who hire workers for these interactive service jobs often expect them to present a particular emotional demeanor as part of performing the job. For example, flight attendants and other workers whose jobs involve contact with customers are expected to be friendly and helpful, and can be disciplined if they fail to display these qualities. Other types of jobs require less pleasurable emotional demeanors. For example, litigators are expected to be aggressive (Pierce 1995) and bill collectors are required to be hostile and confrontational with debtors (Sutton 1991). Emotional labor refers to the effort involved in displaying these characteristics; it involves "the management of feeling to create a publicly observable facial and bodily display" (Hochschild 1983, p. 7).

Emotional labor is a distinctive form of labor, different from physical or mental effort. Emotional labor does not involve primarily the body or mind, but rather involves workers' subjectivity – their sense of self. Jobs that require emotional labor ask a worker to be a certain kind of person on the job and to display certain qualities when interacting with others. As a result of these connections between workers' subjectivity and job requirements, jobs that involve emotional labor may be more gender-typed than others, and jobs that are gender-typed may be more likely than other jobs to require emotional labor.

When jobs are gender-typed as feminine, they are likely to require different kinds of emotional labor than jobs gender-typed as appropriate for males. For example, the occupation of flight attendant – a field traditionally filled by women, but one that has seen increasing numbers of men – requires workers to be sociable and outgoing (Hochschild 1979). Many service jobs are viewed as more appropriate for women than men, largely as a result of being associated with this kind of emotional labor.

MacDonald and Sirianni (1996, p. 3) use the term "emotional proletariat" to refer to the low-paying, low-skill service jobs that require workers to display friendliness and deference to customers. Deference – or the capacity to place oneself in a "one down" position vis-à-vis others – is a characteristic demanded of all those in disadvantaged structural positions, including women, racial-ethnic minorities, and others in subordinate statuses. When deference is made a job requirement, members of structurally disadvantaged groups are likely to be overrepresented in such jobs or even be seen as better suited for the work than members of more advantaged groups. These occupations, while not exclusively female, are often gender-typed as such. Jobs such as waiting tables or receptionist are examples of jobs that require, among other qualifications, that workers display attentiveness to others' needs and concerns.

Not all jobs that require emotional labor are gender-typed as female, however. Many professional and managerial jobs, for example, require a self-presentation designed to convey and wield power. Workers in these occupations, in contrast to those in the "emotional proletariat," exercise authority over those they interact with, rather than having to display deference.

As this discussion of the links between emotional labor and the gender typing of occupations makes clear, gender is incorporated into our understanding of job requirements and characteristics. The gender typing of occupations, jobs, and work tasks is not a random process, however. In particular, we have seen that low-status jobs containing low amounts of power and control over others are much more likely to be gendered female than high-status jobs requiring the exercise of authority. Deference – the capacity to place oneself in a "one down" position vis-à-vis others – is a characteristic demanded of low-status social groups in many circumstances. This capacity may also be expressed as "niceness" or the ability to get along. It is not surprising that, when this capacity is a job requirement, women will be viewed as better qualified than men. Moreover, even when deference may not be a formal job requirement, jobs containing large numbers of women are likely to contain an informal job requirement that encourages this behavior. Conversely, jobs involving the display of authority are more likely to be gendered as male, at least in part because authority in the context of the U.S. is seen as a masculine characteristic. Hence, when jobs require emotional labor – either as deference or authority – they are likely to also be gendered.

Gendered hierarchies and informal work relations

Gender shapes societal expectations of jobs and workers, and it affects how we understand the relations between jobs, including the hierarchical relations that underlie vertical segregation and the informal relations that reinforce horizontal segregation. In his writings on bureaucracy, the classical sociologist Max Weber provided one of the definitive sociological understandings of work hierarchies. For Weber, bureaucratic work arrangements were necessarily hierarchical and involved specialization, a fixed division of labor, and meritocratic rules and regulations (Weber 1946). He viewed the advantages of this system of organization as far outweighing its disadvantages.

One of bureaucracy's primary advantages, in Weber's view, was that it depersonalized organizations. Because bureaucratic authority, in principle, rests in positions not people and is encoded in rules and administrative regulations, bureaucracies are not dependent on the knowledge, expertise, or characteristics of any particular person. In addition, rules, regulations, and offices help insure that the organization's business can be conducted regardless of the nature of the personal ties between organizational members. Weber's faith in bureaucratic systems of administration thus rested heavily on his belief that rules and regulations specifying both the nature of official duties and the relations between positions in the hierarchy increased organizational control over its members' actions.

Weber emphasized the formal aspects of organization and focused on bureaucracy as an "ideal type." By contrast, later scholars turned their attention to the informal workings of bureaucracy and the ways these organizations functioned in fact, rather than in theory. For example, as many have noted, while bureaucracies are notorious for their reliance on rules and regulations, bureaucratic organizations would be less efficient if all members followed all of the rules all of the time. In fact, "working to rule" is an age-old strategy for resisting bureaucratic authority. Studies of informal organization thus have helped complement Weber's analysis of bureaucracy.

For Weber, bureaucracy was a gender-neutral form whose effectiveness stemmed from its decidedly depersonalized character. Gender scholars take issue with this argument, calling attention to the ways that gender shapes patterns of hierarchy and authority in organizations. Women have made inroads into managerial occupations in recent years, yet they remain much less likely than men to have jobs requiring the exercise of authority over resources and/or people.

This lack of access to authority is referred to as a **glass ceiling**. This term was introduced in a 1986 *Wall Street Journal* article to describe the invisible barriers that women and people of color confront as they move closer to the top of the managerial hierarchy. It was later adopted by the U.S. Department of Labor when it created the Glass Ceiling Commission, charged with studying and recommending ways to eliminate "those artificial barriers based on attitudinal or organizational bias that prevent qualified individuals from advancing upward in their organization into management-level positions" (Report on the Glass Ceiling Initiative: U.S. Department of Labor, 1991).

Behind the metaphor of the glass ceiling is an assertion that, as women and minorities attempt to move up the corporate ladder, their chances of doing so gradually decrease. Within managerial occupations, women's progress to the top levels of organizational decision-making has been slow. In 2010, among the largest and most prominent global companies ("The *Fortune Global* 500"), women ran just twelve corporations. That number increases to fifteen if we consider only U.S. firms in the *Fortune 500*. Research suggests that gender (and racial) biases operate at *all* levels of an organization, but may be intensified at the top. In their study of the glass ceiling in eleven European Union countries, Arulampalam, Booth, and Bryan (2007) found that the gender wage gap was higher at the top of the earnings distribution than the middle for both public and private sector workers in most countries.

Women's representation on corporate boards of directors offers another way to examine their access to the top of the managerial hierarchy. Boards of directors play a powerful role in corporate governance. Through their influence on business, members can also be influential in society more generally. Women are a small minority on corporate boards, averaging 15 percent or less in North America and Europe. Terjesen and Singh (2008) found that societal variation in women's representation on boards is related to women's status in the workplace. Women were more likely to serve on corporate boards in countries with smaller gender pay gaps and higher percentages of women in senior management. Countries in which women's political representation was more recent tended to have higher percentages of women on corporate boards than those with longer traditions of women in politics. This finding, which ran counter to the authors' expectations, may reflect a historical tendency for government to be more accessible to women than business.

Who's the boss? Gender and authority   As discussed in the previous section, jobs involving the exercise of authority are often gender-typed as masculine. They are seen as more appropriate for men than women, and men are seen as more qualified to perform the job requirements. This can be clearly seen in the research on leadership, which is an important characteristic expected of managers. Studies of leadership behavior suggest that male and female leaders behave about the same: When found, differences are small, and women and men in leadership positions are rated as equally effective (Heilman 2001; Powell and Graves 1999). Despite these findings, research on people's perceptions of leadership qualities find that most (especially men) view leadership positions as requiring more stereotypically male than female qualities.

When asked if they would rather work for a woman or a man, surveys regularly find a preference for a male boss. Powell and Graves (2003) report that when Gallup asked this question to people in over 22 countries, they found that the preference for a male boss was held worldwide. Although the preference for a male boss seems to have decreased over time, roughly 60 percent of each gender would rather work for a man. Moreover, Powell and Graves (2003, p. 136) note that: "No matter what the comparison, male managers still associate men more than women with the managerial role. They also feel that women managers, when compared to men managers and successful middle managers, are more bitter, quarrelsome, jealous, and obsessed with the need for power and achievement."

Further, according to these researchers, both men and women in Great Britain, Germany, France, and China share these views; only U.S. women associate the managerial role with both genders. One consequence of these deeply held stereotypes is that "women who aspire to management in most societies contend with common stereotypes of their being unfit for the role" (Powell 1999, p. 335).

These perceptions of women in leadership can help to explain the glass ceiling phenomena. In Chapter 3, we discussed status characteristics theory and the processes through which sex categories become the basis for assessments of competence, often disadvantaging women. The effects of these disadvantages on women's ability to reach the next level are cumulative, making each step up the hierarchy more and more difficult (Valian 1998).

Despite these stereotypes and in contrast to the perceptions of subordinate women, increases in the representation of women in management may have positive consequences for subordinate women and for reducing other organizational dynamics that perpetuate gender inequality. For example, Huffman, Cohen, and

Pearlman (2010) found that nonmanagerial women employed in private-sector U.S. workplace were less gender segregated in workplaces with a higher percentage of female managers. They note that increased numbers of women managers can have other positive consequences for organizations as well, including an opportunity to decrease the salience of gender as a status characteristic.

Gender and the informal relations of work   Research on the glass ceiling focuses on women's exclusion from the formal exercise of authority on the job. Gender is also embedded in the informal relations of the workplace. This issue has long been of interest to sociologists of work. Indeed, in a 1949 article on restaurants, William Foote Whyte noted how gender entered into workers' relations with one another on the job and affected the flow of work. Whyte speculated that because most men grow up expecting to be in positions of authority over women, they are uncomfortable when their work requires them to receive orders from women. He identified several strategies male "countermen" (i.e., cooks) used to avoid having to take an order directly from a female waitress.

Almost 30 years after Whyte wrote about gendered interactions between cooks and waitresses, Kanter (1977) examined the gender dynamics inherent in the boss–secretary relationship. She described how women in secretarial positions were expected to function as "office wives." What Kanter (1977, p. 89) referred to as "the marriage metaphor" provided an apt description of the boss–secretary relationship, which included such elements as "greater privileges and less work for women attached to high-status men"; "expectations of personal service, including office 'housework'"; and "an emotional division of labor in which the woman plays the emotional role and the man the providing role."

More recent studies show that gender continues to be embedded in the informal relations between women and men at work. In her research on law firms, for example, Pierce (1995) explored the relations between lawyers (mostly male) and paralegals, a predominantly female occupation. Although the lawyers and paralegals she studied engaged in some of the same kinds of tasks (e.g., legal research and writing) and were very interdependent in many respects, the relations between these positions were highly gendered. As Pierce (1995, p. 86) states: "Structurally, paralegal positions are specifically designed for women to support high-status men, and the content of paralegal work is consistent with our cultural conceptions of appropriate behavior for traditional wives and mothers." Paralegals thus are expected to defer to and serve lawyers, who in turn, rely on paralegals to perform this caretaking labor.

On a broader level, the gender division of labor described above parallels the way relations between women and men are often characterized in other spheres of life, outside the workplace. This division of labor, in many ways, reflects the "doctrine of separate spheres" (Chapter 4), in which men are expected to engage in productive labor, while women are to provide care and support. This relationship is central to the pattern of horizontal segregation described earlier, in which women are assumed to excel in nurturing and support roles and men in more instrumental tasks.

The parallels between gender relations outside and inside the workplace led Nieva and Gutek (1981) to propose the concept of "sex role spillover" as a means to explain the gender typing of work relations. "**Spillover**" is the process whereby gender expectations for behavior emerging outside the workplace creep over into work relations. Spillover thus provides another kind of explanation for gender typing.

Spillover has also been used to account for **sexual harassment** (Welsh 1999; Gutek and Morasch 1982). As a legal matter, sexual harassment is a form of sex discrimination, defined in terms of two types of behavior: Quid pro quo harassment involves using sexual threats as a condition of employment or as a basis for a job decision (e.g., a promotion); hostile environment harassment refers to behaviors that create a hostile or offensive work environment, thus interfering with a person's ability to perform his or her job (Welsh 1999). While both women and men can be victims of sexual harassment, research suggests that women are far more likely to experience this than men (Padavic and Reskin 2002).

The concept of spillover links sexual harassment to the gendered organization of work. For example, work settings containing highly feminized jobs that require workers to provide care and support to male superiors (e.g., secretaries and male bosses) create the conditions for quid pro quo harassment. Harassment may also be engendered by other kinds of highly feminized work situations, where informal work norms require that women be physically appealing to men or where highly sexualized interaction is tolerated or encouraged. For example, consider this description of a catering manager's expectations of her female assistants:

> She "expected" women workers to be able to cope with sexual behavior and attention from men customers as "part of the job." She said that if "the women catering assistants complain, or say things like they can't cope, I tell them it happens all the time and not to worry about it … it's part of the job … if they can't handle it then they're not up to working here." (Williams, Giuffre, and Dellinger 1999, p. 77)

The manager was not necessarily condoning the sexual harassment of her workers, but she certainly expected them to tolerate behaviors that could have been viewed in this way.

At the other extreme, highly masculinized work settings containing few women may create the conditions for sexual harassment as well. By emphasizing women's status as women rather than as workers, some men may use sexual harassment as a tool to put women "in their place." A common element of all of these instances is that women's "femaleness" takes precedence over their other characteristics. Sexual harassment thus can be understood as at least partly a function of the gendered organization of work and the norms that surround it.

The Gender Pay Gap

An important component of vertical segregation in the workplace involves the distribution of salaries and rewards, and the relative values attached to different kinds of work. Societies placing a higher value on males than females carry over this assessment into other institutions. Activities performed by women tend to be viewed as worth less than those performed by men. In the workplace, the relative worth of activities can be assessed economically – in the form of wages – and symbolically – in the form of status and prestige. On both counts, men and masculine activities are more highly valued than women and feminine activities.

An overview of the gender pay gap

Women earn less than men. In the United States, this has been true ever since the country began keeping track of the relative earnings of women and men. Moreover, this wage disparity persists "regardless of how you define earnings (e.g., annual vs. weekly, mean vs. median), in all race/ethnic groups, across educational categories, over the lifecycle, within detailed occupational categories, and across cultures" (Roos and Gatta 1999, p. 95). The **gender pay gap** is most often expressed as a ratio of women's earnings to men's earnings. Typically, this ratio is measured in terms of the median earnings of women and men who work full-time, year-round. In 2009, the gender pay gap in the U.S. was 80.2, meaning that the average woman employed full-time, year-round earned roughly twenty percent less than that earned by average full-time, year-round employed man (Institute for Women's Policy Research, March 2010).

Women in the United States earn less than men in almost every occupation, including those containing high percentages of women. Budig (2002) shows that, even with comparable qualifications, men earn more than women within occupations. Men's advantage with respect to both wages and wage growth is roughly uniform across occupations, regardless of the occupation's sex composition (Budig 2002).

Figure 6.3 shows that the gender wage gap in the U.S. has fluctuated somewhat over time but has declined since 1979. These declines primarily reflect a growth in women's "real" (i.e., adjusted for inflation) earnings relative to men's earnings. Men's real earnings have

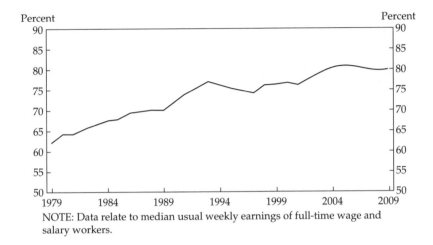

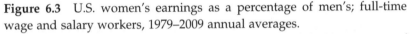

Figure 6.3 U.S. women's earnings as a percentage of men's; full-time wage and salary workers, 1979–2009 annual averages.
Source: Highlights of Women's Earnings in 2009, U.S. Department of Labor, U.S. Bureau of Labor Statistics.

been generally flat since the 1980s, while women's earnings have increased. This is the result of several factors, many of which were discussed in Chapter 5, including a shift away from male-dominated manufacturing jobs to service occupations and increases in women's levels of education. The increase in U.S. women's earning power relative to men can be seen in the increasing numbers of households in which women earn more than their husbands. In 2006, as Figure 6.4 shows, roughly one in four wives earned more than their husbands, an increase of almost ten percentage points from 1987.

The gender wage gap varies with race and ethnicity. Men earn more than women in all racial-ethnic groups. In 2009, however, the gender wage gap was greatest among whites (79 percent) and Asians (82 percent). In contrast, Hispanic women earned 90 percent as much as Hispanic men, while African-American women's earnings were 94 percent as high as African-American men's earnings (U.S. Department of Labor 2010).

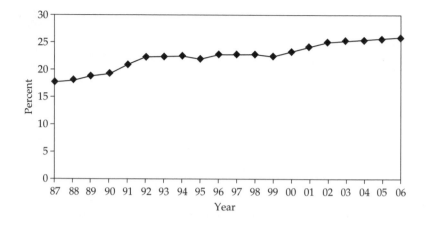

Figure 6.4 Percentage of U.S. wives earning more than their husbands (families where both have earnings), 1987–2006.
Source: TED: The Editor's Desk. U.S. Bureau of Labor Statistics (http:// data.bls.gov/cgi-bin/print.pl/opub/ted/2009/jan/wk1/art05.htm).

The earnings of younger women are closer to the earnings of younger men than is the case among older workers. In 2009, for instance, women between the ages of 25 and 34 (employed full-time, year-round) earned 89 percent of what men in this age group earned, while the gender gap in pay between women and men 35 years or older was 75 percent. These differences stem in part from the fact that younger workers are beginning their careers in a more gender-equal world than the one in which older workers began theirs. In addition, these variations in the gender wage gap in part reflect lifecycle differences in women's and men's careers. Women's and men's earnings may be more similar at the beginning of their careers than later in adulthood after other life events –such as marriage and childbearing – have taken place. Together, these explanations imply that, while gender-based wage discrimination may have decreased, women's and men's earnings continue to be differentially affected by changes over the life course.

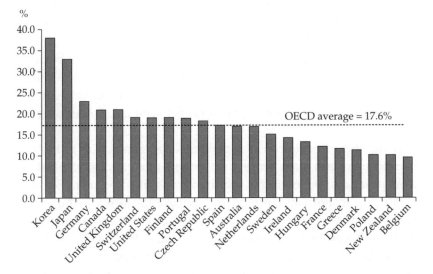

Figure 6.5 Percentage gap between median men's and women's wages for full-time workers by country.
Source: Organization for Economic Cooperation and Development.

Women earn less than men in virtually all countries, but the size of the gender wage gap varies (Figure 6.5). According to the Organization for Economic Cooperation and the Development (OECD), the average wage gap between women and men for OECD countries was 17.6 percent in 2006. (Women earned about 82 percent of what men earned.) Korea and Japan had the largest gender pay gaps, while this gap was smallest in Belgium.

Explaining the Gender Pay Gap

Why do women earn less than men? There is not a simple answer to this question. Part of this gap can be explained by women's and men's different work patterns. For example, in the United States, men are more likely than women to work full-time, year-round. The total number of hours men work in a given year averages

217

more than the total number of hours worked by women. Because wages are influenced by hours worked, these differences in average work hours contribute to women's lower average earnings. However, as noted earlier, women who work full-time, year-round earn only 80 percent of what men earn in these circumstances. This suggests that differences in the work patterns of women and men are only part of the explanation for women's lower average earnings.

A significant portion of the gender wage gap is due to the fact that women and men work in different jobs, and jobs filled by women tend to be lower paying than those filled by men. Sex segregation – in both its vertical and horizontal forms – thus is an important contributor to the gender pay gap. To understand why, we must consider the factors that determine the "value" of a particular job. In general, jobs requiring more investment by workers (e.g., college education, technical training, etc.) pay more than other jobs; higher pay for these jobs thus is a means to compensate workers for their investment. Employers may also consider other factors when setting wages, such as the relative supply of workers available at a given skill level.

Job evaluation and the worth of jobs

Although these factors are important, sociologists argue that the processes through which employers determine a job's worth reflect social as well as economic considerations. This can be seen when we consider studies of job evaluation. **Job evaluation** is a method used by employers to determine how pay is assigned to jobs and to justify (or critique) relative pay rates. Jobs can be evaluated according to several different methods, ranging from a simple ranking of "payworthiness" to more sophisticated systems that assign wages based on a point system (England 1992). All of these methods are based on the belief that it is possible to objectively rank jobs according to their worth to an employer. This ranking may be done by employers or their managers, by outside consulting firms, or by unions and worker representatives.

Although job evaluation is a technique long used by employers, it has also been used to identify and correct a form of gender bias in wage setting called "**valuative discrimination**" (Petersen and Saporta 2004, p. 853). This concept refers to the process whereby "female-dominated occupations are paid lower wages than male-dominated ones, although skill requirements and other wage-relevant factors are the same" (Petersen and Saporta 2004, p. 853). For example, a job evaluation study conducted by an outside consulting firm for a group of public employees in the United States found that predominantly female jobs were systematically paid less than male jobs, even when they received the same number of evaluation points (England 1992).

Although job evaluation has been used extensively to identify and correct valuative discrimination, these methods may contain their own sources of gender bias (Acker 1987; England 1992). One potential source of such bias occurs when predominantly female jobs are given fewer points than they merit, while predominantly male jobs are given a boost in ranking. An example cited by England (1992, p. 199) illustrates the point: "attendants at dog pounds and parking lots (usually men) were rated more highly than nursery school teachers, and zookeepers more highly than day care workers" (see also Steinberg and Haignere 1987). In this instance, the sex composition of the job likely influenced its ranking by evaluators.

That jobs filled with women receive lower average wages than comparable jobs filled by men has become a well-established research finding (Padavic and Reskin 2002; Roos and Gatta 1999; Tomaskovic-Devey 1993). Moreover, both women *and* men suffer wage penalties when they work in predominantly female jobs, and the wages of both genders benefit from employment in jobs held predominantly by men (Tomaskovic-Devey 1993). As this discussion makes clear, gender bias may enter into wage-setting through numerous subtle and unintended ways. Even the practice of job evaluation – intended to identify and correct sources of gender bias – may inadvertently contribute to the devaluing of predominantly female jobs.

219

Welfare regimes, family policies, and the gender pay gap

Much of our discussion of sex segregation and the gender pay gap has focused on the United States, a country that offers few supports for mothers and fathers in the workplace. In contrast, social-democratic regimes tend to offer policies that support mothers' employment and encourage women's labor force participation overall (e.g., extended maternity leaves). Women generally have more responsibility than men for housework and childcare, so these efforts do likely help reduce mothers' work–family conflict. Ironically, however, studies suggest that the gender pay gap is larger in countries with policies designed to attract mothers to the labor market.

In their study of this issue, Mandel and Semyonov (2005) found that all women – not just mothers – suffer economically in countries with policies focused primarily on mothers. Although women in these countries participate in the labor force at high rates, they are more likely to be hired into lower paying, predominantly female jobs, with fewer opportunities for advancement. Employers view all women as "potential" mothers and exclude them from jobs with the most earning potential and opportunities. Under these circumstances, Mandel and Semyonov (2005, p. 965) suggest that: "In the absence of radical changes in gender roles within the family, the aim of reducing labor market equality between men and women may best be served by minimizing the costs to women associated with family-friendly policies while at the same time restructuring the organization of work to reduce the time burden on both genders."

Chapter Summary

Gender shapes the occupational structure and the workplace. Men and women work in different jobs, and sex segregation remains a feature of work in all industrial economies. Sex segregation can be explained by the actions of workers, as well as by processes that occur inside the workplace. Although workers' choices are important, choices about work are shaped by the opportunity structure of the workplace itself.

Gender enters the workplace not only through sex segregation, but through the process of gender typing. Jobs, occupations, work roles, and work relations are laden with gender meanings. In this way, specific work roles, jobs, and occupations come to be seen as more appropriate for one gender than another. Gender typing results from the social processes through which meaning is collectively generated and reinforced. It is external to individuals and imposes itself on them by establishing certain work roles, jobs, and occupations as appropriate for one sex and off-limits to another. It establishes the "way things are" or a set of conventional understandings of who should engage in what type of work. Gender typing thus represents an important aspect of work as a gendered institution.

In addition to shaping the meanings attached to jobs, gender shapes the relative values attached to different kinds of work. The relative worth of jobs can be assessed economically – in the form of wages – and symbolically – in the form of status and prestige. On both counts, gender typing privileges men and masculine activities and penalizes women and feminine activities. Women earn less than men in all industrial societies, though the gender pay gap has diminished over time. Jobs held by women are generally paid less than those held by men. Societies that place a higher value on males than females thus carry over this assessment into other institutions. The gendered aspects of work described in this chapter are often unintended, taken-for-granted, and operate so subtly that they rarely are scrutinized. In this respect, gender is a highly institutionalized feature of the modern workplace.

Further Reading

Charles, Maria, and Grusky, David B. 2004. *Occupational Ghettos: The Worldwide Segregation of Women and Men*. Stanford: Stanford University Press.

Hochschild, Arlie Russell. 1983. *The Managed Heart: The Commercialization of Human Feeling*. Berkeley: University of California.

Williams, Christine. 1995. *Still a Man's World*. Berkeley: University of California.

Key Terms

Sex segregation
Index of dissimilarity
Vertical/horizontal segregation
Allocative discrimination
Statistical discrimination
Internal labor market
Gender-typed job
Emotional labor
Glass ceiling
Spillover
Sexual harassment
Gender pay gap
Job evaluation
Valuative discrimination

Critical Thinking Questions

1   How do the choices of women and men help maintain sex segregation? How are workers' choices affected by the opportunity structure of employment?
2   Policies that support mothers' employment may exacerbate the pay gap between women and men. Why? What policies might help reduce this gap?
3   Why do men *and* women prefer to work for a male boss? How might this contribute to the glass ceiling?

Part III

Epilogue

Chapter 7

Deconstructing Gender Differences and Inequalities

Chapter Objectives

- Review the book's major themes.
- Explain the processes of institutionalization and legitimation as they relate to gender inequality.
- Examine how the ideologies of deference and paternalism have helped to justify gender inequality.
- Explore what is meant by a "degendered" society and consider the prospects for achieving this.

"The future of gender differences is intimately tied to the future of gender inequality" (Kimmel 2000, p. 264)

This book was premised on the position that gender matters. Gender is a multilevel system of social practices that produces distinctions between women and men, and organizes inequality on the basis of

The Sociology of Gender: An Introduction to Theory and Research, Second Edition. Amy S. Wharton.
© 2012 John Wiley & Sons Ltd. Published 2012 by John Wiley & Sons Ltd.

those distinctions. It is a powerful principle of social life that is visible throughout the social world. In this edition, I have used a more expansive understanding of the social world than in the earlier version where my focus was almost exclusively on the United States. I hope readers will agree that providing a cross-national look at gender provides for a richer understanding of its expression and effects on social life. With that focus in mind, I have highlighted three primary levels on which gender operates:

- First, gender is produced at the individual level. Though scholars disagree about the exact processes through which this occurs and the durability of the distinctions that are created, they acknowledge that people are gendered beings.
- Second, gender distinctions and inequalities are produced through social relations and interaction. In this view, gender can best be observed when features of the social context are taken into account.
- Third, gender is produced through organizational arrangements and institutions. To understand gender from this vantage point requires attention to social structure and the policies and practices that sustain it.

In Part I, I discussed these three approaches, beginning with the social practices that produce the gendered person (Chapter 2). In Chapter 3, the focus shifted to interactional and institutional approaches. In Part II, I examined work and family as gendered institutions. Chapter 4 focused on the "big picture," examining these institutions as they have evolved historically, as well as looking at the composition and social organization of these institutions today. Chapters 5 and 6 moved "inside" families and workplaces, exploring how both are structured by gender distinctions and inequalities. In each of these chapters I have discussed the contributions of cross-national perspectives on gender.

In these final pages, I want to reiterate the book's goals and offer some thoughts about the *de*construction of the gender system. My primary goal in writing this book was to provide readers with theoretical and conceptual tools that can help them make sense of gender as it operates in social life. This is a tall order because gender is everywhere and because gender scholars have provided many vantage points from which to examine this issue. I have stressed tools and frameworks rather than specific topic areas, and I have not tried to describe all the ways that gender matters in social life. That would be a very long book indeed. Instead, my goal was more circumscribed: I aimed to show how sociologists have conceptualized gender, focusing particular attention on the different ways they have gone about this task and the different emphases they have placed on various aspects of social life. While the views presented here do not necessarily agree on "where the action is" as far as gender is concerned, together they reinforce the notion that gender is a multilevel system.

With these conceptual tools in hand, the book focused on two important social institutions: family and work. The list could have been expanded to include health, religion, crime, sports, and more, and I urge readers to examine gender in these and other areas of life. Ideally, the conceptual tools acquired here can be used to analyze any area of the gendered world. Can these tools also be used to deconstruct gender and to dismantle gender hierarchies and distinctions? This is the last issue we will explore.

Gender Distinctions and Gender Inequalities

As we have seen, the gender system involves two sorts of processes – the creation of distinctions *and* inequalities based on these distinctions. The previous chapters have described both processes. Regarding gender distinctions, for example, we have seen how forces operating at the individual, interactional, and institutional levels produce a gender-differentiated world. For example, at the individual level, "sex difference" approaches aim to systematically document differences between women and men. For some researchers in this tradition, at least a few of these differences are presumed to have biological or genetic origins. Gender distinctions are also produced through social interaction, as the "doing gender" and status characteristics approaches discussed in Chapter 3 explain. The structures and practices of institutions play a role in the production of gender distinctions as well.

Gender distinctions are inextricably linked to gender inequality. This link is evident at all levels of the social world and can be seen in the uneven patterns of change that have occurred in the gender system during the past half-century. In simplest terms, this link between differentiation and inequality can be seen in the greater societal value and worth attached to maleness *and* to all things masculine, relative to femaleness and things deemed feminine. At the individual level, "traits" and characteristics associated with men and masculinity are accorded more social value than those associated with women and femininity. From an interactionist perspective, as we saw in Chapter 3, the production of difference simultaneously involves the creation of gender hierarchies. Even at the level of organizations and institutions, worth, status, and resources are differentially assigned on the basis of gender. Hence, regardless of the vantage point from which gender distinctions are examined, they provide the underpinnings for inequality.

Inequality and difference are tightly linked, but they are not the same process. Gender inequalities have become less pronounced over time in many respects. There has been a rise in egalitarian beliefs about gender, and gaps between women and men have diminished in areas such as educational attainment, participation in the paid labor force, the household division of labor and more. Despite these changes, however, gender differentiation remains and has intensified in some respects. Disentangling the processes that reduce inequality in some areas while reproducing differentiation in others will be key to making sense of gender in the twenty-first century.

While most gender scholarship focuses on a single level of analysis, it is also important to understand that gender distinctions and inequalities are produced and reproduced at all levels of the social world. Because it is a multilevel system, the gender order has been particularly resistant to change. Gender distinctions and inequalities produced at one level of the social world are often reinforced by social processes operating at other levels.

In order to assess the possibilities for dismantling – or at least systematically challenging – the gender order, we must first look more carefully at how gender is reproduced. I focus on the reproduction of gender *inequality,* but keep in mind that gender distinctions and gender inequalities are interconnected.

The Reproduction of Gender Inequality

Gender inequality is reproduced through two interrelated processes: institutionalization and legitimation. As we explore these processes, we will consider gender inequality in comparison to other kinds of unequal social relations. This comparison helps shed light on why gender inequality has been so difficult to dislodge, and it reveals some of the unique features of gender relations relative to other forms of inequality.

Institutionalizing gender inequality

In Chapter 3, I introduced the concept of gendered institutions. Recall that institutions are comprised of social structures and practices, and they include symbols and beliefs (Friedland and Alford 1991). They are features of social life that seem so regular, so ongoing, and so permanent that they are often accepted as "the way things are." Now, I want to extend this idea by thinking about institutionalization as a *process* that could affect virtually any social relationship or area of social life.

Institutionalization refers to the processes through which social relationships take on the qualities of an institution. From this perspective, we can see that some social relationships are more institutionalized than others. Marriage is an example of a highly institutionalized social relationship (though some would argue that this is less true today than in the past). Though marriage is sometimes referred to as just "a piece of paper" or as strictly a private matter, it is much more powerful than that. Almost everyone expects to marry, and there are widely shared beliefs about the meaning and significance of this social arrangement. In addition, marriage is a legal contract that is recognized by many other important institutions, such as employers, religion, and the government.

Relationships that are highly institutionalized seem almost to reproduce themselves (Berger and Luckmann 1967). They persist without conscious intervention and effort. This means that it is much more difficult to alter something that is highly institutionalized than it is to perpetuate it. As a result, highly institutionalized arrangements do not require coercion to sustain them, making participation appear voluntary and easily justifiable. We can again use the example of marriage to illustrate these qualities: Most people get married and, if their marriage fails, they are likely to get married again. While people may have to justify their choice of a particular marriage partner, adults rarely find themselves having to explain why they are married. *Never married* adults, however, may face questions about their status and have to account for their circumstances.

Social inequalities can also be institutionalized to a greater or lesser degree. Social inequalities are relationships between groups. Slavery, for example, was a highly institutionalized form of inequality in the United States, enshrined in law and enforced by the state. While slavery has disappeared, this has not meant the end of institutionalized inequalities. Though very different from slavery, gender inequality, along with inequalities based on social class and race, are also highly institutionalized. They are long-term, entrenched, and "durable" (Tilly 1999). They are embedded in the structures of and practices of organizations, including workplaces, families, schools, and so on.

Long-term, institutionalized inequalities – like those based on gender, race, and social class – are significantly different from other kinds of unequal social relations in the ways they are experienced and understood (Jackman 1994). These differences affect members of both the dominant and subordinate groups. Most important, institutionalized inequalities are invisible and "depersonalized" to some extent: "When a relationship [of inequality] is regularized and institutionalized, it is simply a case of 'c'est la vie'" (Jackman 1994, p. 8). This may be true both for the subordinate group and for those who benefit from the inequality. Dominant group members not only may fail to acknowledge that inequality exists, but are also unlikely to feel personally responsible or guilty. Subordinate group members may also experience institutionalized inequalities as "just the way things are."

Institutionalized inequalities thus are much more likely to endure than those that are not so stable and routine. This long-term stability provides dominant groups with a strong vested interest in maintaining unequal arrangements. In addition, it has the effect of "stacking the deck" in such a way that subordinate groups feel relatively powerless to challenge their position. The dominant group's vested interest in perpetuating inequality, together with the subordinate group's lack of alternatives, shape the ways both groups make sense of their relationship.

Making sense of gender inequality

Inequalities of all kinds persist in part because people view them (and the processes that generate unequal outcomes) as "legitimate." **Legitimation** refers to the processes through which inequalities are justified – that is, they are understood in ways that make them fair and reasonable. Inequalities may be taken for granted, seen as acceptable, embraced as desirable, or perhaps merely tolerated. They may be invisible or unrecognized. For example, it is well documented that a small minority owns most of the wealth generated in the United States and that this distribution has grown more unequal in recent years (Keister and Moller 2000). Nevertheless, because most people in the United States believe that everyone – including themselves – has the opportunity to get ahead and achieve success, they do not view wealth inequality as unfair or unacceptable (Hochschild 1995).

Americans' views about the availability of economic opportunity and the prospects for achieving success through hard work are part of a powerful ideology commonly understood as "the American

Dream." Although not every group in society equally embraces all tenets of this dream, studies show that all segments of society – including the most poor and vulnerable – believe in it to some degree (Hochschild 1995; Kluegel and Smith 1986). Belief in the American Dream thus helps to legitimate social inequality; wealth disparities are seen as the outcome of a system that provides equal opportunities for all to succeed.

The American Dream is an example of an ideology. **Ideology** refers to a dominant, widely shared worldview that reflects people's understanding of the world around them. Ideologies may contain elements of truth or be entirely false. Their role in reproducing inequality depends less on whether they are true and more on how strongly they are embraced. For example, while studies suggest that race shapes people's ability to amass wealth (Keister and Moller 2000), most whites believe that the American Dream is equally open to everyone. This belief helps explain why whites have been generally unenthusiastic supporters of social policies designed to reduce racial barriers in public life (Hochschild 1995; Kluegel and Smith 1986).

Gender essentialism (see Chapter 3) is another example of an ideology. Central to this view is a belief that women and men are "fundamentally" or "inherently" different from one another. This ideology has undoubtedly weakened over time. However, Charles and Bradley (2009) suggest that gender essentialism remains powerful in industrial societies due to its fit with Western cultural beliefs in individualism and self-expression. Few in these societies endorse the belief that men are innately superior to women. Instead, gender inequalities in men's and women's achievements are likely to be explained in terms of women's and men's "choices" and enduring differences in their worldviews and sense of self.

Gender essentialism is an example of a particular ideology that helps to justify inequalities between women and men. We can better understand how this ideology works if we look carefully at what makes it persuasive to both women and men. Institutionalized, long-term relations of inequality, such as those based on gender, give dominant groups a strong, vested interest in maintaining these arrangements. Doing so requires that they construct ideologies that are benign and flattering towards the subordinate group, rather than hostile and antagonistic. The dominant group must offer the subordinate group an interpretation of their relationship that obscures unequal arrangements. The subordinate group must find this ideology persuasive if the dominant group is to protect its interests.

What strategies of persuasion work best to legitimate gender inequality? In her book, *The Velvet Glove*, Jackman (1994) argues that gender inequality is reproduced through the twin ideologies of paternalism and deference. **Paternalism** referred originally to a traditional father–child relationship, whereby the father cared for and exercised control over his children. In this view, fathers were assumed to love their children, understand their needs, and act in their best interests. Children were seen as less capable and competent than adults and thus were expected to defer to their father's authority and guidance. As Jackman (1994, p. 10) notes, "No arrangement could be more desirable for a group that dominates another." Paternalism is a powerful ideology because it combines positive feelings for the subordinate group with the exercise of social control. **Deference** implies that these positive feelings are reciprocated by the subordinate group, who see no reason to challenge the dominant group's control over them.

When applied to gender relations, paternalism is an ideology that views women as needing the care, protection, and guidance of men (Rothman 2002). Deference implies women's acceptance of this relationship. Insofar as gender relations are interpreted through the lenses of paternalism on the part of men and deference on the part of women, inequalities will be obscured. Not all men or women embrace these ideologies. Nevertheless, Jackman's (1994) research on gender-related beliefs reveals that a majority of women and men adhere to at least some aspects of these belief systems.

In general, women and men do not view each other as adversaries with conflicting interests. Jackman finds instead an "amicable consensus" in how members of both groups assess the gender typing of jobs and the traditional gender division of labor in the home (Jackman 1994, p. 202). For example, roughly two-thirds of her male and female survey respondents saw these arrangements as either positive for the collective, or as benign – neither benefiting nor disadvantaging either group. In addition, her research showed agreement between women and men on each gender's role responsibilities and their support for gender-related social policies. More generally, she found that roughly two-thirds of each gender views the other gender in positive emotional terms; they have warm feelings about the other gender and feel close to them (see also Kluegel and Smith 1986).

Women and men, however, do see each other as *different* in important ways. Both men and women believe that each gender has its own distinctive personality traits. In fact, Jackman (1994) found that only about 12 percent of women and men believe that there are *no* important gender differences. Moreover, women and men generally agree with one another in how they assign these traits; for example, majorities of both genders view women as more talkative and emotional than men. Although both genders believe important differences exist, however, the attributes on which women and men are believed to differ are generally viewed in neutral terms. Women and men generally do not assign positive values to their own group's traits and negative values to those of the other group. Just as in the title of the popular book, *Men are from Mars and Women are from Venus*, women and men tend to regard one another as fundamentally different, but not unequal or differentially valued.

Together, this constellation of beliefs is broadly consistent with the combined ideologies of paternalism and deference: Women and men regard each other positively, agree that each gender has uniquely defined traits and roles, and express relative support for these arrangements. In Jackman's (1994, p. 374) words, "Women are warmly congratulated for their distinctiveness in personal traits that are appropriate to the role they have been assigned."

To understand the significance of these ideologies, compare the attitudes towards one another of whites and blacks in American society and respondents from different social classes. While there is little outright hostility, paternalism and deference are not significant features of race or social class relations. Blacks and whites in the

United States feel more estrangement than warmth towards one another, and they disagree over the desirability of government support for race-related social policies (Jackman 1994; Hochschild 1995). More important, whites tend to attribute more positive personal qualities to their own group than to blacks, while blacks reject these labels. These views are in marked contrast to gender relations, which are characterized by consensus among women and men regarding the extent and neutral character of gender differences. The expressions of conflict and division that permeate whites' and blacks' perceptions are less clearly drawn in the case of beliefs about social classes. Even here, however, there is much less paternalism and deference than in people's beliefs about gender.

Jackman suggests that the proximity and frequency of contact between the genders, as compared to black–white contact and contact between members of different social classes, account for these different patterns of beliefs. Women's and men's lives are often bound together in ways that other unequal groups are not. This fact plays a key role in explaining how gender inequality has been legitimated and why it has not provoked divisiveness and hostility among most women and men – especially when compared to inequalities based on race or social class.

Heterosexual women and men share households, marry, and may have children together. The vast majority of people – regardless of their marital status or sexual orientation – have kinship ties to and perhaps even children of the other gender. This proximity, even intimacy, between the genders in households and family life is much less likely to be present between members of other unequal groups. In the United States, for example, racial segregation in neighborhoods and schools remains high (Massey and Denton 1993; Orfield 2001). While social class divisions may exist within families and households, families and households are much less likely to include members of widely divergent social classes – the very rich and the poor – than members of social classes who are closer in social space (e.g., the middle and working class).

Another angle from which to explore these issues is to examine the interrelations of gender and race, as they together shape people's views of gender inequality. In general, studies suggest that African-Americans in the U.S. are more likely than whites to believe that gender inequality exists, and they are more likely than whites to explain this inequality in terms of social rather than biological factors (Kane 2000). African-Americans are also more likely than whites to support social policies and collective action to reduce gender inequality. These patterns hold when analyses are confined only to women. African-American women are more critical of women's place in society than white women and are more supportive of social policies designed to improve women's status (Kane 2000).

Because of their experiences with racism, African-Americans may be more aware of social inequalities of all kinds than whites. In addition, African-Americans may be more predisposed than whites to support collective action and government intervention to reduce social inequality (Kane 2000). This suggests that African-Americans of both genders may be less influenced by the ideologies of paternalism and deference than white women and men.

Institutions and ideologies

Gender inequality is reproduced through the processes of institutionalization and legitimation. As gender inequality becomes institutionalized, it is built into social structures and the everyday routines that sustain them. One consequence of institutionalization is that gender inequality is depersonalized. This depersonalization extends to both women and men. Gender inequality is legitimated through ideological accounts that emphasize women's and men's differences, but downplay the ways in which those differences generate inequalities. Together, these processes make it difficult to reduce gender inequality.

Challenging Gender Inequality

By focusing on the processes of institutionalization and legitimation, we have highlighted the reproduction of gender inequality.

These issues are important because much of social life – not just in the realm of gender – is stable, ordered, and changes relatively slowly. Given this, we should not underestimate the difficulties associated with deconstructing gender and reducing gender inequality. At the same time, devoting too much time and energy to issues of reproduction may create the opposite problem: a tendency to downplay the possibilities for individuals and groups to make real change and to be unduly pessimistic about the prospects for gender equality.

Many sociologists have sought to understand how social change occurs within deeply institutionalized social processes. These efforts have produced two key insights that are worth remembering as we consider the possibilities for reducing gender inequality. First, even highly institutionalized social relationships are not immune to social change. In fact, social change is inevitable and ongoing, and this is especially true in an increasingly diverse, global world. Of course, most changes to highly institutionalized relationships are unplanned, reactive, and incremental. Moreover, there is nothing automatic about change being in the direction of greater equality. In addition to the ubiquity of social change, we should also understand that it is almost always uneven in its impacts and timing: All parts of the social world do not change at the same time or in the same way. This "unevenness" creates conflict, tension, and disruptions, which have often inspired more far-reaching and self-conscious attempts to alter institutionalized arrangements.

As a multilevel system, the gender order is particularly resistant to radical change or disruption. The social processes that create a world of two genders operate simultaneously at the individual, interactional, and institutional levels. It is difficult to imagine the full-scale dismantling of this system – at least in the short term. Far easier to imagine, however, are openings for smaller-scale, but still significant, challenges to the gender order. These sorts of challenges have already produced change in the direction of greater gender equality and make possible even greater changes to come.

While gender is produced at the individual, interactional, and institutional levels, each level may be somewhat differently impacted by social changes in the larger society. As previous chapters have shown, unevenness of change at these different levels produced significant changes in the gender order during the latter part of the twentieth century. Many men and women raised during the 1960s and 1970s expected to form families where men were primary breadwinners and women had responsibility for home and children. These expectations were reinforced through socialization and reflected in women's and men's gender identities. Changes at the institutional level in both work and family made these expectations unrealizable for many, however. Instead, women and men often found themselves creating lives quite different from those they had imagined (Gerson 1985). Women worked for pay, and men participated in caring for their children and were expected to shoulder at least some of the work of maintaining a household.

In this instance, gender identities at the individual level were at odds with changed institutional realities. Family and work were being reshaped much faster than socialization practices and the gender identities of individuals. This created disruption and conflict both for individuals and for relationships (Hochschild 1989), but it also helped create the foundation for more far-reaching changes in the gender order. This is because uneven social change is destabilizing. Change in one part of the gender order creates openings for changes at other levels. For example, socialization practices for the next generation adjusted to new realities, and the gender identities of young women and men became less anchored in the traditional dichotomy of the male breadwinner and female mother and wife. While gender equality in the family has not been achieved, women's and men's family lives are quite different today than three decades ago. Women have more bargaining power in relationships with men and men are expected to be more involved with family and children. These are real changes that have produced greater equality in the household division of labor and in women's opportunities in the paid workplace.

In the previous example of uneven social change, institutions took the lead, with individuals and interactions changing more slowly. Sometimes, however, individuals change first and create new kinds of relationships that ultimately pressure institutions to respond. Risman (1998) argues that gay and childless heterosexual couples are examples of intimate relationships that challenge gender at the interactional level. Participants in these relationships have urged institutions to change their policies and practices. For example, employers have been encouraged to offer domestic partner benefits to gay couples. Schools have been pressured to acknowledge students' parents, rather than considering only "mothers and fathers." These changes in institutions are not easily achieved; they require unified, sustained, collective action. But they are far from impossible.

As these examples show, social change may be uneven because it affects one level of the gender order sooner or more deeply than another. Another way to think about uneven social change in relation to gender, however, is to consider its differential impact on the lives of women and men. Kimmel (2000, p. 267) argues that we began the twenty-first century with a "half-finished revolution." The first half of this revolution involved significant changes in women's lives. "This century," he notes, "has witnessed an unprecedented upheaval in the status of women, possibly the most significant transformation in gender relations in world history." The changes he cites as evidence for this include women gaining the right to vote, as well as the rights to work in virtually all jobs, to be admitted on the same terms as men to all educational institutions and to join the military. On a smaller scale, we see evidence of this half-finished revolution in the dramatic changes that have occurred in women's work and family lives, relative to the lives of men. This half-finished revolution has not been easy for women, Kimmel suggests, but it has paved the way for the second half of the revolution – changes in men's lives.

All of these examples show evidence of uneven social change creating greater rather than less gender equality. Over the past half-century (in the West, at least), changes in the gender order have generally moved us in this direction. Most gender scholars agree that gender inequality at the individual, interactional, and institutional levels has been reduced across the industrialized world. As this book has shown, however, we are still a long way from a society where gender inequality has been eliminated. In order for that occur, many more far-reaching changes would be necessary. What would that society look like?

Making Gender Matter Less

Sociologists have generally written much more on the topic of inequality than equality. In part, this is because inequality is everywhere; equality has proven to be much more elusive. This is also true in the case of gender, where inequality is institutionalized and legitimated, and gender equality seems a long way in the future. While there is no road map to gender equality, however, sociologists do agree about some of the necessary stops along the way.

In Chapter 1, I argued that gender matters. The path to gender equality is to make gender matter less. This does not mean that we would live in a science fiction-like world where people were all the same. Instead, it means that gender would be significantly less influential as a factor shaping social life than it is today. In certain respects, this has already begun. For example, the social changes cited earlier as evidence for greater gender equality represent successful attempts to make gender matter less in the areas of voting, employment, and education.

A truly degendered society would extend these changes to all areas of social life. Degendering institutions means that their practices, policies, and structures would be indifferent to gender, organized according to other, yet to be discovered, principles. Degendering interaction means that interaction would not depend upon people being identifiable to one another as male or female. Degendering individuals means that gender would no longer be the primary organizer of people's traits, personalities, and identities. Sex categories would be sufficient acknowledgment of the biological distinctions between males and females; there would be no need or reason to make any more of these characteristics.

To more fully understand what this degendered world would look like, reconsider the material discussed in this book. Imagine how personalities and identities would form if gender played a lesser role in shaping what people could become and how they thought of themselves. Consider how social interaction might unfold were people less accountable to gender expectations. Finally, envision families and workplaces as places where gender did not structure the tasks people performed and determine the worth of those activities. For gender equality to be achieved, gender itself must matter less.

These arguments underscore a central theme of this book – the mutually reinforcing ties between gender distinctions and gender inequality. Gender distinctions are the raw material of gender inequality; eroding these distinctions thus is a necessary part of reducing inequality. Reductions in gender inequality, in turn, contribute to a lessening of gender distinctions. As Kimmel (2000) notes, the fact that women and men today are seen as more similar than different reflects not merely a change in people's understanding and perceptions, but rather is a direct consequence of greater gender equality than in the past.

In sum, the forces reproducing gender inequality are deeply entrenched, but this has not prevented some reductions in gender inequality and a lessening of the gender distinctions that support them. By exposing the workings of gender, this book has aimed to help readers analyze its impacts and contribute to its demise.

Chapter Summary

Gender is a powerful principle of social life. It is a multilevel system of social practices that produces distinctions between women and men, and organizes inequality on the basis of those distinctions. Gender operates at the individual, interactional, and institutional levels.

Gender is reproduced through the forces of institutionalization and legitimation. Inequalities based on gender, race, and social class are highly institutionalized. This makes them especially difficult to eliminate; they are taken for granted as "just the way things are." All inequalities must be legitimated; ideologies help provide this by supplying accounts that make inequality seem fair and/or reasonable. Gender inequalities are legitimated through the twin ideologies of paternalism and deference. These ideologies lead men and women to view each other as different in important ways, but they do not necessarily view the other group as an adversary. Gender differences are celebrated, while gender inequalities are downplayed.

Even institutionalized relationships can be changed. These changes are often prompted by changes occurring in the larger society that affect different parts of the gender order in different ways. Uneven social change helps to destabilize the gender system, thus creating the possibility for even more change.

The key to creating gender equality is to make gender a less influential factor in shaping social life than it is today. Reducing the importance of gender will contribute to a lessening of gender inequality. Reducing gender inequality will help reduce gender distinctions.

Further Reading

Deutsch, Francine M. 2007. "Undoing gender." *Gender & Society* 21: 106–27.

Jackman, Mary R. 1994. *The Velvet Glove: Paternalism and Conflict in Gender, Class, and Race Relations*. Berkeley: University of California Press.

Risman, Barbara J. 1998. *Gender Vertigo*. New Haven: Yale University Press.

Key Terms

Institutionalization
Legitimation
Ideology

Gender essentialism
Paternalism/deference

Critical Thinking Questions

1 What is the relationship between gender differences and gender inequality? Can women and men be different *and* equal?
2 What are other examples of deference and paternalism in everyday life?
3 Is a "degendered" world possible? Desirable?

References

Acker, J. 1987. "Sex bias in job evaluation: A comparable worth issue," in Christine Bose and Glenna Spitze (eds.), *Ingredients for Women's Employment Policy*. Albany, NY: SUNY Press.

Acker, J. 1992. "Gendered institutions." *Contemporary Sociology* 21: 565–569.

Alexander, G.M. and Hines, M. 1994. "Gender labels and play styles: Their relative contributions to children's selection of playmates." *Child Development* 65: 869–879.

Allard, M.D. and Janes, M. 2008. "Time use of working parents: A visual essay." *Monthly Labor Review* 131(6): 3–14.

Allmendinger, J. and Hackman, J.R. 1995. "The more, the better? A four-nation study of the inclusion of women in symphony orchestras." *Social Forces* 74: 423–460.

Angier, N. 1999. *Woman: An Intimate Geography*. New York: Houghton Mifflin.

Archer, J. 2006. "Cross-cultural differences in physical aggression between partners: A social-role analysis." *Personality and Social Psychology Review* 10(2): 133–153.

The Sociology of Gender: An Introduction to Theory and Research, Second Edition. Amy S. Wharton.
© 2012 John Wiley & Sons Ltd. Published 2012 by John Wiley & Sons Ltd.

References

Aries, E. 1996. *Men and Women in Interaction*. New York: Oxford University Press.

Arulampalam, W., Booth, A.L., and Bryan, M.L. 2007. "Is there a glass ceiling over Europe? Exploring the gender pay gap across the wage distribution." *Industrial and Labor Relations Review* 60(2): 163–186.

Bandura, A. and Walters, R.H. 1963. *Social Learning and Personality Development*. New York: Holt, Rinehart, and Winston.

Bardwell, J.R., Cochran, S.W. and Walker, S. 1986. "Relationship of parental education, race, and gender to sex role stereotyping in five-year-old kindergartners." *Sex Roles* 15: 275–281.

Barnett, R. and Baruch, G.K. 1987. "Social roles, gender, and psychological distress," in R.C. Barnett, L. Biener and G.K. Baruch (eds.), *Gender and Stress*. New York: Free Press, pp. 122–143.

Batalova, J.A. and Cohen, P.N. 2002. "Premarital cohabitation and housework: Couples in cross-national perspective." *Journal of Marriage and Family* 64: 743–755.

Baxter, J. 1997. "Gender equality and participation in housework: A cross-national perspective." *Journal of Comparative Family Studies* 28: 220–247.

Bellas, M.L. 1992. "The effects of marital status and wives' employment on the salaries of faculty men: The (house) wife bonus." *Gender & Society* 6: 609–622.

Bem, S.L. 1983. "Gender Schema Theory and Its implications for child development: Raising gender-aschematic children in a gender-schematic society." *Signs* 8: 598–616.

Bem, S.L. 1993. *The Lenses of Gender*. New Haven: Yale University Press.

Berger, P.L. and Luckmann, T. 1976. *The Social Construction of Reality*. New York: Anchor Books.

Berk, S.F. 1985. *The Gender Factory*. New York: Plenum.

Bernard, J. 1973a. "My four revolutions: An autobiographical history of the ASA." *American Journal of Society* 78: 773–791.

Bernard, J. 1973b. *The Future of Marriage*. New York: Bantam Books.

Bernard, J. 1992. "The Good-Provider role: Its rise and fall," in Michael S. Kimmel and Michael A. Messner (eds), *Men's Lives*. New York: Macmillan Publishing, pp. 203–221.

Bianchi, S.M. 2000. "Maternal employment and time with children: Dramatic change or surprising continuity?" *Demography* 37: 139–154.

246

Bianchi, S.M., Milkie, M.A., Sayer, L.C., and Robinson, J.P. 2000. "Is anyone doing the housework? Trends in the gender division of household labor." *Social Forces* 79: 191–228.

Bittman, M., England, P., Folbre, N., Sayer, L., and Matheson, G. 2003. "When does gender trump money? Bargaining and time in household work." *American Journal of Sociology* 109(1): 186–214.

Blackless, M., Charuvastra, A., Derryck, A., Fausto-Sterling, A., Lauzanne, K. and Lee, E. 2000. "How sexually dimorphic are we? Review and synthesis." *American Journal of Human Biology* 12: 151–166.

Blair, S.L. and Lichter, D.T. 1991. "Measuring the division of household labor: Gender segregation of housework among American couples." *Journal of Family Issues* 12: 91–113.

Blair-Loy, M. 1999. "Career patterns of executive women in finance: An optimal matching analysis." *American Journal of Sociology* 104: 1346–1397.

Blumstein, P. and Schwartz, P. 1983. *American Couples*. New York: William Morrow & Co.

Booth, A., Johnson, D.R., White, L.K., and Edwards, J.N. 1984. "Women, outside employment, and marital instability." *American Journal of Sociology* 90: 567–583.

Boserup, E. 1970. *Women's Role in Economic Development*. New York: St. Martin's Press.

Boushey, H. 2005. "Are women opting out? Debunking the myth." Center for Economic and Policy Research Reports and Issue Briefs 2005–36.

Breedlove, S.M. 1994. "Sexual differentiation of the human nervous system." *Annual Review of Psychology* 45: 389–418.

Brines, J. 1994. "Economic dependency and the division of labor." *American Journal of Sociology* 100: 652–688.

Britton, D.M. 2000. "The epistemology of the gendered organization." *Gender & Society* 14: 418–434.

Buchmann, C., DiPrete, T.A., and McDaniel, A. 2008. "Gender inequalities in education." *Annual Review of Sociology* 34: 319–337.

Budig, M.J. 2002. "Male advantage and the gender composition of jobs: Who rides the glass escalator?" *Social Problems* 49: 258–277.

Budig, M.J. and England, P. 2001. "The wage penalty for motherhood." *American Sociological Review* 66: 204–225.

Buss, D.M. 1995. "Psychological sex differences." *American Psychologist* 50: 164–168.

References

Cahill, S.1986. "Language practices and self-definition: The case of gender identity acquisition." *Sociological Quarterly* 27: 295–311.

Calás, M.B., Smircich, L., Tienari, J., Ellehave, C.F. 2010. "Editorial: Observing globalized capitalism: Gender and ethnicity as an entry point." *Gender, Work & Organization* 17(3): 243–358.

Cancian, F. 1987. *Love in America: Gender and Self-Development*. Cambridge: Cambridge University Press.

Cancian, F. 1989. "Love and the rise of capitalism," in Barbara J. Risman and Pepper Schwartz (eds), *Gender in Intimate Relationships*. Belmont, CA: Wadsworth Publishing Co., pp. 12–25.

Casper, L.M. and Bianchi, S.M. 2002. *Continuity and Change in the American Family*. Thousand Oaks, CA: Sage Publications.

Ceci, S.J. and. Williams, W.M. 2010. *The Mathematics of Sex: How Biology and Society Conspire to Limit Talented Women and Girls*. New York: Oxford University Press.

Charles, M. 1992. "Cross-national variation in occupational sex segregation." *American Sociological Review* 57: 483–502.

Charles, M. and Bradley, K. 2009. "Indulging our gendered selves? Sex segregation by field of study in 44 countries." *American Journal of Sociology* 114: 924–976.

Charles, M. and Grusky, D.B. 2004. *Occupational Ghettos: The Worldwide Segregation of Women and Men*. Stanford: Stanford University Press.

Cherlin, A. 2010. "Demographic trends in the United States: A review of research in the 2000s." *Journal of Marriage and Family* 72(3): 403–419.

Chodorow, N. 1978. *The Reproduction of Mothering*. Berkeley: University of California Press.

Chodorow, N. 1995. *The Power of Feelings: Personal Meaning in Psychoanalysis, Gender, and Culture*. New Haven: Yale University Press.

Cohany, S.R. and Sok, E. 2007. "Trends in labor force participation of married mothers of infants." *Monthly Labor Review* (February): 9–16.

Cohn, L.D. 1991. "Sex differences in the course of personality development: A meta-analysis." *Psychological Bulletin* 109: 252–266.

Collins, R., Saltzman Chafetz, J., Blumberg, R.L., Coltrane, S., and Turner, J.H. 1993. "Toward an integrated theory of gender stratification." *Sociological Perspectives* 36: 185–216.

Coltrane, S. 1989. "Household labor and the routine production of gender." *Social Problems* 36: 473–490.

Coltrane, S. 1998. *Gender and Families*. New York: Rowman & Littlefield.

Coltrane, S. 2000. "Fatherhood and marriage in the 21st century." *National Forum*, 80: 25–28.

Connell, R.W. 1995. *Masculinities*. Berkeley: University of California Press.

Cooke, L.P and Baxter, J. 2010. "'Families' in international context: Comparing institutional effects across western societies." *Journal of Marriage and Family* 72: 516–536.

Correll, S.J., Benard, S., and Paik, I. 2007. "Getting a job: Is there a mother-hood penalty?" *American Journal of Sociology* 112: 1297–1338.

Cowan, R.S. 1983. *More Work for Mother*. New York: Basic Books.

Dalton, S.E. and. Bielby, D.D. 2000. "That's our kind of constellation: Lesbian mothers negotiate institutionalized understandings of gender within the family." *Gender & Society* 14: 36–61.

Davids, T. and van Driel, F. (eds). 2005. *The Gender Question in Globalization: Changing Perspectives and Practices*. Hants, England: Aldershot Publishing Ltd.

Davis, S.N. and Greenstein, T.N. 2009. "Gender ideology: Components, predictors, and consequences." *Annual Review of Sociology* 35:88–105.

Deaux, K. 1984. "From individual differences to social categories: Analysis of a decade's research on gender." *American Psychologist* 39: 105–116.

Deaux, K. and Major, B. 1990. "A social-psychology of gender," in Deborah L. Rhode (ed.), *Theoretical Perspectives on Sexual Difference*. New Haven: Yale University Press, pp. 89–99.

Deutsch, F.M. 2007. "Undoing gender." *Gender and Society* 21: 106–127.

DeVault, M.L. 1991. *Feeding the Family: The Social Organization of Caring as Gendered Work*. Chicago: University of Chicago Press.

Dunne. G.A. (ed.). 1998. *Living 'Difference': Lesbian Perspectives on Work and Family Lives*. New York: Harrington Park Press.

Eagly, A.H. 1987. *Sex Differences in Social Behavior: A Social Role Interpretation*. Hillsdale, NJ: Lawrence Erlbaum Associates.

Eagly, A.H. 1995. "The science and politics of comparing women and men." *American Psychologist* 50: 145–158.

Eagly, A.H. and Crowley, M. 1986. "Gender and helping behavior: A meta-analytic review of the social psychological literature." *Psychological Bulletin* 100: 283–308.

Eagly, A.H. and Steffen, V.J. 1986. "Gender and aggressive behavior: A meta-analytic review of the social psychological literature." *Psychological Bulletin* 100: 309–330.

References

Ehrenreich, B. and Hochschild, A.R. 2002. *Global Woman: Nannies, Maids and Sex Workers in the New Economy*. New York, NY: Henry Holt & Co., LLC.

England, P. 1992. *Comparable Worth: Theories and Evidence*. New York: Aldine de Gruyter.

England, P. 1998. "What do we mean when we say something is gendered?" Newsletter of the Organizations, Occupations, and Work Section of the American Sociological Association. Fall: 1.

England, P. 2001. "Review of *The Case for Marriage: Why Married People are Happier, Healthier, and Better Off Financially*." *Contemporary Sociology* 30: 564–565.

England, P. and Folbre, N. 1999. "The cost of caring." *Annals of the American Academy of Political and Social Science* 561: 39–51.

England, P. and Farkas, G. 1986. *Households, Employment, and Gender: A Social, Economic, and Demographic View*. New York: Aldine De Gruyter.

Epstein, C. 1988. *Deceptive Distinctions: Sex, Gender, and the Social Order*. New York: The Russell Sage Foundation.

Esping-Andersen, G. 1990. *The Three Worlds of Welfare Capitalism*. New Jersey: Princeton University Press.

Fagot, B.I. and Leinbach, M.D. 1991. "Gender-role development in young children: From discrimination to labeling." *Developmental Review* 13: 205–224.

Fagot, B.I. and Hagan, R. 1991. "Observations of parent reactions to sex-stereotyped behaviors: Age and sex effects." *Child Development* 62: 617–628.

Fagot, B.I., Leinbach, M.D., and O'Boyle, C. 1992. "Gender labeling, Gender stereotyping, and parenting behaviors." *Developmental Psychology* 28: 225–230.

Farley, R. 1996. *The New American Reality: Who We Are, How We Got Here, Where We Are Going*. New York: Russell Sage Foundation.

Feingold, A. 1993. "Cognitive gender differences." *Sex Roles* 29: 91–112.

Feingold, A. 1994. "Gender differences in personality: A meta-analysis." *Psychological Bulletin* 116: 429–456.

Fernandez, R.M. and Sosa, M.L. 2005. "Gendering the job: Networks and recruitment at a call center." *American Journal of Sociology* 111: 859–904.

Ferree, M.M. 1990. "Beyond separate spheres: Feminism and family research." *Journal of Marriage and the Family* 52: 866–884.

Ferriman, K., Lubinski, D., and Benbow, C.P. 2009. "Work preferences, life values, and personal views of top math/science graduate students and the profoundly gifted: Developmental changes and sex differences during young adulthood and parenthood." *Journal of Personality and Social Psychology* 97: 517–532.

Fincham, F.D. and Beach, S.R.H. 2010. "Marriage in the new millennium: A decade in review." *Journal of Marriage and Family* 72(3): 630–649.

Fisher, K., McCulloch, A., and Gershuny, J. 1999. "British fathers and children." Working paper. University of Essex: Institute for Social and Economic Research.

Freese, J. 2008. "Genetics and the social science explanation of individual outcomes." *American Journal of Sociology* 114: S1–S3.

Freese, J., Allen Li, J.-C., and Wade, L. 2003. "The potential relevances of biology to social inquiry." *Annual Review of Sociology* 29: 233–256.

Freese, J. and Shostak, S. 2009. "Genetics and social inquiry." *Annual Review of Sociology* 35: 107–128.

Friedland, R. and Alford, R.R. 1991. "Bringing society back in: Symbols, practices, and institutional contradictions," in Walter W. Powell and Paul J. DiMaggio (eds), *The New Institutionalism in Organizational Analysis*. Chicago: University of Chicago Press, pp. 232–265.

Fuwa, M. 2004. "Macro-level gender inequality and the division of household labor in 22 countries." *American Sociological Review* 69: 751–767.

Garfinkel, H. 1967. *Studies in Ethnomethodology*. Englewood Cliffs, NJ: Prentice-Hall.

Gauthier, A.H., Smeeding T.M., and Furstenberg, Jr., F.F. 2004. "Are parents investing less time in children? Trends in selected industrialized countries." *Population and Development Review* 30(4): 647–671.

Gerson, K. 1985. *Hard Choices: How Women Decide About Work, Career, and Motherhood*. Berkeley: University of California Press.

Gerson, K. 1993. *No Man's Land: Men's Changing Commitments to Family and York*. New York: Basic Books.

Gilligan, C. 1982. *In a Different Voice: Psychological Theory and Women's Development*. Cambridge, MA: Harvard University Press.

Goldscheider, F.K. 2000. "Men, children and the future of the family in the Third Millennium." *Futures* 32: 527–538.

Goldscheider, F.K., and Waite, L.J. 1991. *New Families, No Families? The Transformation of the American Home*. Berkeley: University of California Press.

References

Gornick, J.C., Meyers, M.K. and Ross, K.E. 1998. "Public policies and the employment of mothers: A cross-national study." *Social Science Quarterly* 79(1): 35–54.

Gose, B. 1998. "The feminization of veterinary medicine." *Chronicle of Higher Education*. April 24, pp. A55–A56.

Granovetter, M. 1974. *Getting a Job: A Study in Contacts and Careers*. Chicago: University of Chicago Press.

Guiso, L., Monte, F., Sapienza, P., and Zingales, L. 2008. "Culture, gender and math." *Science* 320(5880): 1164–1165.

Gutek, B.A. and Morasch, B. 1982. "Sex ratios, sex role spillover, and sexual harassment of women at work." *Journal of Social Issues* 38: 55–74.

Guttentag, M. and Secord, P.F. 1983. *Too Many Women? The Sex Ratio Question*. Newbury Park, CA: Sage Publications.

Hall, R.H. 2002. *Organizations: Structures, Processes and Outcomes*, 8th edn. Upper Saddle River: Prentice-Hall.

Harding, S. 1986. *The Science Question in Feminism*. Ithaca, NY: Cornell University Press.

Hare-Mustin, R.T. and Marecek, M. 1988. "The meaning of difference: Gender theory, postmodernism, and psychology." *American Psychologist* 43: 455–464.

Hareven, T.K. 1990. "A complex relationship: Family strategies and the processes of economic and social change," in Roger Friedland and A.F. Robertson (eds), *Beyond the Marketplace: Rethinking Economy and Society*. New York: Aldine de Gruyter, pp. 215–244.

Harkness, S. and Waldfogel, J. 1999. "The family gap: Evidence from seven industrialised countries." CASE paper 29, Centre for Analysis of Social Exclusion, London.

Harris, K.M., Furstenberg, F.F., and Marmer, J.K. 1998. "Parental involvement with adolescents in intact families: The influence of fathers over the life course." *Demography* 35: 201–216.

Harris, K.M. and Morgan, S.P. 1991. "Fathers, sons and daughters: Differential paternal involvement in parenting." *Journal of Marriage and the Family*: 531–544.

Hawkesworth, M. 1997. "Confounding gender." *Signs* 22: 649–713.

Heilman, M.E. 2001. "Description and prescription: How gender stereotypes prevent women's ascent up the organizational ladder." *Journal of Social Issues* 57: 657–674.

Henson, K.D. and Rogers, J.K. 2001. "Why Marcia, you've changed!" Male clerical temporary workers doing masculinity in a feminized occupation." *Gender & Society* 15: 218–238.

Heymann, S.J. and Earle A. 2010. *Raising the Global Floor: Dismantling The Myth that We Can't Afford Good Working Conditions For Everyone.* Stanford University Press.

Hirschfeld, Lawrence A. 1996. *Race in the Making: Cognition, Culture, and the Child's Construction of Human Kinds.* Cambridge: The MIT Press.

Hochschild, A. 1979. "Emotion work, feeling rules, and social structure." *American Journal of Sociology* 85: 551–575.

Hochschild, A.R. 1983. *The Managed Heart: The Commercialization of Human Feeling.* Berkeley: University of California.

Hochschild, A. 1989. *The Second Shift: Working Parents and the Revolution at Home.* New York: Viking Penguin Inc.

Hochschild, J.L. 1995. *Facing Up to the American Dream: Race, Class, and the Soul of the Nation.* Princeton, NJ: Princeton University Press.

Hodson, R. and Sullivan, T.A. 1990. *The Social Organization of Work.* Belmont, CA: Wadsworth.

Hollander, J.A. and Howard, J.A. 2000. "Social psychological theories on social inequalities." *Social Psychology Quarterly* 63: 338–351.

Hook, J. 2006. "Care in context: Men's unpaid work in 20 countries, 1965–2003." *American Sociological Review* 71(4): 639–660.

Hook, J. 2010. "Gender inequality in the welfare state: Task segregation in housework, 1965–2003." *American Journal of Sociology* 115(5): 1480–1523.

Howard, J. 2000. "Social psychology of identities." *Annual Review of Sociology* 26: 367–393.

Hoyenga, K.B. and Hoyenga, K.T. 1993. *Gender-Related Differences: Origins and Outcomes.* Boston: Allyn and Bacon.

Huffman, M., Cohen, P., and Pearlman, J. 2010. "Engendering change: Organizational dynamics and workplace gender desegregation, 1975–2005." *Administrative Science Quarterly* 55: 255–277.

Hyde, J.S. 2005. "The gender similarities hypothesis." *American Psychologist* 60: 581–592.

Hyde, J.S. and Linn, M.C. 2006. "Gender similarities in mathematics and science." *Science* 314(5799): 599–600.

Hyde, J.S. and Mertz, J.E. 2009. "Gender, culture, and mathematics performance." *Proceedings National Academy Sciences USA* 106: 8801–8807.

References

Institute for Women's Policy Research. 2010. "The gender wage gap: 2009". March 2010.

Jackman, M.R. 1994. *The Velvet Glove: Paternalism and Conflict in Gender, Class, and Race Relations*. Berkeley: University of California Press.

Jencks, C. 1992. *Rethinking Social Policy: Race, Poverty, and the Underclass*. Cambridge, MA: Harvard University Press.

Jepperson, R.L. 1991. "Institutions, institutional effects, and institutionalism," in Walter W. Powell and Paul J. DiMaggio (eds), *The New Institutionalism in Organizational Analysis*. Chicago: University of Chicago Press, pp. 143–163.

Johnson, M.M. 1988. *Strong Mothers, Weak Wives: The Search for Gender Equity*. Berkeley: University of California Press.

Jones, C.M., Braithwaite, V.A. and Healy, S.D. 2003. "The evolution of sex differences in spatial ability." *Behavioral Neuroscience* 117: 403–411.

Jurik, N. and Siemsen, C. 2009. "Doing gender as canon or agenda." *Gender & Society* 23: 72–75.

Kane, E.W. 2000. "Racial and ethnic variations in gender-related attitudes." *Annual Review of Sociology* 26: 419–439.

Kane, M.J., and Lenskyj, H.J. 1998. "Media treatment of female athletes: Issues of gender and sexualities," in L. Wenner (ed.), *MediaSport*. New York: Routledge, pp. 186–201.

Kanter, R.M. 1977. *Men and Women of the Corporation*. New York: Basic Books.

Keister, L.A., and Moller, S. 2000. "Wealth inequality in the United States." *Annual Review of Sociology* 26: 63–81.

Kennelly, I., Merz, S.N., and Lorber. J. 2001. "Comment: What is gender?" *American Sociological Review* 66: 598–604.

Kessler, S.J. 1990. "The medical construction of gender." *Signs* 16: 3–26.

Kessler, S.J. 1998. *Lessons from the Intersexed*. New Brunswick, NJ: Rutgers University Press.

Kessler, S.J. and McKenna, W. 1978. *Gender: An Ethnomethodological Approach*. Chicago: University of Chicago Press.

Kessler, S. J. and McKenna, W. 2000. "Gender construction in everyday life: Transsexualism." *Feminism & Psychology* 10: 11–29.

Kestnbaum, E. 2003. *Culture on Ice: Figure Skating and Cultural Meaning*. Middletown, CT: Wesleyan University Press.

Kimmel, M.S. 2000. *The Gendered Society*. New York: Oxford University Press.

Kluegel, James R., and Smith, E.R. 1986. *Beliefs about Inequality: American's Views of What Is and What Ought to Be*. New York: Aldine de Gruyter.

Kohlberg, L.A. 1966. "A cognitive-developmental analysis of children's sex role concepts and attitudes," in E.E. Maccoby (ed.), *The Development of Sex Differences*. Stanford: Stanford University Press.

Kurdek, L. 1995. "Lesbian and gay couples," in Anthony R. D'Augelli and Charlotte J. Patterson (eds), *Lesbian, Gay, and Bisexual Identities Over the Lifespan*. New York: Oxford University Press.

Landry, B. 2000. *Black Working Wives: Pioneers of the American Family Revolution*. Berkeley: University of California Press.

Lee, M.A. and Mather, M. 2008. "U.S labor force trends." *Population Bulletin* 63(2).

Lemert, C. 1997. *Social Things: An Introduction to the Sociological Life*. New York: Rowman and Littlefield Publishers, Inc.

Lenski, G., Nolan, P., and Lenski, J. 1995. *Human Societies: An Introduction to Macrosociology*, 7th edn. New York: McGraw-Hill, Inc.

Lin, N. 1999. "Social networks and status attainment." *Annual Review of Sociology* 25: 467–487.

Lippe, T. van der and van Dijk, L. (eds) 2001. *Women's Employment in a Comparative Perspective*. New York: Aldine De Gruyter.

Lorber, J. 1994. *Paradoxes of Gender*. New Haven: Yale University Press.

Lytton, H. and Romney, D.M. 1991. "Parents' differential socialization of boys and girls: A meta-analysis." *Psychological Bulletin* 109: 267–296.

Maccoby, E.E. 1992. "The role of parents in the socialization of children: An historical overview." *Developmental Psychology* 28: 1006–1017.

Maccoby, E.E. 1998. *The Two Sexes: Growing Up Apart, Coming Together*. Cambridge, MA: Harvard University Press.

Maccoby, E.E. and Jacklin, C. 1974. *The Psychology of Sex Differences*. Stanford: Stanford University Press.

Maccoby, E.E., Snow, M.E., and Jacklin, C.N. 1984. "Children's dispositions and mother–child interaction at 12 and 18 months: A short-term longitudinal study." *Developmental Psychology* 20: 459–472.

Macdonald, C.L., and Sirianni, C. 1996. "The service society and the changing experience of work," in Cameron Lynne Macdonald and Carmen Sirianni (eds), *Working in the Service Society*. Philadelphia: Temple University Press, pp. 1–26.

Mandel, H. and Semyonov, M. 2005. "Family policies, wage structures, and gender gaps: Sources of earning inequality in 20 countries." *American Sociological Review* 70: 949–967.

References

Marini, M.M. and Shu, X. 1998. "Gender-related change in the occupational aspirations of youth." *Sociology of Education* 71: 43–67.

Marsden, P.V. 1987. "Core discussion networks of Americans." *American Sociological Review* 52: 122–131.

Martin, G. and Kats, V. 2003. "Families and work in transition in 12 Countries, 1980–2001," *Monthly Labor Review*, September 2003: 3–31.

Martin, C.L., Eisenbud, L., and Rose, H. 1995. "Children's gender-based reasoning about toys." *Child Development* 66: 1453–1471.

Massey, Douglas S. and Denton, N.A. 1993. *American Apartheid: Segregation and the Making of the Underclass*. Cambridge: Harvard University Press.

Mayer, J.D. and Schmidt, H.M. 2004. "Gendered political socialization in four contexts: political interest and values among junior high school students in China, Japan, Mexico, and the United States." *Social Science Journal* 41(3): 393–407.

McIllwee, J.S. and Robinson, J.G. 1992. *Women in Engineering: Gender, Power, and Workplace Culture*. Albany, NY: State University of New York Press.

McLoyd, V.C., Cauce, A.M., Takeuchi, D., and Wilson, L. 2000. "Marital processes and parental socialization in families of color: A decade review of research." *Journal of Marriage and the Family* 62: 1070–1093.

McMahon, M. 1995. *Engendering Motherhood: Identity and Self-Transformation in Women's Lives*. Toronto: Guilford Press.

McPherson, J.M., Popielarz, P.A. and Drobnic, S. 1992. "Social networks and organizational dynamics." *American Sociological Review* 57: 153–170.

McPherson, J.M. and Smith-Lovin, L. 1986. "Sex segregation in voluntary associations." *American Sociological Review* 51: 61–79.

Messner, M.A. 1992. *Power at Play: Sports and the Problem of Masculinity*. Boston: Beacon Press.

Messner, M.A. 2009. *It's All for the Kids: Gender, Families and Youth Sports*. Berkeley, CA: University of California Press.

Milkman, R. 1987. *Gender at Work: The Dynamics of Job Segregation by Sex during World War II*. Urbana, IL: University of Illinois Press.

Miller, E.M. and Costello, C.Y. 2001. "The limits of biological determinism." *American Sociological Review* 66(4): 592–598.

Mills, M. and Begall, K. 2010. "Preferences for the sex-composition of children in Europe: A multilevel examination of its effect on progression to a third child." *Population Studies* 64(1): 77–95.

Mischel, W. 1970. "Sex-typing and socialization," in Paul H. Mussen (ed.), *Carmichael's Manual of Child Psychology*, Vol. 2, 3rd edn. New York: John Wiley & Sons, Inc.

Misra, J., Budig, M., and Moller, S. 2007. "Employment, wages, and poverty: Family policies and gender equity." *Journal of Comparative Policy Analysis* 9: 135–155.

Misra, J., Moller, S., and Budig, M. 2007. "Work–family policies and poverty for partnered and single women in Europe and North America." *Gender & Society* 21: 804–827.

Moen, P. and Roehling, P. 2005. *The Career Mystique: Cracks in the American Dream*. Lanham: Rowman and Littlefield.

Moore, G. 1990. "Structural determinants of men's and women's personal networks." *American Sociological Review* 55: 726–735.

Moore, D.S., and Johnson, S.P. 2008. "Mental rotation in human infants: A sex difference." *Psychological Science* 19: 1063–1066.

Mosisa, A. and Hipple, S. 2006. "Trends in labor force participation in the United States." *Monthly Labor Review* 129(10): 35–57.

Munch, A., Miller, M., and Smith-Lovin, L. 1998. "Gender, children, and social contact: The effects of childrearing for men and women." *American Sociological Review* 62: 509–520.

Nieva, V.F. and Gutek, B.A. 1981. *Women and Work: A Psychological Perspective*. New York: Praeger Publishers.

O'Connor, J., Orloff, A., and Shaver, S. 1999. *States, Markets, Families: Gender, Liberalism and Social Policy in Australia, Canada, Great Britain, and the United States*. New York, Cambridge, and Melbourne: Cambridge University Press.

Oliver, M.B. and Shibley Hyde, J. 1993. "Gender differences in sexuality: A meta-analysis." *Psychological Bulletin* 114: 29–51.

Orfield, G. 2001. *Schools More Separate: Consequences of a Decade of Resegregation*. Report prepared for The Civil Rights Project. Cambridge, MA: Harvard University.

Padavic, I. and Reskin, B. 2002. *Women and Men at Work*. Thousand Oaks, CA: Pine Forge Press.

Park, C.B. and Cho, N.-H. 1995. "Consequences of son preference in a low-fertility society: Imbalance of the sex ratio at birth in Korea." *Population and Development Review* 21(1): 59–84.

Penner, A.M. 2008. "Gender differences in extreme mathematical achievement: An international perspective on biological and social factors." *American Journal of Sociology* 114: S138–S170.

References

Petersen, T. and Saporta, I. 2004. "The opportunity structure for discrimination." *American Journal of Sociology* 109(4): 852–901.

Pew Research Center. 2010. "Gender equality universally embraced, but inequalities acknowledged." Global Attitudes Project. 22-Nation Pew Global Attitudes Survey.

Piaget, J. 1932. *The Moral Judgment of the Child*. London: Routledge & Kegan Paul.

Pierce, J. 1995. *Gender Trials: Emotional Lives in Contemporary Law Firms*. Berkeley: University of California Press.

Pomerleau, A., Bolduc, D., Malcuit, G., and Cossette, L. 1990. "Pink or blue: Environmental stereotypes in the first two years of life." *Sex Roles* 22: 359–367.

Popielarz, P. 1999. "(In)Voluntary association: A multilevel analysis of gender segregation." *Gender & Society* 13: 234–250.

Portes, A. 1998. "Social capital: Its origins and applications in modern sociology." *Annual Review of Sociology* 24: 1–24.

Powell, G.N. 1999. "Reflections on the glass ceiling: Recent trends and future prospects," in G.N. Powell (ed.), *Handbook of Gender and Work*. Thousand Oaks, CA: Sage.

Powell, G.N. and Graves, L.M. 1999. *Women and Men in Management*, 2nd edn. Thousand Oaks, CA: Sage.

Powell, G.N. and Graves, L.M. 2003. *Women and Men in Management*, 3rd edn. Thousand Oaks, CA: Sage.

Raag, T. and Rackliff, C.L. 1998. "Preschoolers' awareness of social expectations of gender: Relationships to toy choices." *Sex Roles* 38: 685–700.

Raffaelli, M. and Ontai, L.L. 2004. "Gender socialization in Latino/a families: Results from two retrospective studies." *Sex Roles: A Journal of Research* 50: 287–299.

Raley, S. and Bianchi, S. 2006. "Sons, daughters, and family processes: Does gender of children matter?" *Annual Review of Sociology* 32: 401–421.

Reskin, B.F. 1999. "Racial and ethnic occupational segregation among women," in I. Browne (ed.), *Latinas and African American Women in the Labor Market*. New York: Russell Sage, pp. 183–204.

Reskin, B. and Padavic, I. 1994. *Women and Men at Work*. Thousand Oaks, CA: Pine Forge Press.

Reskin, B.F. and Roos, P.A. 1990. *Job Queues, Gender Queues: Explaining Women's Inroads into Male Occupations*. Philadelphia: Temple University Press.

Ridgeway, C.L. 1993. "Gender, status, and the social psychology of expectations," in Paula England (ed.), *Theory on Gender/Gender on Feminism*. New York: Aldine de Gruyter, pp. 175–198.

Ridgeway, C.L. 1997. "Interaction and the conservation of gender inequality." *American Sociological Review* 62: 218–235.

Ridgeway, C.L. and Correll, S.J. 2004. "Unpacking the gender system: A theoretical perspective on gender beliefs and social relations." *Gender & Society* 18(4): 510–531.

Ridgeway, C.L. and Diekema, D. 1992. "Are gender differences status differences?" in Cecelia L. Ridgeway (ed.), *Gender, Interaction, and Inequality*. New York: Springer-Verlag, pp. 157–180.

Ridgeway, C.L. and Smith-Lovin, L. 1999. "The gender system and interaction." *Annual Review of Sociology* 25: 191–216.

Rinehart, R. 2005. " 'Babes' & boards: Opportunities in New Millennium sport?" *Journal of Sport and Social Issues* 29(3): 232–255.

Risman, B.J. 1998. *Gender Vertigo*. New Haven: Yale University Press.

Risman, B.J. 2001. "Calling the bluff of value-free science." *American Sociological Review* 66(4): 605–611.

Roos, P.A. and Gatta, M.L. 1999. "The gender gap in earnings: Trends, explanations, prospects," in Gary N. Powell (ed.), *Handbook of Gender and Work*. Thousand Oaks, CA: Sage, pp. 95–123.

Ross, H. and Taylor, H. 1989. "Do boys prefer Daddy or his physical style of play?" *Sex Roles* 20: 23–33.

Ross, L. 1977. "The intuitive psychologist and his shortcomings: Distortions in the attribution process," in L. Berkowitz (ed.), *Advances in Experimental Social Psychology*. New York: Academic Press, pp. 174–221.

Rossi, A.S. 1977. "A biosocial perspective on parenting." *Daedalus* 106: 1–31.

Roth, L.M. 2004. "The social psychology of tokenism: Status and homophily processes on Wall Street." *Sociological Perspectives* 47(2): 189–214.

Rothman, R.A. 1998. *Inequality and Stratification in the United States*. Englewood Cliffs, NJ: Prentice-Hall

Rothman, R.A. 2002. *Inequality and Stratification: Race, Class, and Gender*, 4th edn. Upper Saddle River, NJ: Prentice Hall.

Rotolo, T. and Wharton, A.S. 2003. "Living across institutions: Exploring sex-based homophily in occupations and voluntary groups." *Sociological Perspectives* 46: 59–82.

References

Rubin, J.Z., Provenzano, F.J., and Luria, Z. 1974. " 'The eye of the beholder': Parents' views on sex of newborns." *American Journal of Orthopsychiatry* 44: 512–518.

Ryan, J. 1995. *Little Girls in Pretty Boxes*. New York: Warner Books.

Sandberg, J.F. and Hofferth, S.L. 2001. "Changes in children's time with parents, U.S. 1981–1997." *Demography* 38(3): 423–436.

Sayer, L.C., Gauthier, A.H., and Furstenberg Jr., F.F. 2004. "Educational differences in parents' time with children: Cross-national variations." *Journal of Marriage and Family* 66(5): 1152–1169.

Schrock, D. and Schwalbe, M. 2009. "Men, masculinity, and manhood acts." *Annual Review of Sociology* 35: 277–295.

Shavit, Y., Arum, R., Gamoran, A. and Menahem, G. (eds) 2007. *Stratification in Higher Education: A Comparative Study*. Palo Alto: Stanford University Press.

Shelton, B.A., and John, D. 1996. "The division of household labor." *Annual Review of Sociology* 22: 299–322.

Siegal, M. 1987. "Are sons and daughters treated more differently by fathers than by mothers?" *Developmental Review* 7: 183–209.

Smith, D. 1974. "Women's perspective as a radical critique of sociology." *Sociological Inquiry* 44: 7–13.

Smith-Doerr, L. 2004. *Women's Work: Gender Equality vs. Hierarchy in the Life Sciences*. Boulder, CO: Lynne Rienner Publishers.

Smith-Lovin, L. and McPherson, J.M. 1993. "You are who you know: A network approach to gender," in Paula England (ed.), *Theory on Gender/Feminism on Theory*. New York: Aldine de Gruyter, pp. 223–251.

Smock, P. and Greenland, F.R. 2010. "Diversity in pathways to parenthood: patterns, implications, and emerging research directions." *Journal of Marriage and Family* 72(3): 576–593.

Song, S., and Burgard, S.A. 2008. "Does son preference influence children's growth in height? A comparative study of Chinese and Filipino children." *Population Studies* 62(3): 305–320.

Spelman, E.V. 1988. *Inessential Woman*. Boston: Beacon Press.

Spence, J.T. 1984. "Masculinity, femininity, and gender-related traits: A conceptual analysis and critique of current research," in B.A. Maher and W. Maher (eds.), *Progress in Experimental Research*. San Diego: Academic Press, pp. 2–97.

Stacey, J. 1996. *In the Name of the Family: Rethinking Family Values in the Postmodern Age*. Boston: Beacon Press.

Stack, C.V. 1974. *All Our Kin*. New York: Harper & Row.

Steele, C. 1997. "A threat in the air: How stereotypes shape intellectual identity." *American Psychologist* 52: 613–629.

Steinberg, R.J. and Haignere, L. 1987. "Equitable compensation: Methodological criteria for comparable worth," in Christine Bose and Glenna Spitze (eds), *Ingredients for Women's Employment Policy*. Albany, NY: SUNY Press, pp. 157–182.

Stempel, C. 2006. "Televised sports, masculinist moral capital, and support for the U.S. invasion of Iraq." *Journal of Sport and Social Issues* 30(1): 79–106.

Stern, M. and Hildebrandt Karraker, K. 1989. "Sex stereotyping of infants: A review of gender labeling studies." *Sex Roles* 20: 501–522.

Stier, H. and Lewin-Epstein, N. 2003. "Time to work: A comparative analysis of references for working hours." *Work and Occupations* 30(3): 302–326.

Stockard, J. and Johnson, M.M. 1992. *Sex and Gender in Society*. Englewood Cliffs, NJ: Prentice Hall.

Stone, J. and Horne, J. 2008. "The print media coverage of skiing and snowboarding in Britain: Does it have to be downhill all the way?" *Journal of Sport and Social Issues* 32(1): 94–112.

Su, R., Rounds, J., and Armstrong, P.I. 2009. "Men and things, Women and people: A meta-analysis of sex differences in interests." *Psychological Bulletin* 135: 859–894.

Sullivan, O., Coltrane, S., McAnnally, L. and Altintas, E. 2009. "Father-friendly policies and time-use data in a cross-national context: Potential and prospects for future research." *Annals of the American Academy of Political and Social Science* 624: 234–254.

Sutton, R.I. 1991. "Maintaining norms about expressed emotions: The case of bill collectors." *Administrative Science Quarterly* 36: 245–268.

Sweet, S. and Meiksins, P. 2008. *Changing Contours of Work: Jobs and Opportunities in the New Economy*. Thousand Oaks: Pine Forge Press.

Tanner, N. and Zihlman, A. 1976. "Women in evolution. Part I: Innovation and selection in human origins." *Signs* 1: 585–608.

Terjesen, S. and Singh, V. 2008. "Female presence on corporate boards: A multi-country study of environmental context." *Journal of Business Ethics* 83(1): 55–63.

Thomas, W.I. 1966. *W.I. Thomas on Social Organization and Social Personality* (ed. Morris Janowitz). Chicago: University of Chicago.

References

Thorne, B. 1982. "Feminist rethinking of the family: An overview," in Barrie Thorne and Marilyn Yalom (eds), *Rethinking the Family: Some Feminist Questions*. New York: Longman, pp. 1–24.

Thorne, B. 1993. *Gender Play: Girls and Boys in School*. New Brunswick, NJ: Rutgers University Press.

Thorne, B. 1995. "Symposium: On West and Fenstermaker's 'Doing Difference.'" *Gender & Society* 9: 497–499.

Tilly, C. 1999. *Durable Inequality*. Berkeley: University of California Press.

Tilly, L.A., and Scott, J.W. 1978. *Women, Work and Family*. New York: Holt, Rinehart and Winston.

Tomaskovic-Devey, D. 1993. *Gender and Racial Inequality at Work*. Ithaca, NY: ILR Press.

Tomaskovic-Devey, D., Zimmer, C., Stainback, K., Robinson, C., Taylor, T., and McTague, T. 2006. "Documenting desegregation: Segregation in American workplaces by race, ethnicity, and sex, 1966–2003." *American Sociological Review* 71(4): 565–588.

Torsheim, T., Ravens-Sieberer, U., Hetland, J., Välimaa, R., Danielson, M., and Overpeck, M. 2006. "Cross-national variation of gender differences in adolescent subjective health in Europe and North America." *Social Science & Medicine* 62(4): 815–827.

Tsui, A.S. and Gutek, B.A. 1999. *Demographic Differences in Organizations*. Lanham, MD: Lexington Books.

Tsui, A.S., Egan, T.D., and O'Reilly III, C.A. 1992. "Being different: Relational demography and organizational attachment." *Administrative Science Quarterly* 37: 549–579.

Turner, S.S. 1999. "Intersex identities: Locating new intersections of sex and gender." *Gender & Society* 13: 457–479.

Udry, J.R. 2000. "Biological limits of gender construction." *American Sociological Review* 65: 443–457.

U.S. Department of Education. 2010. *Digest of Education Statistics, 2009*. Washington, DC: National Center for Education Statistics.

U.S. Department of Labor. 1991. "Report on the Glass Ceiling Initiative." Glass Ceiling Commission.

U.S. Department of Labor. 2010. "Highlights of women's earnings in 2009," Report 1025, June. U.S. Bureau of Labor Statistics.

Valian, V. 1998. *Why So Slow? The Advancement of Women*. Cambridge, MA: MIT Press.

References

Van de Velde, S., Bracke, P., Levecque, K., and Meuleman, B. 2010. "Gender differences in depression in 25 European countries after eliminating measurement bias in the CES-D8." *Social Science Research* 39(3): 396–404.

Van der Lippe, T. and Van Dijk, L. 2002. "Comparative research on women's employment." *Annual Review of Sociology* 28: 221–241.

Voyer, D., Voyer, S. and Bryden, M.P. 1995. "Magnitude of sex differences in spatial abilities: A meta-analysis and consideration of critical variables." *Psychological Bulletin* 117: 250–270.

Waite, L.J. and Gallagher, M. 2000. *The Case for Marriage.* New York: Doubleday.

Webber, G.R. and Williams, C.L. 2008. "Part-time work and the gender division of labor." *Qualitative Sociology* 31:15–36.

Weber, M. 1946. "Bureaucracy," in H.H. Gerth and C. Wright Mills (eds), *Max Weber: Essays in Sociology.* New York: Oxford University Press, pp. 196–244.

Welsh, S. 1999. "Gender and sexual harassment." *Annual Review of Sociology* 25: 169–190.

West, C. and Fenstermaker, S. 1993. "Power, inequality and the accomplishment of gender: An ethnomethodological view," in Paula England (ed.), *Theory on Gender/Feminism on Theory.* New York: Aldine De Gruyter.

West, C. and Fenstermaker, S. 1995. "Doing difference." *Gender & Society* 9: 8–37.

West, C. and Zimmerman, D.H. 1987. "Doing gender." *Gender & Society* 1: 125–151.

West, C. and Zimmerman, D.H. 2009. "Accounting for doing gender." *Gender & Society* 23: 112–122.

Whiting, B.B. and Edwards, C.P. 1988. *Children of Different Worlds: The Formation of Social Behavior.* Cambridge, MA: Harvard University Press.

Whitley, B.E., Jr., Nelson, A.B., and. Jones, C.J. 1999. "Gender differences in cheating attitudes and classroom cheating behavior: A meta-analysis." *Sex Roles* 41(9): 657–680.

Whittington, K.B. 2007. *Employment Structures as Opportunity Structures: The Effects of Location on Male and Female Scientific Dissemination.* Stanford, CA: Department of Sociology, Stanford University.

References

Whittington, K.B. and Smith-Doerr, L. 2008. "Women as inventors in context: Disparities in patenting across academia and industry." *Gender & Society* 22: 194–218.

Whyte, W.F. 1949. "The social structure of the restaurant." *American Journal of Sociology* 54: 302–310.

Williams, C. 1989. *Gender Differences at Work: Women and Men in Nontraditional Occupations*. Berkeley: University of California Press.

Williams, C.L. 1992. "The glass escalator: Hidden advantages for men in the 'female' professions." *Social Problems* 39: 253–267.

Williams, C. 1995. *Still a Man's World*. Berkeley: University of California.

Williams, C.L., Giuffre, P.A. and Dellinger, K. 1999. "Sexuality in the workplace." *Annual Review of Sociology* 25: 73–93.

Williams, J. 2000. *Unbending Gender: Why Work and Family Conflict and What to Do About it*. New York: Oxford University Press.

Index

Page numbers referring to figures are in italic; page numbers referring to tables are in bold.

The Sociology of Gender: An Introduction to Theory and Research, Second Edition. Amy S. Wharton.
© 2012 John Wiley & Sons Ltd. Published 2012 by John Wiley & Sons Ltd.